AGAINST CONSTITUTIONALISM

AGAINST CONSTITUTIONALISM

Martin Loughlin

HARVARD UNIVERSITY PRESS

Cambridge, Massachusetts, & London, England

2022

First printing

Cataloging-in-Publication Data is available from the Library of Congress
ISBN: 978-0-674-26802-9 (alk. paper)

For Laurie & Nye

CONTENTS

PREFACE

More than at any other time in modern history, the place of the constitution in the political and social life of the nation has become a matter of intense interest. No longer merely a document that establishes the framework for government, we look to the constitution for answers to our most intractable political controversies. Yet how can a document drafted at a specific moment in time, generally in exceptional circumstances, serve as an enduring symbol of the collective identity of the people? The answer is not obvious, but the theory of constitutionalism provides the key.

The problem is that constitutionalism, though often extolled, is rarely defined. It certainly expresses a belief that order, freedom, and justice are best promoted in a regime whose main characteristics are defined by a founding text elevated above the ordinary cut and thrust of politics. Beyond that basic assumption, its meaning remains obscure. The few works devoted to the study of constitutionalism invariably concede that the theory is "evocative and persuasive in its connotations yet cloudy in its analytic and descriptive content."[1]

Given how much has been written about other ideologies that occupy a central place in modern political and legal thought, this is a surprising gap. Compare, for example, the many studies devoted to nationalism, conservatism, liberalism, and socialism. Aspirations commonly associated with constitutionalism are, of course, easy to identify and have been much analyzed. Crucial elements are those of imposing curbs on the exercise of arbitrary power, advancing "the rule of law," establishing a regime of limited government, and ensuring that the citizen's basic rights are protected. But having paid lip service to these primary objectives, studies of constitutionalism tend to veer off in various directions, conflating constitutionalism with constitutional government, with a medley of liberal values, or simply with having adopted a modern type of constitution.[2]

This protean quality might serve the interests of its many advocates, but it must surely leave others dissatisfied. The apparent ubiquity of its professed ideals now renders the concept alarmingly vacuous. Constitutionalism was first formulated in the eighteenth century as an expression of the values of those who aspired to overthrow regimes of arbitrary rule and set in place a system of limited government that maximized individual liberty. But far from lingering on as a set of rhetorical tropes of increasing irrelevance to today's challenges, it has continued to evolve in ways not contemplated by those eighteenth-century aspirations. Constitutionalism is now an over-powerful theory of state-building, rapidly becoming the world's most influential contemporary philosophy of government.

These developments demand that the concept be subjected to close critical analysis. This is the main objective of this book, but it is not the only one. I propose to show that constitutionalism is not some vague amalgam of liberal values but a specific and deeply contentious governing philosophy. Constitutionalism has become the primary medium through which an insulated elite, while paying lip service to the claims of democracy, is able to perpetuate its authority to rule.

It is accepted that modern democracies are sustained by institutions through which popular opinion is sifted, refined, and converted into effective policy and action. That is the chief feature of constitutional democracy. The burden of my argument will be to show that, contrary to the claims of many, constitutionalism should not be equated to constitutional democracy. Arguing that constitutionalism is an aberrant mode of governing that must be overcome if faith in a constitutional democracy is to be maintained, this book makes the case for constitutional democracy *against* constitutionalism.

This is not written as a direct assault on the citadel of contemporary constitutionalism. My method has been to show how constitutionalism was constructed and how it has evolved so that the weaknesses of its foundations are exposed. This requires me to situate constitutionalism within an account of the development of modern constitutional thought. To that end, I divide the work into three distinct parts. The first part shows that constitutionalism in its classical formulation is incompatible with the demands of modern government. The second indicates how, despite being widely conflated with constitutional democracy, the two are structurally dissonant philosophies. The third, which analyzes the contemporary significance of constitutionalism, explains how it has recently undergone a remarkable transformation and now exerts a worldwide influence that is as powerful as it is contentious.

AGAINST CONSTITUTIONALISM

INTRODUCTION

What Is Constitutionalism?

CONFUSION about the meaning of constitutionalism derives from ambiguity about the very idea of a constitution. In modern understanding, a constitution is a consciously constructed artifact. A constitution is a document adopted in the name of the people that defines the powers of government, specifies the basic rights of citizens, and regulates the relationships between the established institutions of government and their citizens. By extension, constitutionalism expresses the conviction that the exercise of political power in that regime must be subject to the disciplinary constraints imposed by that special text.

This elementary point is not universally accepted. In a celebrated account, Charles Howard McIlwain maintains that constitutionalism long predates that modern meaning. It is fundamentally a "set of principles embodied in the institutions of a nation and neither external to these nor prior to them."[1] The idea, therefore, does not derive from some formally adopted text; it is an expression of the rights and liberties that constitute the lifeblood of the political nation. In all its successive phases, McIlwain concludes, constitutionalism has only one essential quality: it imposes "a legal limitation on government" and in this respect it is "the antithesis of arbitrary rule; its opposite is despotic government, the government of will instead of law."[2]

It is not difficult to feel the force of McIlwain's argument. The belief that constitutionalism rests on values that express the character of a people has long persisted. When Edward Corwin explained that the supremacy of the Constitution and "its claim to be worshipped" is founded on "the belief in a law superior to the will of human governors," he was expressing the importance of this continuity of beliefs and values.[3] And when Francis Wormuth argued that "the tradition of constitutionalism begins in ancient Athens and has had a long, interrupted, and irregular history" that now finds its expression in the "auxiliary precautions" advocated by the framers of the American Constitution, he too was celebrating that continuous lineage.[4] Yet these claims are not specifications of constitutionalism as such; they are elaborations of the values of constitutional government.

For constitutionalism to be accorded a clear meaning, it must be acknowledged as a purely modern concept. Constitutionalism did not exist before the idea that the basic terms of the governing relationship could be defined in a foundational document. Searching for the intellectual origins of constitutionalism, scholars commonly arrive at the pioneering mid-eighteenth-century work of Montesquieu. Again, this is an error. While extolling the values of constitutional government, Montesquieu believed that no universal solution to the tension between order and liberty could be found. Concluding that each regime must determine its own form of constitutional government, taking into account factors like climate, geography, economy, and political traditions, he maintained that the success of its constitution depended on the vibrancy of its political culture, or what he called "the spirit of the laws."[5] Montesquieu gives us a theory of relativity; constitutionalism, by contrast, is a universalist philosophy. The true foundational text of constitutionalism is James Madison, Alexander Hamilton, and John Jay's *Federalist Papers*, published in 1787.

Constitutionalism, then, is a theory concerning the role, standing, appropriate institutional form, and telos of a purely modern invention: the documentary constitution. It maintains that the form of government established by the constitution rests its authority on two great pillars.

The first pillar is that of *representative government*. In *Federalist* 63, Madison explains that this principle requires "the total exclusion of the people in their collective capacity" from the business of governing and the delegation of that task to a small number of citizens elected by the rest. "The people" are acknowledged as the authors of the constitution and the ultimate source of governmental authority. But, as he notes in *Federalist* 10, in order to "refine and enlarge the public views," the actual tasks of governing must be entrusted to a representative body "whose wisdom may best discern the true interest of their country and whose patriotism and love of justice will be least likely to sacrifice it to temporary or partial considerations."

The second pillar requires the establishment of institutional mechanisms for limiting, dividing, and balancing the powers of government. This need for *institutional differentiation* is often presented as the doctrine of the separation of powers, a doctrine that Maurice Vile claims as "the most useful tool for the analysis of Western systems of government" and "the most effective embodiment of the spirit which lies behind those systems."[6]

Although the institutional architecture of constitutionalism rests on these two crucial pillars, the concept of constitutionalism is not reducible to a specific institutional configuration. So we should not get hung up on the fact that in *Federalist* 51 Madison veers between advocating checks and balances on governmental powers and promoting a separation of powers. As Hamilton notes in *Federalist* 66, once the true purpose of institutional separation is appreciated, a "partial intermixture is . . . not only proper but necessary to the mutual defense of the several members of the government against each other." Rather than reducing it to a doctrine concerning the institutional distribution of powers, constitutionalism is a theory that promotes a certain ethos of governing. The differentiation of functions and the imposition of checks and balances are both designed to constrain governmental power and maximize individual liberty.

If constitutionalism were conceived as a set of institutional safeguards to limit government, the criticism that it is an eighteenth-century theory reflecting the values of a bygone era would be compelling. After all, we no longer live in a world of limited government. Across the world and irrespective of the character of the regime, there is scarcely an area of civic life in which government's reach is not felt. The challenges of limiting and directing government today are much more profound than those presented by a hereditary ruler exercising arbitrary power. And it is precisely because of the complexity of these challenges that constitutionalism has evolved and is now becoming so influential. Constitutionalism presents itself today as a method of advancing liberty in a world of total government.

What, then, is its basic template? The most rudimentary requirement of constitutionalism is that the exercise of political power is subjected to the discipline of a *text*. That text, the constitution, is drafted in the name of the people and designed to be *comprehensive*. It must contain the essential principles on which government is founded, the method by which it will be organized, and the powers it will possess—in short, noted Thomas Paine, "everything that relates to the complete organization of a civil government, and the principles on which it shall act, and by which it shall be bound."[7] The scheme is not random: it aims to ensure that government sticks to its proper purposes and protects liberty. But the theory extends beyond these basic requirements in three important respects.

The first supplement is that the constitution is intended to establish a *permanent framework* of government. One remarkable attribute of constitutionalism is that, although it founds the constitution's authority on the fact that "the people are the only legitimate fountain of power," there are "insuperable objections against the proposed recurrence to the people." Madison's objection to such recourse, he explains in *Federalist* 49, is that the constitution would thereby be deprived of "that veneration which time bestows on everything, and without which perhaps the wisest and freest governments would not possess the requisite stability." Regular recourse to the people would only excite the passions and disturb the public peace. The constitution must therefore be established as a permanent framework because only then can "the reason, alone, of the public . . . control and regulate the government."

But how exactly is the "public reason" that controls and regulates government to be discerned? The answer is provided by a second requirement: that the constitution takes effect as the *fundamental law* of the regime. This was the major innovation of the American settlement. It provided an institutional solution to the problem of how to render the exercise of the powers of rulers, including their powers to legislate, compliant with the principle of the rule of law. The remedy was to establish the constitution as a type of higher-order law and to entrust to the judiciary the responsibility of acting as its guardian.

No legislative act contrary to the constitution could be valid, it was claimed, because the latter, expressing the authentic will of the people, must take priority over the former. This is the logic of delegated authority. To deny this, Hamilton explained in *Federalist* 78, "would be to affirm that the deputy is greater than his principal; that the servant is above his master; that the representatives of the people are superior to the people themselves." It therefore falls to the judiciary to police all governmental action to ensure its compliance with the constitution. To the objection that this assumes the superiority of the judiciary over the legislature, Hamilton answers that it merely supposes that "the power of the people is superior to both." Unlike the other branches of government, the judiciary possesses neither force nor will but only judgment and is disciplined by being "bound down by strict rules and precedents which serve to define and point out their duty in every particular case that comes before them."

Hamilton's arguments appear less compelling once placed alongside Madison's point that the constitution must establish a permanent framework. Claiming the constitution as the authoritative expression of the will of the people might be convincing with respect to those citizens who consented, but what of the will of subsequent generations? If the judiciary is indeed to be bound by strict rules and precedents, then constitutionalism begins to look like what Paine called "the manuscript-assumed authority of the dead."[8] How can the "requisite stability" be maintained while at the same time accommodating social evolution?

The second remarkable feature of constitutionalism, then, is not just that it establishes the constitution as fundamental law: it also entrusts to the judiciary an altogether novel task. The judiciary, mandated to follow precedents according to common law and to adhere to strict rules of interpretation in compliance with legislative will, is now also invested with the authority to discern what public reason dictates. Liberty, declaims Hamilton in *Federalist* 78, "can have nothing to fear from the judiciary," which, in asserting its constitutional jurisdiction, is established as "the citadel of the public justice and the public security." Constitutionalism leads to the emergence of a new species of law, that of *constitutional legality*. By virtue of this innovation, the rule of law is converted from the rule of rules into the rule of reason.

The third additional requirement builds on these first two elements. Constitutionalism is commonly thought of as differentiating between governmental tasks in order to establish a system of "limited government" and therefore as a theory about the design of the office of government. But it harbors much grander ambitions. Devised in a world where public and private, state and society, were just emerging as distinct from each other, constitutionalism evolves as a theory that aspires ultimately to transcend those divisions. And in the course of that evolution, it presents itself as a theory not just to limit institutions of the state but also to regulate the entire society. Constitutionalism advances a conception of collective self-government that transforms the very idea of democracy. Democracy is no longer to be conceived as an expression of the collective *will* of a people; it is reconfigured as an expression of the collective *identity* of a people and, critically, an identity that is permanently inscribed into the foundational principles of the constitution.[9] According to the theory of constitutionalism, the constitution created by an exercise of democratic will comes to determine the very meaning of democracy within that regime.

In pursuit of this ambition, the constitution is converted from a political pact into a medium of societal self-organization. This shift, rarely articulated, has profound significance. It is most boldly expressed in Jed Rubenfeld's book *Freedom and Time*. Acknowledging the ambition underpinning the theory of constitutionalism, Rubenfeld maintains that democratic self-government can no longer be realized either "by way of a politics of popular voice" or "by declaring new constitutional rules perfectly congruent with our present collective will." This is because the constitution "continues to gather up generation upon generation of Americans into a single political subject" such that the people must now be conceived as the constitution's trustees. Freedom comes to be understood simply as adherence to the fundamental commitments expressed in the constitution as interpreted and memorialized over time. "We can achieve liberty," he concludes, "only by engaging ourselves in a project of self-government that spans time." In this manner, Rubenfeld claims to have solved the counter-majoritarian problem. His solution requires us to treat constitutionalism *as* democracy.[10]

Democracy, Karl Marx once suggested, "is the resolved mystery of all constitutions."[11] Rubenfeld now trumps this with the claim that constitutionalism is the resolved mystery of all democracies. His argument most surely captures the world-historical significance of constitutionalism but, as I aim to show, it does so at the cost of eviscerating the modern idea of democracy.

These elements can now be drawn together to give a more precise specification of the concept. Closely associated with the emergence of modern documentary constitutions, constitutionalism identifies the model characteristics of, and ideal aspirations behind, the adoption of a constitution. The constitution, it is suggested, (1) establishes a comprehensive scheme of government, founded (2) on the principle of representative government and (3) on the need to divide, channel, and constrain governmental powers for the purpose of safeguarding individual liberty. That constitution is also envisaged (4) as creating a permanent governing framework that (5) is conceived as establishing a system of fundamental law supervised by a judiciary charged with elaborating the requirements of public reason, so that (6) the constitution is able to assume its true status as the authoritative expression of the regime's collective political identity.

Constitutionalism or Constitutional Government?

Constitutionalism is a discrete concept expressing a specific philosophy of governing. It should not be conflated with more general themes revolving around constitutional government or constitutional democracy. The promotion of constitutional government has a much longer history. McIlwain and Wormuth identify many of these practices but wrongly confuse them with constitutionalism. The practices of constitutional government continue to exert a guiding influence over many contemporary systems of government, including those of France, Sweden, and the United Kingdom, which do not adhere to the precepts of constitutionalism. Neither should constitutionalism be conflated with constitutional democracy. Attempts have been made to show that constitutional and democratic values are reconcilable, but so long as these values are in perpetual and productive tension with one another and recognized to be accommodated politically, constitutional democracy must be treated as a quite distinct regime. For similar reasons, the use of certain adjectival qualifiers, such as "popular constitutionalism," "political constitutionalism," and even "authoritarian constitutionalism," are misnomers: their advocates advance arguments either about popular political agency or an authoritarian regime's use of these instruments that are antithetical to the actual meaning of constitutionalism.[12]

Constitutionalism, then, can be understood only when treated as a singular philosophy of governing of universal significance. This contrast between the pluralism of constitutional government and the universalism of constitutionalism was keenly felt from the moment of birth of the modern constitution. It is thrown into relief by contrasting the *Federalist* arguments with those contemporaneously expressed by Thomas Jefferson. Adhering to the principle of popular sovereignty, Jefferson believed that since "the earth belongs to the living and not to the dead," the people must retain the power regularly to review the Constitution and reaffirm their consent. He therefore proposed that the US Constitution contain a sunset clause according to which it must be renewed every generation, which—following the then

accepted calculations—meant every nineteen years. If the regime's fundamental law is indeed founded on the will of the people, then one generation
should not possess the power unilaterally to bind another; to seek to do so
would amount to "an act of force, and not of right." Jefferson later explained
that he was not advocating "frequent and untried changes in laws and constitutions." Rather, he insisted that the powers and purposes of governmental
institutions "must go hand in hand with the progress of the human mind."
The Constitution should not be held in "sanctimonious reverence" and regarded as "too sacred to be touched."[13]

Jefferson foresaw the inevitability of constitutional innovation, recognizing
that for the Constitution to retain its legitimacy it must be regularly ratified
by popular assent. In this respect, he was asserting a basic principle of constitutional democracy, one that—contrary to constitutionalism—does not
permit the elevation of the constitution from its useful role in establishing a
stable governmental framework into a fixed object of worship. Whether the
Federalist authors fully understood this is uncertain. They maintained that
the Constitution rests on popular consent, forcefully asserting that the entire system rests on "the vigilant and manly spirit which actuates the people
of America—a spirit which nourishes freedom, and in return is nourished by
it."[14] But they also felt that Jefferson's intervention could undermine the stability needed to establish and maintain the Constitution's authority. Innovation through judicial interpretation, they implied, was a more secure means
of adjusting to changing conditions, not least because—rather than fueling
the passions—this method relied on "public reason."

In contrast to a regime of constitutional democracy, the US Constitution
is the original model of constitutionalism. This does not mean that it lacks
democratic elements. Rather, it suggests that it was established and has
evolved in accordance with the six basic criteria of constitutionalism. It has
now imposed its authority as a comprehensive, fixed scheme of government
in which the Supreme Court, through constitutional interpretation, is the
principal medium of constitutional innovation and the Constitution itself is
the most important symbol of national political identity. Whether this model
of constitutionalism is sufficiently robust to maintain "the vigilant and [civic]
spirit" needed to sustain constitutional government is a question for further
consideration. But we should be in no doubt that it expresses a distinctive
method of reconciling order and freedom in modern government.

The Project of Constitutionalism

In the late eighteenth century, the forces of industrialism, nationalism, and liberalism in an ever-quickening process of change shaped certain powerful social and political movements that have left an indelible imprint on the modern world. The modern concept of the constitution was one of their creations. Invented during this first phase of universal history, the constitution was a product of the late eighteenth-century Enlightenment revolutions in America and France. But because the French failed to contain their revolutionary momentum in any fixed constitutional form, it was only in America that the associated concept of constitutionalism took hold.

One reason for Europe's relative failure to establish constitutionalism was its history of feudalism and absolutism. These legacies were so deeply inscribed in European societies that the struggles to establish new orders founded on liberty, equality, and solidarity were both long and intense. Consider only post-1789 France, whose history involved a continuous conflict between the forces of Revolution and Restoration, the outcome of which was only resolved after 1877 when the parliamentary advocates of the Third Republic prevailed over the will of a royalist president.[15] Of more general significance is that the Enlightenment challenge to imperial forms led to the emergence of the modern nation-state, an entity that spawned a different relationship between state and constitution.

The modern nation-state, a corporate entity with a deeper and broader foundation than monarchy and feudalism, was constructed from a new type of national sentiment that derived from commonalities of territory, traditions, language, and religion.[16] As much a cultural as a political phenomenon, the growth of nationalism invested the emerging idea of the "sovereign people" with a common political identity. And the cohesive power of nationalism created what in effect was a constitutional order of the state. Because these emancipatory nationalist movements enabled the people to acquire a clearer sense of themselves as a collective entity before their governmental arrangements had been drafted, the constitution was regarded as a phenomenon of secondary importance.

Circumstances in North America were rather different. The express purpose of early settlers to Britain's North American colonies had been to escape feudalism and monarchical authority. Migrating as free people, they were imbued with the belief that they brought with them not just the ancient rights of the common law but also a long tradition of Anglo-Saxon liberties. Having successfully established settler regimes founded on Protestantism and republican ideals of self-government, they found the stability of their world undermined when the British Crown, seeking to manage its expanding empire more effectively, proclaimed imperial authority over its colonies. Maintaining that the assertion of hierarchical authority frustrated their rights as British subjects of Anglo-Saxon lineage, the colonists argued that the mother country had broken an implicit compact and had left them with no alternative but to vindicate their claims through a war of independence.

It was this fight for independence that launched the American experiment with constitutionalism. Given the challenge of uniting thirteen very different colonies in a novel federal arrangement, they were obliged to specify the terms of their union in a foundational document. And it is only in these unique circumstances that one could say the Constitution founded a nation and created a federal republic, a union of states that was not at that moment a state.[17]

The scale of their task should not be underestimated. Tensions had been heightened as early as 1772 when Lord Mansfield, Chief Justice of the King's Bench, ruled that slavery was incompatible with the traditions of the English common law. If it were permissible in the colonies, this could only be because, as conquered territories, they derived their law not from the common law but from the Crown's prerogatives. This ruling, notes Aziz Rana, challenged "both the future of slavery as a social institution and the vision of settlers as culturally superior to non-Anglo subjects."[18] Independence was felt necessary to ensure the continuation of a unique republican project that had been founded on conquest,[19] and consolidated through slavery.[20] The Constitution devised in this first phase of universal history thus sought not only to institute a republican model of government but also to legitimate the rule of conquerors,[21] to protect a mode of human exploitation,[22] and to advance what Jefferson called "the empire of liberty."[23]

In a recent study, Paul Kahn has described how during the nineteenth century the American constitutional imagination was transformed from project to system. The revolutionary break was the moment when a new political order was envisioned as a constitutional *project*. The Constitution, drafted by an assembly and authorized by the political community, was conceived as the product of a collective political decision to shape the future. But if the aim of the Constitution was to establish a comprehensive system of government and realize the telos of constitutionalism, the specific intent of its original authors eventually had to fade into the background. "It makes no sense to speak of authorship with respect to a systemic order," explains Kahn, because "systems are not the end of any particular subject's actions."[24] Once its authority is consolidated, a *system* operates according to its own immanent principles of order and, having the capacity of self-regulation, can maintain itself against disturbance. A *project* speaks in the language of "we the people," whereas a *system* jettisons authorial intention in favor of maintaining the integrity of a regime.

It would be wrong to think of this tension between project and system as a problem that can be entirely resolved. "The social scientist's imagination of system," suggests Kahn, "can no more displace our experience of project than the natural scientist's imagination of causation can displace our experience of freedom."[25] But that is not to diminish the significance of the American ambition. The Constitution is conceived as a *project* to establish the authority of a *system*. As an expression of freedom, the project subordinates the social to the political, but once the Constitution's authority is consolidated, the political must be subordinated to the social. The Constitution is drafted as a political project to create a governing order, but once its authority is established the Constitution becomes a self-sustaining system. Its guardians, the constitutional lawyers, need no longer see their role as discerning the Framers' intentions; their task becomes one of making curative adjustments to maintain the system's equilibrium.

The great pioneer of this project to establish a system was John Marshall. Serving as chief justice for over three decades until his death in 1835, Marshall became the dominating force in crafting the Constitution as a system of fundamental law.[26] But this venture hit the buffers in the 1860s when a gulf was exposed between a *project* that protected slavery and an evolving *system* that acknowledged the implications of social and economic change. The Civil War that followed was not just another revolutionary upheaval. That it was mainly perceived as a conflict over competing interpretations of the Constitution indicates just how far the project had already advanced.[27] By the end of the century, the sense that the Constitution was a systemic order evolving through experience had gained broad acceptance. And once the Constitution is conceived as the dynamic order of an evolving society rather than an authoritative text adopted by its founders, the basic ideals of constitutionalism have been realized.

During the first half of the twentieth century, constitutionalism was recognized as America's unique contribution to the art of governing. By the end of that century Rubenfeld was promoting it as a universal theory, but during its first half it stood alone. Other states had adopted written constitutions but, as the US diplomat David Jayne Hill wrote in 1916, "In their attempts to imitate our system they have neglected to adopt the two really original and distinctive features of it, namely our renunciation of the absolute power of majorities over individual rights and liberties, and our idea of judicial authority as a means of preventing the overthrow of constitutional guarantees by mere majority legislation."[28] A further round of extensive constitution-making was undertaken by many of those engaged in the First World War, but with less than uplifting results: by the end of the 1930s, of the seventeen constitutional democracies formed from the entrails of European empires, the majority had collapsed and reverted to authoritarianism.[29]

Yet American constitutionalism itself was not immune from the social, political, economic, and technological changes of the times. In the interwar period, it faced a second crisis in which the tension between project and system resurfaced. "Believing in the approximate perfection of our system," Hill had proclaimed in 1916, "the people of the United States have, in general, desired to maintain the stability of the Constitution, and so far it has been subjected to very little change."[30] But Roosevelt's New Deal placed severe strains on that system's commitment to limited government and free markets.

The New Deal ushered in fundamental changes to both governmental relations and the constitutional meaning of liberty, but for two reasons it did not bring about major structural change to the constitutional system. First, constitutionalism is not reducible to an institutional doctrine of the separation of powers and, second, even though it originally advanced a conception of liberty as the absence of external constraints, once established as a system, this conception of liberty could no longer limit its aspirations. Constitutionalism requires the Constitution to be a permanent, comprehensive scheme of government that maintains institutional differentiation and protects liberty. But to maintain its symbolic status as an expression of collective political identity, its judicial guardians must also be authorized to reinterpret meaning in the light of changing conditions. Like the Civil War, the New Deal was a dispute over constitutional interpretation.

Under the New Deal, the Constitution was reaffirmed neither as a "lawyer's contract" nor a "layman's document." Capable of absorbing basic social and political change without formal amendment, the Constitution was acknowledged as a "charter of general principles" of "enduring wisdom." The New Deal's lasting impact was to strengthen both the Constitution's permanence as a system and, *pace* Roosevelt's criticisms of conservative judicial rulings, the Supreme Court's vital guardianship function.[31]

Sowing the Seeds of Constitutionalism

In the aftermath of the Second World War, the seeds of constitutionalism were scattered not only over depleted European states but also across newly established postcolonial regimes. Most fell on infertile ground, but in two cases, those of Germany and India, the seeds managed to germinate and produce fruit. Their achievements are both impressive and instructive.

After the interwar experience, in which newly established constitutional regimes rapidly descended into totalitarianism, postwar constitutional reconstruction in Europe was a deliberative and reactive affair. In divided and demoralized Germany, responsibility for drafting the Basic Law—the Federal Republic's provisional constitutional document—was entrusted to an assembly of delegates of the Länder. Working under the tutelage of the Allies, the document they produced was then ratified by the Länder governments alone. Determined to ensure that the failed experiment of Weimar was not repeated, drafters proposed a federal system, a more formal separation of powers, and a comprehensive catalog of basic rights. They also ensured that the core of the regime—the federal system and the protection of basic rights—was made invulnerable to constitutional change.[32]

The template of the Basic Law bore all the hallmarks of constitutionalism. It established a regime of "constrained" democracy that abolished the plebiscite and declared unconstitutional any political parties seeking "to undermine or abolish the free democratic basic order or to endanger the existence" of the state.[33] It also made a significant innovation. Concerned that ordinary courts imbued in the formal traditions of civilian jurisprudence might not be sufficiently active in protecting constitutional values, the Basic Law established a

Federal Constitutional Court charged with the task of guaranteeing the integrity of the system. This Court quickly gained authority as guardian of the order. Promoting the Basic Law as an "order of values" that through its "radiating effect" overcame the public-private division and shaped the character of the entire regime,[34] it later became a model that many states transitioning to constitutional government would seek to emulate.

Under the Court's supervision, the Basic Law quickly established itself as the most important symbol of the Federal Republic's collective political identity. There is no clearer indication of the success of this project in constitutionalism than the fact that in 1989 the Basic Law was simply extended by treaty to encompass a reunited Germany. Conceived as a provisional measure that "shall cease to apply on the day on which a constitution freely adopted by the German people takes effect,"[35] the authority of the Basic Law was such that it was felt to be too unsettling for the regime at the moment of reunification to expose the character of this German constitution to popular deliberation.[36]

Attempts at transplanting constitutionalism in the first wave of postcolonial states also had varying success.[37] But one remarkable success story is that of India. The task of drafting a constitution for a vast subcontinent of over 350 million people, the great majority of whom were poor and illiterate and divided not only by territory but also by language, religion and caste, was immense. It was entrusted to a Constituent Assembly comprising delegates of provincial legislatures constituted on a restricted franchise. The outcome was a constitution that, running to 395 articles and eight schedules, is the world's longest. This Constitution was adopted without ratification and entered into force in January 1950.

According to the catechism of American constitutionalism, the constitution should fix only a general framework and articulate certain basic principles; it should not "form a detailed legal code" because that type of document "could never be understood by the public."[38] But conditions in India were rather different. Reflecting these unique conditions, the Indian constitutional project rested on three fundamental objectives.

First, a strong centralized state apparatus able to provide leadership was felt to be required for the purpose of creating an Indian nation. Formally, a federal scheme was adopted, but the central government held the essential powers. Those responsible for drafting the new Constitution were mindful of the challenges they confronted in seeking to establish a democracy based on universal suffrage in a society whose members had not yet made the transition from subjects to citizens. They recognized both that the people had to be guided and that their legislative representatives remained in need of strong governing leadership. It was from this requirement of a high degree of centralization of power that the second objective followed.

The drafters were conscious of the problems entailed in adopting too detailed a code. Jawaharlal Nehru, who was to become India's first prime minister, expressed concern that this would make the Constitution so rigid it could not adapt to change and would therefore be unlikely to endure. But B. R. Ambedkar, the chair of the drafting committee, explained its underlying rationale. "It is only where people are saturated with constitutional morality," he clarified, "that one can take the risk of omitting from the constitution details of administration and leaving it for the legislature to prescribe them." He emphasized that "constitutional morality," by which he meant "a paramount reverence for the forms of the constitution," was something that "our people have yet to learn."[39] The detail included in the constitutional text, Madhav Khosla explains, was intended to be "an instrument of political education" and a way "to liberate Indians from existing forms of thought and understanding."[40] That task included educating legislators on the limits of their powers. The second objective, of adopting the Constitution as a detailed code, was therefore felt to be necessary for the purpose of making Indians democrats.

The third objective of the new Constitution was to construct an image of the political subject as an individual rights-bearing citizen. This identity could perhaps be assumed in enacting a new constitution for a secularized Western regime at an advanced stage of social and economic development. In a traditional society shaped by religious and caste identities, it could not. The Constitution had therefore to assist with the task of liberating citizens from communal identities. This required not just the enunciation of civil and political rights but also action to address material conditions of social and economic disadvantage. It is for this reason that the Constitution included "Directive Principles of State Policy," principles that provided guidance to both the legislature and executive on how they should discharge their responsibilities.

The Indian Constitution thus established a centralized system of authority founded on a differentiation of powers and a platform of basic rights of the citizen. In contrast to the rigidity of the US Constitution, it included a simpler amendment procedure, a provision that has been used more than a hundred times. But it is the realization of an additional—fourth—objective that provides the strongest evidence of the underlying project of constitutionalism. Not only has the Indian Constitution achieved its standing as a relatively comprehensive and permanent settlement, but its Supreme Court—affirming that the power of amendment cannot offend the Constitution's "essential features" of democracy, equality, federalism, the rule of law, secularism, and socialism—has assumed the critical role of guardian of its "basic structure."[41] In India, "a vast range of political, administrative, and judicial matters have become constitutional questions that are routinely brought to the courts." Indian constitutional law, the editors of *The Oxford Handbook of the Indian Constitution* conclude, "is interesting precisely because it has constitutionalized so much of Indian life."[42]

Germany and India illustrate how in the postwar period and in very different conditions the seeds of constitutionalism were sown and grew into modern regimes in which the constitution becomes a crucial symbol of national political identity. The social, political, economic, and cultural conditions of these regimes could scarcely be more different. But these cases share one important feature: in each, the constitution was drafted at a critical moment of rupture in the history of the state. This is a moment at which either there was no prior history of self-rule on which to draw or it was politically impossible to derive guidance from earlier practices of self-rule. When a clean break with the past was required, the project of constitutionalism offered a path to a new world.

The Age of Constitutionalism

Germany and India were indicative of postwar possibilities, but it is only in the last three decades that constitutionalism truly has come of age. This period has seen a dramatic growth in the number of constitutional democracies. One reason has been the disintegration of authoritarian regimes in Central and Eastern Europe following the collapse of the Soviet Union in 1989. Together with the downfall of dictatorships in Latin America and, to a lesser extent, in Asia and Africa, these changes led to new constitutions being drafted at an unprecedented rate. Over the last thirty years, most of the world's constitutions have either been newly adopted or radically amended.[43] And as regimes have striven to renew their authority, they have sought to burnish their credentials as constitutional democracies.[44] Since 1989, the number of regimes adopting written constitutions that institute a separation of powers, commit to the principle of the rule of law, provide for the protection of individual rights, and require the holding of free and fair elections has almost doubled. Almost two-thirds of the 193 United Nations (UN) member states are now classified as constitutional democracies.[45]

But this new wave of constitution-making is not the only, nor the most important, reason for the wider embrace of constitutionalism across the world. In both new and well-established constitutional regimes, the range of constitutional judicial review has extended dramatically and strengthened in intensity.[46] Across the world, judges are now reviewing contentious public policy questions that a generation ago were assumed to be beyond their competence. This has been spearheaded by enhanced rights protection, especially with respect to issues of ethnicity, gender, language, and religion. But the jurisdictional reach of courts extends far beyond individual rights protection; the judiciary is now bidden to adjudicate a broad range of disputes touching on fundamental aspects of collective identity and national character. The constitutional court has now emerged in many parts of the world as the key institution for resolving many of their most contentious political controversies.

This movement, which affects both established and new constitutional democracies, is a novel phenomenon. Its purpose has been to subject ever more aspects of governmental decision-making to the structural constraints, processes, principles, and values of the constitution. It aspires to bring the practices of constitutional government adopted across a range of regimes into alignment with the precepts of constitutionalism. This signifies the emergence of a new movement: that of *constitutionalization*. This term expresses the ways in which the variable practices of constitutional government are reshaped in accordance with the universal precepts of constitutionalism.[47]

In his 2004 study of these developments, Ran Hirschl identified six "scenarios of constitutionalization" that have emerged since the Second World War: *reconstruction* (in Germany, but also Japan and Italy); *decolonization* (India, but also affecting many former British colonies in Africa and Asia); *transition from authoritarianism* to democracy (Greece, Portugal, and Spain in Europe; many Latin American states; South Africa in Africa); *dual transitions* to market economy and democracy (post-Soviet bloc states in Central and Eastern Europe); the *incorporation of international standards* into domestic law (Denmark, Sweden, Britain); and a residual category of *no apparent transition scenarios* in which constitutional reforms have been introduced without basic changes to the political regime (Mexico, New Zealand, Israel, Canada).[48] Hirschl's work shows not just the increased pace of constitution-making but also how ever more extensive aspects of social and political life are being regulated by the principles and values of constitutionalism.

This is an extraordinary development. In 1979, Gordon Schochet introduced an influential collection of essays on constitutionalism by noting that, because the notion of "limited government" is of marginal relevance to contemporary challenges of governing, constitutionalism had ceased to be an important field of political study. "Expanding population coupled with growing economic disparities, the need to conserve natural resources, and the regulation of deadly technologies," he explained, "require more decisive and resolute action than limited constitutional government can provide."[49] The scale of these challenges has certainly increased since Schochet wrote but, remarkably, so too has the perceived importance of constitutionalism as a solution. And the reason is that constitutionalism is no longer seen as a useful institutional fix in establishing a system of limited government; it is now recognized as a distinctive, ambitious, and wide-ranging philosophy of governing.

What explains this dramatic reversal of fortunes? Any explanation requires a broader analysis. In his great trilogy on "the long nineteenth century," Eric Hobsbawm wrote an account of European history ranging from the *Age of Revolution* (1789–1848), through the *Age of Capital* (1848–1875), to the *Age of Empire* (1875–1914). Drawing on a remarkable range of economic, social, and political material, Hobsbawm's periods run in parallel to those of the American founding, the Civil War crisis, and the Reconstruction. They therefore span the period from the adoption of the Constitution as a project to establish an "empire of liberty" to its establishment as the immanent order constituting the political identity of the American Empire. Hobsbawm later supplemented this work by writing a "short history of the twentieth century," designated the *Age of Extremes* (1914–1991).[50] This spans two distinct periods in the history of constitutionalism: the first, running to the end of the Second

World War, in which America stands alone in the world as a constitution-alist regime, and the second, the postwar period in which the seeds of constitutionalism are scattered and propagated in a small number of states.

Hobsbawm's historical survey stops at the contemporary period: the fifth age. This age, opening in 1989, marks the era in which constitutionalism comes into its own. In labeling the contemporary period the *Age of Constitutionalism,* my account does not accord with Hobsbawm's scale, nor does it accept all the assumptions of his analysis.[51] The point is to provoke reflection on the contemporary significance of constitutionalism by situating it in a broader context and noting that constitutionalization is associated with a series of profound social and economic developments.

What I am calling the age of constitutionalism is attributable to developments in the second phase of modernity. By modernity, I mean a mode of organized social life that emerged in Europe during the eighteenth century and which, by extending its influence across much of the world, marks the first phase of universal history. Generated by the processes of industrialization and urbanization and extended by colonialization, modernity eroded many of our traditional ways of social life. Max Weber called this a process of "disenchantment" in which metaphysics was demystified by science, religion was displaced by secularism, customary ways were suppressed by bureaucratization, and the imagination was supplanted by rationalism.[52] Modernization led to the consolidation of the authority of the nation-state and, following revolutionary ruptures, to the emergence of the constitution as the key instrument for constraining the state's powers and enhancing its authority.[53]

If modernity is signified by a questioning of established ways, the process is likely to eventually provoke questions about the foundations of modern societies. This questioning quickens in pace after 1989 and leads to the emergence of a new phenomenon—that of "reflexive modernization."[54] In this second phase of modernity, many solid structures of modern societies are shaken. Economic security bolstered by industrial regulation and full employment, social security provided by a welfare state, cultural security protected by the distinction between citizens and others, stable family structures, and vibrant political parties based on established class structures—all enter a state of flux. Even the founding political principles of modernity—liberty, equality, and solidarity—become objects of reevaluation and disenchantment.[55] And not surprisingly some of the basic premises of the modern constitution, such as its template of institutional differentiation and its promotion of negative freedom, are caught up in this process.

The impact of these political changes is most visible in the effects of globalization on the standing of the nation-state. The accelerating expansion of global trade, investment, technology, and communication networks erodes the authority of government as the capacity of nation-states to regulate their own economies is diminished. As states become locked into rapidly developing global networks, they are obliged to participate in the work of international regulatory institutions whose rule systems impose structural constraints on them. Consequently, the enhanced constitutionalization of domestic governmental action commonly takes place at precisely the moment when more and more governmental action is conducted in transnational, supranational, or international arenas. Constitutionalization intensifies just as the proportion of domestic governmental action affected by it diminishes. Far from signaling an age of constitutionalism, then, it might be argued that these trends mark its twilight.[56]

But this would be to overlook another dimension of change. Continuous modernization leads to a conviction that, wherever it is located, governmental action must be constitutionally authorized if it is to be legitimate. Globalization has been tracked by movements advocating the constitutionalization of such international institutions as the UN, the World Trade Organization (WTO), and the European Union (EU). During the second phase of modernity, this leads to the fixed coordinates of constitutionalism being loosed from their moorings. Nurtured in the crucible of the modern American republic, constitutionalism extends its horizons and becomes a set of self-sustaining principles that legitimate all forms of governmental decision-making. In this second phase, the six basic precepts of constitutionalism—comprehensiveness, representation, power differentiation, enduring framework, judicial guardianship, and expression of a regime's identity—become reflexive.

If the driving force of constitutionalism during the first phase of modernity was liberalism, that of its second phase is neoliberalism. The liberal model had focused on the powers of the modern state, specifically on the powerful Western states which, through imperialism and their dominant influence on the global economy, controlled the governments of much of the rest of the world. Constitutional government with liberal principles disciplined the powers of Western governments at home while leaving them free to exert hierarchical authority over dependent states abroad. With the gathering pace of decolonization in the postwar period, however, this liberal project had to be extended to incorporate constitutional constraints into the governing structures of newly independent states. Constitutionalism became a double-edged philosophy. Promising the transformation of these societies by instituting values of liberty, equality, and solidarity,[57] it sought at the same time to ensure a regime that protected property and the institutions of the market.[58]

Liberalism was supplanted by neoliberalism once its advocates realized that markets, far from being self-regulating organisms, required strong governmental institutions to flourish. In this second phase, the project became that of establishing constitutionalism on a worldwide scale. This ambitious institution-building project depended on the promotion of constitutionalism as a system within nation-states. It needed to establish the constitution of a representative democracy as a comprehensive structure of institutionally differentiated governmental agencies ruled by a body of fundamental law and policed by the judiciary, a development that gave voice to the progressive notion of aspirational constitutionalism. But worldwide constitutionalism also required the establishment of a global network of institutions to advance both liberal values and the market conditions underpinning them. This network—which includes the UN, the International Monetary Fund, the World Bank, the WTO, an increasing number of independent central banks, and regional bodies like the EU and the North American Free Trade Agreement—operates reflexively to institute a cosmopolitan regime of what might be called Ordo-constitutionalism. Recognizing that markets do not evolve spontaneously but require supportive governmental action to thrive, Ordo-constitutionalism seeks to ensure that all institutions exercising governmental power—whether national or international, public or private—adhere to liberty-preserving constitutional values. It aspires to uphold the basic values of classical constitutionalism in a globalized and extensively governed world.

Democratization has therefore tended to be accompanied by the constitutionalization of political regimes. Constitutionalism, devised as a set of principles for a new republic founded neither on "accident or force" but on "reflection and choice," has evolved into a set of principles instituting a global order founded on rather abstract principles of rationality, subsidiarity, and proportionality. This global project has yet to establish its authority as a system and remains a contentious undertaking. Indeed, in some regimes it is experienced not as a matter of choice but of force and necessity.[59] For those in the vanguard, it is advocated as the only method of ensuring that the democratic impetus does not lead to a disintegration of the world.[60] But there can be no doubt that in this reflexive form, constitutionalism has become the most powerful philosophy of governing shaping the world today.

Constitutionalism, I have suggested, has been widely perceived as a positive phenomenon largely because it has never been closely analyzed. It continues to circulate as both abstract and venerated, not least because it can be inscribed with whatever values the heart desires. In seeking a more precise specification, I identify constitutionalism as a governing philosophy that must be distinguished from the general values underpinning constitutional government. The concept was formulated at the founding of the American republic, steadily gained in authority through the development of the American empire, and came to be recognized as America's unique contribution to modern constitutional thought.

Had it remained a distinctively American experiment in government then, peculiar though it might seem to outsiders, that governing philosophy would be more difficult to criticize. To each their own, we might say; if it works for Americans, then it is not for others to denounce its practices. Over the last seventy years, however, the precepts of constitutionalism have gained a more wide-ranging influence, and during the last three decades an altogether new impetus.[61] Constitutionalism has been rejuvenated, acquiring in this new reflexive form the capacity to reshape regimes across the world. It is this aspiration to extend constitutionalism beyond the patrimony of a particular regime and to repackage it as a universal philosophy that must be closely examined. Presenting one window onto reality, constitutionalism is converted into an abstract ideology, a striving for power.

This is the basic argument of the book. Its objective is not so much to examine social and economic developments that have shaped these changes; important though they may be, my primary aim is to capture the *spirit* of constitutionalism. I therefore focus on the implications of these changes in the meaning of constitutionalism on legal thought and political practice. Their significance, I suggest, cannot be fully appreciated without situating these innovations in modern historical context.

Part I, therefore, explains how constitutionalism first emerged as an influential theme in modern political thought. Designed as the centerpiece of an Enlightenment philosophy of governing, the modern constitution was fashioned as a liberal ideology that sought to protect established rights by instituting a system of limited government (Chapter 1). These aims were nevertheless threatened by structural changes in government following the expansion of the franchise; the rise of democracy, it appeared, signaled the decline of constitutionalism (Chapter 2). Having been designed to impose restraints on government, it was soon realized that the constitution could maintain its authority only by drawing on more basic narratives of the collective political identity of "the people," an insight that confounded the ambitions of constitutionalism's original advocates (Chapter 3). Consequently, attempts to revive the values of constitutionalism in the face of continuous governmental growth revealed its unrealistic character: either the role of the state must be limited to that of a custodian of a formal rule system or the entire modern worldview of political organization had to be overthrown. These radical consequences have been avoided only by reconceiving constitutionalism as a project to discipline government by requiring it to protect markets and individual freedoms (Chapter 4).

As classically formulated, constitutionalism is incompatible with mass democracy. But is it possible that its core values can still be realized in a world of administrative government? Many who believe so advocate the virtues not of constitutionalism as such but of constitutional democracy. Part II, therefore, examines the concept of constitutional democracy. Its two basic correlative principles—which express the competing values of public autonomy and private autonomy, of democracy and rights, and of will and reason—are first assayed separately as constituent power (Chapter 5) and constitutional rights (Chapter 6). Whether they are reconcilable is then directly addressed (Chapter 7). The conclusion reached is that the two principles can be reconciled only when constitutional democracy is reconstructed as constitutionalism. But such a rights-based reconstruction, I argue, renders constituent power redundant, and for constitutional democracy to remain distinct, not just the equal importance but also the irreconcilable character of these two principles must be acknowledged. Only then can the regime's open, dynamic, and indeterminate qualities be maintained. And the fact that this tension must be managed prudentially through political deliberation and accommodation and cannot satisfactorily be reconciled in law signifies that constitutional democracy is a discrete regime that differs from constitutionalism.

Part III, then, examines how, with the rejuvenation of constitutionalism in the second phase of modernity, the role of the constitution is transformed from that of an instrument of collective decision-making into a symbolic representation of collective political identity (Chapter 8). This development is driven by a "rights revolution" that subjects governmental action to comprehensive review through abstract principles (Chapter 9) and this engenders novel methods of interpretation as courts give meaning to the regime's "invisible constitution" (Chapter 10). This idealized, invisible, and totalizing constitution dissolves the boundary between constitutional reason and political necessity, between norm and exception, leading to the emergence of a new species of law that draws as much on political as on legal rationality (Chapter 11). Revealing the constitution as a particularity masquerading as a universal, this transformation also drives a quest for inclusion advanced through constitutional litigation (Chapter 12). And as constitutionalism's universal aspirations acquire prominence, its principles are harmonized across states, extended to international institutions, and presented as a self-sustaining system of values (Chapter 13).

The book concludes with reflections on why constitutionalism has been reinvigorated, how constitutional democracy is being degraded, and why constitutional democracy remains our best hope of maintaining the conditions of civilized existence.

PART I

Origins of Constitutionalism

Chapter 1

CONSTITUTIONS

Traditional and Modern

MANY constitutional controversies are attributable to ambiguities over the meaning of the term "constitution." The word derives from the Latin noun, *constitutio,* used by ancient Romans to denote an enacted law, and in its plural version, *constitutiones,* laws promulgated by the emperor. This is quite different from what we now understand as a constitution. Far from signifying a set of laws made by the ruler as an instrument of power, a constitution is now regarded as imposing constraints on those who exercise power.

This modern meaning was inspired by late eighteenth-century revolutionary achievements. Some contend that this was not an organic development but a radical break, signifying the shift from an empirical to a normative phenomenon.[1] There can be no doubt that the politics of the period procured a change in the meaning of the term, and this was commonly associated with a more fundamental change in the character of the association we now call the state. But we risk distorting that modern meaning if we invest it with unjustified normative significance. It would be better to say that the traditional and modern conceptions of constitution each carry normative authority but that they draw on different sources of normativity.

Our concern is with the modern concept. But we should begin by considering the traditional idea of a constitution, not least because it is from this idea that an influential set of discourses about the character of constitutional government derives.

Constitutional Government

The practice of constitutional government long predates the modern idea of the constitution. The ancient Greeks used the term *politeia* to denote the constitution, though for them it was a purely descriptive term referring to the established form of political order. *Politeia* comprises "all the innumerable characteristics which determine that state's peculiar nature, and these include its whole economic and social texture as well as matters governmental in our narrower modern sense."[2] In this respect, constitution simply meant the form of order assumed by a political regime.

A stronger normative inflection emerged during the Middle Ages with the formation of certain practices of governing that came to be called "medieval constitutionalism." This label was applied to practices of "mixed government," a term indicating that "the major interests in society must be allowed to take part jointly in the functions of government, so preventing any one interest from being able to impose its will upon the others."[3] Inspired by the works of Aristotle, this ancient idea of mixed government was restated by Aquinas and his followers primarily to strengthen the standing of representative institutions. The most secure method of avoiding arbitrary rule, they maintained, is to establish institutional arrangements that differentiate between the various functions of government.[4]

This argument was reinforced by early modern jurists who asserted that rulers must comply with the "fundamental law." Resonant though it sounds, this concept was intensely contested, being inextricably bound up with the ideological struggles of the period.[5] Invoked to remind rulers of their obligation to rule according to established practices, the concept mainly drew its authority from strict adherence to the ways of the past.[6] These inviolable customs, the rights protected by fundamental law, in reality protected the privileges of the few. By imposing restraints on a ruler's powers, however, they also carried within them the kernel of a more general claim that governments must act in accordance with settled law and practice. Established as the privileges of a landed class, over time these practices presented themselves as national characteristics of the governing regime.

Such a conception of constitutional government now seems thoroughly conservative. If a deviation from traditional ways is deemed "arbitrary," then strict adherence to fundamental law imposes significant restraints on innovation. Once rulers were forced to innovate because of social and economic change, a crisis of constitutional government became inevitable. The language through which it was expressed is graphically illustrated by the fate of the Stuart kings of England. When in 1649, following civil war, Parliament put

Charles I on trial, the king was charged with possessing "a wicked design totally to subvert the ancient and fundamental laws and liberties of this nation, and in their place to introduce an arbitrary and tyrannical government." And when the Whig aristocracy stood opposed to the policies of his son, James II was deemed to have abdicated and, in an eerie echo from forty years before, was also charged with "having violated the fundamental laws."[7] The language of lawful conduct evidently remained closely wrapped up with the precepts of medieval constitutionalism.

Yet in the period between the demise of Charles I and the downfall of James II there are signs that the meaning of the term "constitution" was beginning to change. Sentencing Charles, the High Court of Justice held that he was guilty of overthrowing the "rights and liberties of the people" according to "the fundamental constitutions of this kingdom,"[8] a usage quite clearly consistent with the ancient Roman meaning. By contrast, the charge sheet against James maintained that he had "endeavoured to subvert the constitution of the kingdom," which adopts the modern sense of the term. This modern formulation had begun to make fitful appearances earlier in the century, though its invocation in 1689 marks the first time it had been used in official documentation.[9]

The modern formulation had appeared fitfully in English civil war pamphlets. An anonymous tract of 1643 in defense of the rights of Parliament, for example, systematically used "constitution" to mean the laws, customs, and practices that shape the political formation of the state. Entitled *Touching the Fundamentall Laws, or Politique Constitution of this Kingdom*, its author argues that fundamental laws not only regulate the relationship between the king and the people; they are also "things of constitution . . . giving such an existence and being by an externall polity to King and Subjects, as Head and Members, which constitution in the very being of it is a Law held forth with more evidence, and written in the very heart of the Republique, farre firmlier than can be by pen and paper."[10] Here, the author is plainly using "constitution" to mean much more than merely the rights and responsibilities of governing officers; it signifies the manner of the makeup of the entire polity.

In medieval usage, then, the term "constitution" commonly followed the Roman meaning, retaining a clear distinction between formal enactment and customary source.[11] The seventeenth century was a period of transition in which "constitution" was used in both senses without either meaning

becoming authoritative. Consequently, despite its earlier, more modern invocation, the 1653 constitution of the Commonwealth of England, Scotland,
and Ireland was called "The Instrument of Government."[12] And when John
Locke drafted a framework of government for North Carolina in 1669, he employed the traditional Roman usage in designating his 120 regulations "The
Fundamental Constitutions of Carolina."[13] It was not until the eighteenth
century in Britain that the term "constitution" was regularly employed to explain the manner and conditions of governing. And it was not until the
middle of that century that the expression "unconstitutional" first made an
appearance in political discourse.[14]

Traditional usage of the term lingered even longer in continental European regimes, with "constitution" (*constitutio* or *Konstitution*) designating a
law promulgated by the Holy Roman Emperor until the late eighteenth
century. By contrast, the term commonly applied to laws and customs regulating the exercise of political power remained that of "fundamental laws"
(*leges fundamentales* or *Grundgesetze*).[15] In France, it was Emer de Vattel who
first gave it a modern meaning when, in 1758, he defined "constitution" as
"the fundamental regulation (*le règlement fondamental*) that determines the
manner in which public authority is to be executed."[16]

That the early eighteenth century marks the period of transition in European discourse is exemplified by the influential essays of Henry St. John, Viscount Bolingbroke. Writing in 1733, Bolingbroke defined constitution as
"that assemblage of laws, institutions and customs, derived from certain fixed
principles of reason, directed to certain fixed objects of public good, that com-
pose the general system, according to which the community hath agreed to
be governed." He goes on to explain that constitutional government is established when "the whole administration of public affairs is wisely pursued,
and with a strict conformity to the principles and objects of the constitution."[17]
Rationalizing the traditional while gesturing toward the modern, Bolingbroke's definition encapsulates the sense of a term in flux.

Montesquieu: The Link between Traditional and Modern

The story of constitutional government reaches its apogee in Montesquieu's
The Spirit of the Laws of 1748. His monumental survey of the history of governmental forms employed a standard typology of the main forms of

government—republican, aristocratic, monarchical, and despotic. But he was mainly concerned with explaining the principles through which they work: virtue in republics, moderation in aristocracies, honor in monarchies, and fear in despotisms. And the strength of each regime depended on the degree to which form and principle were conjoined.[18]

Montesquieu's overall ambition was to discover the constitutional arrangement in which order and liberty are best reconciled. Republican constitutions might seem most likely to fit the bill, but he doubted they could realize their objectives in the modern world. Depending for their authority on the maintenance of a virtuous citizenry, republican constitutions work best in small, homogeneous, and well-integrated societies, which was not the type of world that was unfolding. Ancient republics were too small to protect themselves from external aggression, and modern republics were too big to protect themselves against internal vice.[19] Accepting that "any man who has power is led to abuse it," he maintained that the most important function of a constitution is to protect against this threat: "power must check power by the arrangement of things."[20]

In pursuit of that ambition, Montesquieu concluded that there is "one nation in the world whose constitution has political liberty for its direct purpose."[21] This was that of modern England. The English constitution embodied this purpose because it provided for the distribution of power between the legislative, the executive, and the judicial: "When legislative power is united with executive power in a single person or in a single body of the magistracy, there is no liberty. . . . Nor is there liberty if the power of judging is not separate from the legislative power and from executive power." These three powers must be formed so that "as they are constrained to move by the necessary motion of things, they will be forced to move in concert."[22]

Montesquieu was not describing the realities of eighteenth-century English government; he was presenting what Max Weber would call an ideal type of a constitutional form that could reconcile order and liberty. In this respect, his work is the pivot between traditional practices and modern ideas, between the governing arrangements that establish a basis for constitutional government and the modern idea of constitutionalism.

The Spirit of the Laws may have taken the form of a historical study of systems of government, but its focus was on the modern world then emerging. This indicates its lasting value. Montesquieu provided us with the blueprint of a new constitutional order that is neither a classical republic nor a noble aristocracy, and certainly not a feudal monarchy. His study of the history of governmental forms and principles is directed toward outlining the essential characteristics of the modern constitutional state. In signaling this shift from traditional to modern, Montesquieu converted the medieval practices of the mixed constitution into a modern institutional template based on a separation of powers. He achieved this only by an idealized reconstruction of British constitutional arrangements, but in doing so, as Judith Shklar surmises, he effectively made "the equivalent of a first draft available to constitution-makers on a distant continent."[23]

The Modern Idea of Constitution

The idea of the constitution as a written text that establishes and limits the powers of government is an invention of the late eighteenth century. It was devised and implemented in North America, adopted in revolutionary France, from where it was extended to much of the European continent and subsequently across the world.

Constructed by the emerging bourgeoisie as a tool for overthrowing hereditary monarchies, the constitution became a key symbol of modernity. For liberals the struggle for a modern constitution was the great political issue of nineteenth-century Europe. "Such high expectations were attached to it," explains Dieter Grimm, "that innumerable people were prepared to risk their careers, their property, their freedom and even their lives for it." That process reached its culmination at the end of the First World War, when, following the collapse of European empires, the adoption of a modern type of constitution prevailed across much of the continent and subsequently extended to "parts of the world subject to European influence."[24] Such was the prestige attached to the concept that during the twentieth century even socialist states formed in revolutionary circumstances recognized the benefits of adopting it. Only in the country that inspired Montesquieu's reflections on the virtues of constitutional government have its attractions been resisted.

Yet this synopsis conceals a more complicated history. Even before late eighteenth-century revolutionary upheavals, documentary constitutions had been adopted in many states. Some were "scraps of parchment dependent from day-to-day upon a king's pleasure"; others were "compacts between citizens of free communities"; and between these two poles were "a welter of charters, statutes, bulls, treaty clauses, political testaments, pragmatic sanctions, manifestoes and mere undertakings that had managed to stick like burrs to the body politic on its way down the ages."[25] Often, these documents were struck off as concessions made by rulers at moments of crisis. Far from signaling comprehensive reconstruction, they were mostly mere modifications to the old order.

Even after 1789, the picture across Europe remained messy.[26] In the decade that followed its revolutionary upheaval, France became an elaborate laboratory of constitutional experiment but one that culminated in Napoleon's coup d'état of 1799 and his coronation as emperor in 1804. What followed was the conversion of much of Europe into dependent republics and subservient monarchies.[27] And although the principle of the written constitution was generally accepted after the Bourbon Restoration of 1814, few nineteenth-century European constitutions were free acts of the people; in reality, they amounted to not much more than concessions wrested from authoritarian rulers. Such "legitimist" constitutions sought in effect to reestablish order while staving off the twin evils of revolution and republicanism.[28] Consequently, modern constitutional democracies were not established on any significant scale until the creation of nation-states from the bowels of collapsed empires at the end of the First World War.

The basic principle of the modern constitution is that it is drafted by elected representatives of the people meeting in a constituent assembly with the purpose of establishing a regime of limited government that respects the fundamental rights of the individual. This modern type was widely instituted only in the twentieth century. It was commonly drafted at moments of crisis when discontent was being expressed not just about the character of the ruler but also about the entire system of rule. The constitution thus sought to rejuvenate the political life of the nation on new founding principles.

Like the early modern proponents of fundamental law who argued that the commonwealth was based on some original contract by which the people bestowed a limited authority on the ruler,[29] the drafters of modern constitutions also gained inspiration from the works of social contract thinkers. But whereas the former sought to restore some mythical ancient constitution,[30] the latter looked to the future for the realization of their ambitions. And whereas the former invoked natural rights to measure the legitimacy of the law, the latter sought to convert ideal principles into positive constitutional law.

This last innovation has had the most profound impact. The enactment of a modern constitution inscribed a hierarchical principle in the legal order. Whereas law had once been defined as the commands of the sovereign authority—in the ancient meaning, the ruler's "constitutions"—those commands were now subservient to the rules of the constitution. Once the constitution determines the competencies of the institutions of government, including those of the law-making power, then that law-making power must ipso facto be limited. And to be effective, that constitution must be legally binding.

The modern constitution takes effect as fundamental law. Promulgating a set of norms about the legitimate scope of norm-making, it takes precedence over all other forms of law. Once this principle is established, so too is the principle of constitutional jurisdiction. That is, the judiciary is entrusted with the responsibility of acting as "guardian of the constitution." In Montesquieu's worldview, the judges were "only the mouth that pronounces the words of the law, inanimate beings who can moderate neither its force nor its rigor."[31] Once judges acquire the power of review to nullify the effects of laws made by the legislature on the basis that they infringe the rules and principles of the constitutional text, however, their role is transformed. In effect, the judiciary emerges as a new type of political actor.

These juridical innovations show why the modern idea of the constitution is not simply a rationalizing mechanism, a device by which the terms of legitimate governing are specified in documentary form. This innovation marks a much more fundamental shift in the foundations of political authority. The constitution, no longer regarded as an inheritance, is now the product of momentous decision, a decision by "the people" who by an act of "constituent power" have authorized the very terms by which they are to be governed. It is at this moment, when the people are acknowledged as the ultimate source of constitutional authority, that "the state" acquires its modern meaning as the regulatory idea in which the people of a defined territory, through its established apparatus of rule, governs itself.

This modern worldview distinguishes between public and private, between what is of collective interest and what remains a matter of private responsibility. The boundary between public and private remains one of continuous contestation that cannot easily be resolved by constitutional texts. But having brought new clarity and precision to the forms of government, the modern constitution leads to that issue gradually being fought out through competing theories of constitutional interpretation.

Constitutional Authority

It is tempting to treat the modern constitution as marking a clean break with the traditional idea of a constitution as an evolving set of customary practices. Yet this cannot be assumed. The constitution might proclaim that the state's authority rests on a body of general liberal democratic principles inscribed in that text, but the constitution itself cannot guarantee their realization. The degree to which those principles are made real depends on the extent to which dominant political actors accept that the constitution has normative force.

This explains why idealized normative claims made of the constitution have often been met with skepticism. In the 1790s, a powerful attack on the entire enterprise was launched by the French counter-revolutionary thinker Joseph de Maistre. Pondering over the essential features of the constitution specified in what he called Paine's "evil book on the rights of man," he declaimed that "it would be difficult to get more errors into fewer lines." The belief that "a constitution can be made as a watchmaker makes a watch," he asserted, was one of the greatest errors of Enlightenment thought, not least because "the constitution of a nation is never the product of deliberation."[32] For de Maistre, the break marked by such an exercise in reconstitution could never establish anything new; at best, it could only amount to a formal declaration of rights that were already present within the regime.

These arguments were controversial, not least because they were tied to his firm belief in divine power and an objective sense of the good. But even without the theology, his arguments have force. The constitution of a state, de Maistre was arguing, expresses the political unity of a people, a sense of unity that is revealed through the actual practices of governing rather than in the formal rules and principles of some text.

Similar arguments were made by Edmund Burke and G. W. F. Hegel. Burke also defends the traditional conception of the constitution as a set of customary practices, though he does not grant it authority merely because of its longevity. Claiming that any constitution must derive its authority from the good outcomes it produces, he maintains that a constitution most worthy of respect has proved its value over many generations. In a metaphor also adopted by de Maistre, he suggests that "an ignorant man, who is not fool enough to meddle with his clock, is however sufficiently confident to think he can safely take to pieces, and put together at his pleasure, a moral machine of another guise, importance and complexity, composed of far other wheels, and springs, and balances, and counteracting and co-operating powers."[33]

Recognizing the value—indeed the necessity—of continuous innovation, Burke sees the importance of constitutional renewal while ruling out the possibility of radical change.[34] Hegel makes a similar claim, stating that it is impossible to "make" a constitution because, properly understood, a constitution "only develops from the national spirit."[35] Adhering to the traditional conception of a constitution, these writers emphasize that a political constitution must continue to evolve, just as the way of life of "a people" or "a nation" evolves. Constitutions, they maintain, can no more be made than language is made.

There is a core of good sense in Burke and Hegel's arguments. We need only consider Germany's first experiment in social democratic constitution-making following its defeat in the First World War and the abdication of the kaiser. On paper, the Weimar Constitution of 1919 is a social democratic model from which many states have subsequently borrowed. But in the turbulent political and economic conditions of the 1920s, it spectacularly failed to establish its authority. Destined to be an idea seeking to become a reality, the constitution appeared to have established a republic without republicans, a constitution without constitutionalists, and a democracy without democrats— at least in sufficient numbers to establish its authority as a constitutional and democratic republic. And thirteen years later, following Hitler's appointment as chancellor in 1933, it was entirely subverted through constitutional means. In 1967, the German jurist, Ernst-Wolfgang Böckenförde, wrote, "The liberal, secularized state draws its life from presuppositions that it cannot itself guarantee."[36] Widely debated in German constitutional circles, the Böckenförde dictum expresses the critical point that de Maistre, Burke, and Hegel had earlier emphasized.

The evolution of the term, we might conclude, shows that traditional and modern conceptions of a constitution have different meanings and orientations and draw on different sources of normative authority. The traditional focuses on the ethos of a people, the modern on the will expressed in their power to make a constitution. The traditional draws its authority from continuity with the past, while the modern marks a rupture and looks toward the future. As the pace of social, economic, and technological change accelerates, the authority of the traditional conception diminishes. But in seeking to break with the past, the modern is obliged to acknowledge that it cannot establish its authority unless its subjects, many of whom have absorbed the earlier traditions, accept its proclaimed principles.

Yet criticism of the modern idea of the constitution does not just come from traditionalists. It has also been critiqued by radical scholars who attribute the invention of this new piece of political technology to underlying changes in economic power relations. In the nineteenth century, such claims were powerfully advanced by Henri de Saint-Simon, Lorenz von Stein, and Ferdinand Lassalle, who in their various ways all argued that constitutional innovation was a mere surface phenomenon and that the real basis of the constitution was the material conditions of society and its system of property relations.[37] And in the early twentieth century, exponents of the new discipline of political science explained this innovation as a method of legitimating changes in coercive political power relations that were leading toward centralization, unification, and uniformity.[38]

Such materialist critiques might be important, but they cannot fully capture the significance of this change. The emergence of the modern constitution cannot be satisfactorily explained without going beyond material factors and considering change in symbolic representation. Such changes are brought about not only by developments in the means of production or in the techniques of coercion but also in the methods of interpretation and techniques of ideological reproduction.

Chapter 2

THE IDEOLOGY OF CONSTITUTIONALISM

CONSTITUTIONALISM is a method by which we shape a cluster of beliefs and cultural symbols into a meaningful arrangement, thereby making it available for purposive action. In this respect, like liberalism and nationalism, constitutionalism is an ideology.[1] The ideology of constitutionalism was a key element of eighteenth-century Enlightenment philosophy, becoming the driving force of liberals for whom the struggle to establish a constitution was the great political issue of the nineteenth century. Their aspirations have been eloquently expressed by Giovanni Sartori. Arguing that the struggle was not just for a document recording the basic form of government, he maintains that what these popular movements were demanding was clear. For them, the constitution meant "a fundamental law, or a fundamental set of principles, and a correlative institutional arrangement, which would restrict arbitrary power and ensure a 'limited government.'"[2] Following its invention in the late eighteenth century, the constitution became intrinsically linked to the ideology of constitutionalism.

From this enlightened perspective, "constitution" is an evaluative notion incorporating the positive and highly emotive properties of freedom, justice, and democracy. In the century following its invention, Sartori argues, this normative conception was well understood and widely accepted. A constitution, in this sense, contains two essential elements: a framework of government and a charter of rights. Any document establishing a framework of government without such a charter is not a constitution. Critical to the concept is its purpose, its *telos*, which is to protect basic liberties. The institutional arrangements of government must therefore be so configured as to secure their protection, an arrangement reinforced by defining those liberties in a charter. Once that purpose is apparent from the institutional arrangement, the constitution can be established as the fundamental law. The very concept of the constitution, he maintains, incorporates this essential *garantiste* element.

During the early decades of the twentieth century, Sartori argues, this accepted understanding of the constitution was lost. One reason is due to the growing influence of legal positivism in late nineteenth-century European jurisprudence. Continental jurists, "anxious to put their rationalistically trained juridical consciences at ease by finding a 'universal' definition of constitution," found it expedient to separate the universal trait—the form of government—from the *garantiste* component. Once adopted as a matter of legal science, "constitution" became detached from constitutionalism. The impact of this rupture was reinforced by the political changes of the 1920s. In this environment, so-called feeble politics gave way to intense politics or, from a different angle, "the peaceful-legalitarian approach to political relationships was giving way to a warlike view of politics." Political terminology became abused and corrupted, and the concept of a constitution was converted into an ambiguous term with two very different meanings.[3]

Sartori might be right about the significance of the political changes of the early twentieth century, but he fails to explain that what he calls the era of "intense politics" was also the period when European regimes were democratized. This development throws into relief the ambivalent relationship between constitutionalism and democracy. Constitutionalism—and constitution in Sartori's understanding—is exposed as a bourgeois liberal ideology that protects established rights against the will of enfranchised majorities. A constitution, he explains, "is neither an arbitrary stipulation, nor something to be discovered in the 'popular mind' of semi-literate majorities."[4]

The objective of Sartori's study is to restore the bond between the term "constitution" and the ideology of constitutionalism. He emphasizes that the term must have a precise normative meaning, revealed by historical experience combined with rational argument. Warning us not to confuse a homonymy with a homology, "the noun with the concept, or . . . the Latin *constitutio* with our 'constitution,'" he claims that the modern meaning of the word only begins in the eighteenth century when "constitution" begins to stand for the principle of "limited government." The term "was re-conceived, adopted and cherished not because it merely meant 'political order,' but because it meant much more, because it meant 'political freedom.'"[5] Constitution refers to the adoption of a framework of government organized through law for the purpose of restraining the exercise of arbitrary power.

Because the twentieth century brought confusion leading to the loss of the constitution's normative meaning, adjectival qualifiers must apparently now be appended. Sartori distinguishes between three types: *garantiste,* nominal, and façade constitutions. Only the former is a constitution properly so called. Nominal constitutions simply express the form of government of a state; they organize but do not restrain the exercise of political power. They simply describe the system of government. Façade constitutions are even more dangerous. Offering no reliable guide to how power is actually exercised, they are merely for show. Since their *garantiste* aspects are ignored, the regime might have adopted a constitution, but it will lack the practice of constitutional government.[6] So too, Sartori suggests, does a regime with a nominal constitution. If that constitution confers arbitrary powers on the government, then a law-governed regime has not been established. Constitution without constitutional government is meaningless.

Writing in the 1960s, Sartori was warning that contestation over the very concept of "constitution" meant losing sight of its precise normative connotation. Whenever the term loses its link to constitutionalism, it is corrupted.

The Rule of Law and the *Rechtsstaat*

The modern idea of the constitution, Sartori argues, was prescribed by the Enlightenment philosophy of constitutionalism. Its overriding purpose was to protect and promote individual liberty by ensuring that the coercive powers of government are strictly confined. The method of achieving this objective has been to adopt a constitution that ensures that governing authorities act in accordance with known general rules. By virtue of institutional design, we establish a "government of laws, not of men."[7] Constitutionalism thus seeks to preserve individual liberty by promoting "the rule of law."

But the rule of law is a highly ambiguous notion. Coined during the nineteenth century and extolled by Albert Venn Dicey as a defining characteristic of the British constitution, the term was invoked to explain the importance of certain English governing practices that run counter to the modern idea of the constitution. Acknowledging that the rule of law expressed such liberal principles as equality before the law and the necessity of promulgating law as general rules of conduct, Dicey also emphasizes that it was the distinguishing feature of Britain's unique and superior constitutional arrangements.

The great strength of the British constitution, he explains, is that its general principles are the product of "judicial decisions determining the rights of private persons in particular cases." Its unique character rests on the fact that it is a "judge-made constitution," that its principles are generalizations inferred from judicial decisions and that, contrary to the modern constitution, in which rights are assumed to derive from the text, these rights are inductions that are "inherent in the ordinary law of the land." These practices might not have been codified in a document specifying "those declarations or definitions of rights so dear to foreign constitutionalists" but that it had evolved and "gradually framed the complicated set of laws and institutions we now call the constitution" conferred distinct benefits. Obliged by the stress of circumstances to advocate a modern constitution, foreign constitutionalists had become preoccupied with specifying rights in texts and were insufficiently attentive to the necessity of ensuring effective remedies. The English Habeas Corpus Acts, by contrast, might "declare no principle and define no rights, but they are for practical purposes worth a hundred articles guaranteeing individual liberty."[8]

Dicey recognizes that maintaining a close link between rights and remedies need not be inconsistent with the adoption of a modern constitution. The problem arises because once rights are felt to exist only when declared in a written document, they can all too easily be suspended. Where, by contrast, "the right to individual freedom is part of the constitution because it is inherent in the ordinary law of the land, the right is one that can hardly be destroyed without a thorough revolution in the history and manners of the nation."[9] Adherence to the traditional idea of a constitution, he concludes, offers the best guarantee of rights protection.

These ambiguities are compounded when one compares the analogous German concept of *Rechtsstaat*. This concept came into common usage during the first half of the nineteenth century but in rather different political circumstances. In most Continental countries, explains Friedrich Hayek, "two hundred years of absolute government had, by the middle of the eighteenth century, destroyed the traditions of liberty." By the time liberal ideas of governing according to law had developed into a political movement, a powerful centralized administrative machinery had already been built, and this "bureaucracy concerned itself much more with the welfare . . . of the people than the limited government of the Anglo-Saxon world either could or was expected to do."[10] The concept of *Rechtsstaat* was invented by German jurists to reconcile modern demands for individual liberty with an already established tradition of authoritarian government.

The liberal idea of *Rechtsstaat* was inspired by the work of Immanuel Kant. In his *Rechtslehre,* Kant argues that the three basic powers of the state—legislative, executive, and judicial—can be likened to the three propositions in a practical syllogism. The major premise expresses the law enacted by sovereign will, the minor premise comprises the executive command to act according to the law, and the conclusion contains the legal judgment as to the rights and wrongs of each particular case. Kant's claim is that legislative and executive acts are mere sources of law: "true" law was to be found in the synthesis of judicial decision.[11] He, in effect, offers a rationalized sketch of the underlying logic of what was later to be Dicey's account of the rule of judicature. But the practical challenges facing German jurists were far removed from Kant's idealized presentation.

These challenges led to competing conservative and liberal expressions of the *Rechtsstaat* principle. The conservative version sought only to ensure that the state is organized according to formal rational principles; it was therefore open to the criticism that *Rechtsstaat* principles were simply placing the cloak of legitimation around an authoritarian regime. Liberals, by contrast, argued that rational organization of the state was not sufficient; its policies and practices must also ensure the protection of liberty, security, and property.[12] Tensions between these variants came to a head in the 1848 revolution. The Paulskirche national assembly, which proposed a modern constitution, saw the *Rechtsstaat* as the embodiment of Enlightenment constitutionalism. But following the failure of that movement, the idea of the *Rechtsstaat* that circulated during the latter half of the century became an ambiguous compromise between liberalism and monarchical authoritarianism.

The basic values of the *Rechtsstaat* were further compromised by the growing dominance of legal positivist jurisprudence. In this, the state was conceived as a legal person embodying sovereign authority, an idea anathema to any notion that rights-bearing individuals might impose limits on the state's authority. Once rights were regarded as the creation of objective law, the concept of the *Rechtsstaat* became subsumed in a broader concept of *Staatsrecht*. The *Rechtsstaat* principle thus implied only that the state and its agencies must act in accordance with the promulgated rules. To the extent that a broader, liberal conception lived on in German jurisprudence, it could only take the form of political aspiration.[13]

A further important distinction must be drawn between common law and continental conceptions. For Dicey, the rule of law means the rule of ordinary law: equality before the law means equal subjection to one law equally administered by the ordinary courts. It means that "every official, from the Prime Minister down to a constable or a collector of taxes, is under the same responsibility for every act done without legal justification as any other citizen."[14] However, throughout continental Europe, officials were subject to an evolving administrative jurisdiction rather than accountable to the ordinary courts. This was justified on the grounds that "disputes over administrative acts require a knowledge both of branches of law and fact which the ordinary judge . . . cannot be expected to possess." But it was also believed, explains Hayek, that "disputes about the lawfulness of an administrative act cannot be decided on as a pure matter of law, since they always involve issues of government policy or expediency."[15] For Dicey, this continental notion of administrative law "rests on ideas foreign to the fundamental assumptions of our English common law, and especially to what we have termed the rule of law."[16]

It was already apparent at the time he wrote that Dicey had grossly underestimated the extent to which Continental administrative jurisdiction had been regularized as a special system of law.[17] Yet he resolutely stuck to his argument long after the emergence of evidence contradicting his claims. He also held on to his romanticized beliefs in the constitutional value of the rule of law long after he admitted they no longer matched the governmental conditions of his time. In his lectures on law and public opinion in England, published twenty years after *Law of the Constitution,* he charts a shift from the era of individualism (1825–1870) to collectivism (1865–1900). He characterizes this as one of steady decline in which "faith in *laissez faire* suffered an eclipse," and the mechanisms for protecting individual liberty were eroded.[18] In the extended introduction to his last edition of *Law of the Constitution* in 1915, the implications of this for the rule of law became clear. Veneration of the rule of law, he concludes, is now suffering "a marked decline" because English law is being "officialised" by legislation passed under the influence of "socialistic ideas."[19]

Dicey had to concede that the rule of law, that genius of traditional English constitutional practice, was being undermined by structural changes in government. Only modern constitutional reconstruction could preserve the values that the rule of law sought to uphold. Dicey poured scorn on the benefits of modern constitutional arrangements, on charters of rights and jurisdictions that sought to establish a liberal *Rechtsstaat*. But this could not prevent an emerging liberal consensus that in the modern world of democratic government this was the sole means of promoting constitutionalism.

The Doctrine of the Separation of Powers

Montesquieu's great achievement was to have based the justification for modern liberal government on an institutional doctrine concerning the need for separated powers. This doctrine had a profound influence on American and French revolutionaries. Having asserted that all political power emanates from the people, their revolutionary task was to design a system of government on the principles of delegated authority and the accountability of officeholders to the people. The republican solution was the doctrine of the separation of powers. But revolutionaries soon found that the apparent simplicity of this doctrine was deceptive.

Separation of powers had been devised as the alternative to the idea of mixed government. Mixed government, a central theme of what had been called "medieval constitutionalism," was the idea that the institutional arrangements of government should ensure that all major interests in society were represented. Revolutionaries rejected this on the ground that it would mean the retention of power by monarchical and aristocratic factions. Being antithetical to republicanism, mixed government was off the agenda.

Some in the revolutionary vanguard did suggest establishing a regime of balanced government rather than a strict separation of powers. But their proposals were opposed by republicans who felt that the idea that institutions of government would provide a series of checks and balances on one another effectively introduced an aristocratic principle into modern constitutionalism. In postrevolutionary debates, these theories of balanced government and separation of powers presented themselves as rivals for the mantle of American constitutionalism.

In 1776, the doctrine of the separation of powers represented republicanism in its purest form. It expressed a new type of constitutional design that, rather than being inherited from the traditions of British government, was devised to accord with first principles. Separation of powers arose from the principle that governmental power must be susceptible to control by the people. Each branch of government—legislative, executive, and judicial—must acquire its mandate from the people, each must keep within its constitutionally conferred powers and, since they acquired authority from delegation by the people, each must be elected and subject to regular recall.

This doctrine was enunciated in several state constitutions and declarations of the period. In 1776, the framers of the Constitution of Virginia, for example, declared: "The legislative, executive and judiciary departments shall be separate and distinct, so that neither exercise the powers properly belong to the other: nor shall any person exercise the powers of more than one of them at the same time."[20] Yet this constitutional theory was soon superseded by the idea that instead of complete separation, a constitutional order should establish a system of checks and balances.

The main problem with the separation of powers doctrine was to determine the limits of legislative power. Legislative power was to be supreme in that its decisions could not be challenged by any other institution of government. But it was also accepted that, if constituent power was vested in the people, the legislature exercised a delegated power that must necessarily be limited. It was, after all, in opposition to the British assertion of the absolute legislative authority of the Crown-in-Parliament that American independence was asserted. How, then, might a supreme but limited legislature be constituted?

The solution was the theory of checks and balances. Balancing the three powers against one another would prevent arbitrariness in government and secure liberty. The theory was developed by the Federalists in opposition to the republican theory of separation. It is most clearly articulated by Madison in *Federalist* 47, who notes that one of the republican objections to the 1787 Constitution was its supposed violation of the separation of powers. That objection arose because, in the Constitution, the several departments "are distributed and blended in such a manner as at once to destroy all symmetry and beauty of form," and this exposes some parts of the edifice to "the danger of being crushed by the disproportionate weight of the other parts." Madison avers that this notion of strict separation misconstrues Montesquieu's argument, whose true meaning was that "where the *whole* power of one department is exercised by the same hands which possess the *whole* power have another department, the fundamental principles of a free constitution are subverted."[21]

The critical disagreement was over judicial review. In the republican doctrine of the separation of powers, no one branch has the authority to intervene in the functions of another. On this basis, judicial review, like the power of the executive to veto legislation, is impermissible. The principle of separated powers is therefore a necessary but not sufficient basis for the doctrine of judicial review. As Hamilton explains in *Federalist* 78, judicial review can be justified only by modifying the doctrine of a pure separation of powers according to the Federalist principle of balanced government. If the Constitution is to be established as higher-order law, it seems incumbent on the judiciary to disapply or refuse to enforce laws that conflict with the Constitution. Tellingly, such a principle is not universally accepted by modern regimes establishing constitutions on the principle of the separation of powers.

The federal Constitution of 1787 represented the victory of the theory of the balanced constitution over the republican doctrine of separation of powers.[22] The American model established a moderated system of separated powers reinforced by checks and balances built into the Constitution. During the early nineteenth century, this was contested by Jeffersonian republicans asserting that the balanced constitution introduced elements of restraint that, independent of popular power, could yet impose restrictions on the direct representatives of that power. Republicanism, Jefferson had explained, meant the control of the people over their government, and mechanisms like judicial review were incompatible with a republican constitution that affords each branch of government equal power. If the people are the only legitimate agency of control, all branches of government must be popularly elected and subject to regular recall.[23] This debate rumbled on; it was not until after the Civil War of the 1860s that the Federalist principle could truly be said to have triumphed.

The American experience of constitutional design can be contrasted with the French. In the American case, the main objective had been to break from the authority of the British Crown, resulting in the adopted Constitution bolstering an already-established social order. But the purpose of the French Revolution had as its much more radical aim the eradication of the old order in its entirety. The *Declaration of the Rights of Man and the Citizen* had enunciated the principles on which the new order was to be established, albeit with juridical implications that then were only latent. With respect to constitutional design, Montesquieu's doctrine of the separation of powers was also a powerful influence, evident in the *Declaration,* announcing in Article 16 that "any society in which the guarantee of rights is not assured, nor the separation of powers secured, has no constitution." But unlike in the United States, Rousseau's ideas were equally important. Law, he argued, is an expression of the general will, by which he meant a "common interest" that unites the sovereign people. This sovereign will of the people is exercised through legislative power. Rousseau recognized that the executive powers of government could and should be differentiated, and also that legislative power is absolute and inviolable.[24] He therefore rejected theories of balanced government if that meant that institutions were invested with the power to check the legislature. And this meant that Montesquieu's theory could only be accepted in its pure republican form.

Rousseau's ideas on popular sovereignty had a powerful influence on French revolutionary thought, though with the significant modification that in a modern state—unlike Rousseau's ideal of a small city republic—power had necessarily to be exercised by a representative assembly. Emmanuel-Joseph Sieyes, the main architect of this modification, accepted that, as the sovereign power, the nation "cannot alienate or prohibit its right to will" but must entrust this power to its representatives. Sieyes distinguished between two categories of power: the legislative power to make laws and the constituent power to determine the constitutional form of the state. The nation is the source of that power in both cases, but the ability of "extraordinary representatives" acting as "a surrogate for an assembly of that nation" to make the constitution must be differentiated from the ordinary representatives of the people who are "entrusted with exercising, according to constitutional forms, that portion of the common will that is necessary for good social administration."[25]

In other respects, Rousseau's influence prevailed. French courts were not invested with the power to review legislation, nor could the civil courts engage in the review of administrative action.[26] But the authority of these republican constitutional arrangements proved difficult to establish in the postrevolutionary context. After a turbulent decade, the path was prepared for the imperial ambitions of Napoleon.

Following Napoleon's downfall, theories of balanced government were entertained, most notably in the *Charte* of 1814 and through the influence of such jurists as Benjamin Constant, Pierre Royer-Collard, and François Guizot.[27] But the basic principles of constitutionalism that continued to be debated in nineteenth-century France were then threatened by social, economic, and political changes. Leading to the extension of democracy and the growth of governmental powers, these changes undermined the authority of the principles of both the separation of powers and balanced government.[28] In the process, the Enlightenment philosophy of constitutionalism, so influential with late eighteenth-century revolutionaries, came to be seen as the philosophy of an earlier era with little relevance to a new world of administrative government.

The Limitations of Enlightenment Constitutionalism

The coming of democracy in the twentieth century gave rise to what Sartori called "intense politics" and Dicey the "era of collectivism." In this world of party government organized through the administrative delivery of public services, constitutionalism seemed an obsolete eighteenth-century philosophy. Born of the conflict between the emerging liberal bourgeoisie and absolute monarchy, its attempt to establish limited, law-bounded, and liberty-preserving government through the medium of institutional design seemed singularly unsuited to contemporary requirements.

It had long been accepted that the republican doctrine of the separation of powers could only work when governmental functions were restricted to defense, law and order, and the preservation of individual liberty. But as social conditions rapidly changed, so had the essential constitutional task. The challenge was no longer to fix the boundaries of a preexisting hierarchically ordered regime; it was to create conditions that could enable a democratic regime to flourish. In this environment, the range of governmental responsibilities extended greatly, transforming the task of maintaining a balance between legislature, executive, and judiciary. Founded on the assumption that the legislature posed the greatest threat to liberties, the ideology of constitutionalism was upended when the so-called executive branch—the government—began to absorb many of the tasks of the other two. The two pillars of classical constitutionalism—separation and balance—had been erected on foundations of sand.

The task of subjecting government to law was also affected. The driving principle of the *Rechtsstaat* had force when the powers of the executive were limited by a legislature formed as a representative assembly of the people. But when the executive was also established on popular lines and, especially in parliamentary systems, came to control the legislature, restraints on governmental action diminished. Even Dicey's paean to the common law rang hollow: the rule of judicature, he suggested, could not be undermined without a revolution in "the history and manners of the [political] nation." This is precisely what the coming of democracy brought about.

Constitutionalism, in short, was the expression of a bourgeois liberal philosophy of governing that could not survive the age of mass democracy. In his defense of the ideology in the 1960s, Sartori acknowledges that assumptions about the fixity of its written form had to be revised. In an age of interpretation, the idea of the "living constitution" had to be acknowledged but provided the telos of the document was maintained, constitutionalism could be adapted to these new circumstances. But Sartori was very concerned about more recently adopted constitutions. These, he argues, are invariably "bad constitutions technically speaking" in that they include "unrealistic promises and glamorous professions of faith on the one hand, and numberless frivolous details on the other." Most importantly, some are "so 'democratic' that . . . they are no longer constitutions," because the constitution must limit "the 'will of the people' concept of democracy just as much as it limits the will of the power holders."[29]

Sartori was not alone in this assessment. During the twentieth century, the belief that the rise of democracy signaled the decline of constitutionalism was widespread.[30] Given the recent ubiquity of constitution-making, this might suggest that the constitution, having lost its historic purpose of limiting power, now merely performs the function of legitimating power. But is it possible that constitutionalism has been able to survive the era of mass democracy by jettisoning its classical doctrines of institutional design and reinventing itself? Just as the meaning accorded to political freedom changes with each age, so too might the meaning of constitutionalism. Can the ideology of constitutionalism evolve and engage effectively with the challenge of specifying conditions of legitimate rule in the era of big government? This is the issue that is taken up in Chapter 4, but first the nature of the political association that the constitution aspires to regulate must be considered.

Chapter 3

THE CONSTITUTION
OF WHAT?

CARL Schmitt began his treatise *Constitutional Theory* by noting that although each entity has a constitution, no constitutional theory can be derived from this fact. A proper grasp of the subject requires the meaning of the term "constitution" to be restricted to that of the constitution of the state. Our accounts of constitution and constitutionalism have proceeded on this assumption, but the nature of the state has been taken for granted. We must now examine the nature of the association which the constitution purports to constitute.

For a deeper understanding of constitutionalism, it is not enough to assume that the state is the supreme authority, holding the means of coercion and the allegiance of its subjects. If the constitution is intended to impose a sense of right ordering over the exercise of public power, we cannot avoid examining the distinctive way in which the state itself organizes public power. This aspect is often overlooked in discussions of constitutionalism, not least because, owing to the unusual circumstances leading to the formation of the United States—the regime in which constitutionalism is most firmly inscribed—the Constitution was commonly assumed to have determined the character of its political association we now call the state. But the US experience is thoroughly atypical. To examine this issue more rigorously, European debates must be considered.

Elements of a General Theory of the State

The abstraction we call "the state" is the product of what Hobbes called "Powers Invisible," by which humans "stand in awe of their own imaginations."[1] The state creates a world of meaning comprising a regime of rights, duties, powers, and liabilities. In common with the many institutions that shape modern life—the family, the church, the school, our system of monetary exchange, and even our common language—we learn to organize our thoughts and actions with reference to them. And because they are such basic parts of the regular furniture of social life, we commonly act without being conscious of their founding assumptions.

Conjured into existence through these assumed meanings, the state possesses the capacity to exert a powerful performative influence on the lives of its subjects, not least through powers of coercion that range from the imposition of tax liabilities to imprisonment for criminal behavior. Yet the state should not be equated with its coercive powers, these being mere effects of its existence. And it is this melding of idea and impact that led Georg Jellinek to conclude that the state has two essential aspects: the normative (*Recht:* right) and the material (*Macht:* power). In combination, these two aspects establish what Jellinek called "the normative power of [political] reality."[2]

The state is the notion that must be presupposed to envision a modern political reality. It enables us both to make sense of a political world created through a collective act of imagination and to express this materially as an institutional configuration that organizes a territorially defined mode of association. This conjunction yields "the constitution of the state." As a constituted order, the state has three main elements: *territory,* the state as an independent and bounded land area; *people,* the state as an aggregation of members of the association—subjects / citizens—within that territory; and *ruling authority,* the state as the institutional apparatus of rule that secures its powers to govern the subjects of that territory.

The first element asserts that the state exists by acquiring control over a defined portion of the earth's area (*Staatsgebiet*). The entire land area of today's world is divided up between two hundred or so states, each of which claims an exclusive governmental jurisdiction within a defined area. Without this territorial jurisdiction, there is no state; sovereign authority is territorially bounded. Tracing the historical evolution of state formation, Schmitt argues that the process began with a land grab: "Not only logically, but also historically, land-appropriation precedes the order that follows from it." After this, the land was divided into parcels of property, providing the foundation for productive activity. His point is that in its original meaning *nomos* signified the constitution of "the original spatial order," and this is "the source of all further concrete order and all further law."[3]

Territory, then, is an essential aspect of the state. But does it follow that the state's territorial boundaries are inviolable? This claim was explicitly advanced in the constitutions of postrevolutionary France. The Constitution of 1791 asserted that "the kingdom is one and indivisible," a claim strengthened in 1792 by a unanimous vote of the National Convention declaring that "whoever should propose or attempt to break the unity of the French republic . . . should be punished by death."[4] Such expressions fix the territory with an almost sacred character. But although this tells us something about the idea of the state in the French political imagination, it cannot be held up as a general principle of statehood for the simple reason that, as historical experience shows, state territories have been endlessly formed and reformed by processes of annexation, secession, and disintegration.[5]

The second element of state theory concerns subjects of the state (*Staatsvolk*). As an institution that organizes relations between people, the state does not exist unless there are people within that territory. Just as we assume that the state is a bounded territory, we also imagine the state as an expression of the political unity of its people. In this respect, the state is "the people." But the set of relations formed by the people is complicated. In one sense, "the people" is the ultimate source of authority in the state, a principle most clearly visible whenever a constitution is drafted. When its preamble proclaims that "We the People . . . do ordain and establish this Constitution," it refers to the people *as* the state. This is complicated for two main reasons. The first is that the authors of the constitution are also those over whom authority is to be exercised and who are bound in ties of allegiance to the state. This is the paradox of the founding, and it is not overcome by appealing to some general principle of "collective self-government." The second is that the claim is largely symbolic; when this was proclaimed in 1787, for example, there was no suggestion that all the inhabitants of the North American colonies formed part of "the people."

One way to finesse such difficulties has been to distinguish between "the people" as an ideal expression of collective political unity and "the nation" as the actual group bound by common ties of race, language, customs, or history. This brings Jellinek's two aspects of the state into closer alignment.

Viewed as a normative construct, the idea of the state as the people is the source of constitutional authority. But as a political reality, whatever authority that constitution acquires depends on the way in which common sentiment can be distilled from the social practices of ordinary life. Constitutional authority is formally asserted in the name of "the people," but it is actually derived from the way that common language, shared customs, similarities of racial or religious identities, and collective historical consciousness bind the population of a defined territory in political unity.

Many studies have explained the ways in which these bonds are forged and reinforced. Scholars have suggested that a population conceives of itself as a nation by establishing "a large-scale solidarity, constituted by the feeling of the sacrifices that one has made in the past and of those that one is prepared to make in the future"; that is, they become part of an "imagined community." Such studies show that there is no naturalistic principle determining the territorial boundaries of states. Nations are made by political will. Or, as Ernest Gellner expressed it: "It is nationalism which engenders nations, and not the other way round."[6] On the principle that the idea creates the political reality, it might be said that the state makes the people.

The third element is the state as an expression of the institutions that make authoritative decisions. This is the state as the government, the set of institutions established by the constitution and through which the will of the state is formulated and executed. The office of government is, in this sense, the machinery of the state. Its officers, those who assume legislative, executive, or judicial tasks, exercise sovereign powers as agents of the state.

This office of government must be distinguished from any particular administration. Although the personnel of government regularly changes, whether through the election of a new administration or appointment of new officials, the office persists. But as the US Supreme Court emphasized in *Poindexter v. Greenhow* (1885), the distinction between the government of a state and the state must also be observed. The Court emphasized that, although often treated synonymously in common speech, "the state itself is an ideal person, intangible, invisible, immutable" and must be distinguished from the government, which is only its agent.[7] That ruling reinforced a decision the Court had earlier handed down in *Texas v. White* (1868), in which the acts of secession of southern states that led to the Civil War in 1861 were held to be unlawful acts of usurping governments of the states and not acts of the states themselves. The Union of the States, Chase C.J. explained, was not an artificial contrivance: "It began among the Colonies, and grew out of common origin, mutual sympathies, kindred principles, similar interests, and geographical relations."[8]

In the late nineteenth century, German jurists sought to redefine this idea of the state by claiming that the state, understood as the union of the elements of territory, people, and ruling authority, possessed a special type of corporate personality.[9] This effectively equated the concept of the state with the third element, that of *Staatsgewalt.* Drawing a distinction between "state" and "society," they conceived the state as the institutional apparatus that regulates social forces and maintains political unity from social diversity.[10] This positivist conception of the state as a legal person, a peculiarity of German state development, has been adopted by many jurists and political scientists, often with unfortunate consequences.

Whenever the idea of the state is reduced to any one of its three elements, it is impoverished. The state is not just a synonym for the office of government—it is an abstraction that remains distinct from both government and governed. As an abstract entity encompassing territory, ruling power, and people, the state expresses the autonomy of the political worldview. It opens up a distinctive way of viewing the world, one comprising citizens and subjects who are impressed with rights and duties and who adopt a particular manner of acting, reasoning, and calculating. That is, the state gives us access to a political world of institutions and practices formed as an autonomous set of politicolegal relations. The contours of this scheme—the ways in which the state is constituted—are continually contested, but there cannot sensibly be an ongoing argument about meaning and significance without first positing the idea of the state.

Sovereignty

Sovereignty is a correlative expression of the state. The state and sovereignty are codependent: state as intelligible scheme and sovereignty its authority. And just as there is about the state, so too is there confusion about the meaning of sovereignty. This results from a failure to differentiate between the concrete and the abstract, or between sovereign and sovereignty. Just as the meaning of state—from the Latin *status*, expressing a condition of stability—has evolved, so too has the concept of sovereignty.

The term "sovereign" was coined to denote the office of a ruler. A sovereign ruler was not legally obligated to any other power. The ruler's "sovereignty" indicated the absolute character of the legal relationship between ruler and subject. This is a modern innovation: while medieval jurists had a clear sense of hierarchy, they lacked the abstraction that Jean Bodin was to call sovereignty.

In using this terminology, early modern jurists recognized that, whatever deference was paid to the king's majesty, the ruler was not exercising personal power but occupying a representative office. The implications of this only emerged gradually. First, the monarchical image of the sovereign ruler was idealized. It was accepted that "the king can do no wrong," but an idealization of the office of the king led to its institutionalization. If the king could do no wrong, errors must be attributable to "evil counsellors." The king might be beyond reproach, but his advisers must be rendered accountable. The next step was to acknowledge that "the king's will" was an institutional will: the king spoke authoritatively through his council. In this way, the sovereign came to be seen not as a person but as a corporate office with the "sovereign" powers of government no longer inhering directly in the person of the ruler. These powers were to be exercised variously through the king-in-parliament, the king-in-council, the king's ministers, and the king's courts.

Institutionalization, internal differentiation, and corporatization of the office of the sovereign ultimately led to a distinction emerging between the sovereign powers of rule and the concept of sovereignty itself. Specifically, the powers of rule could be divided, but sovereignty—expressing the absolute authority of the ruling power—could not. In 1576, Bodin marked this development, explaining that there is a "great difference between the state and the government of the state," that is, between sovereignty and the sovereign powers of government. The distinction, he suggested, "seems to me more than necessary for the good understanding of the state of every commonwealth, if a man will not cast himself headlong into an infinite labyrinth of errors."[11] Contemporary confusion comes from a failure to grasp this elementary point.

The significance of Enlightenment revolutions can now be explained. Overthrowing the claim that sovereign right is bestowed from above by God, they asserted that it was conferred from below by "the people." But, as with the idea of the state, the people can exist qua "the people" only when the "sovereign" office of government has been established. Since it is difficult to vindicate the "sovereignty of the people" as a matter of historical fact, early modern social contract theorists, such as Hobbes, Locke, and Rousseau, sought a way out of the paradox by changing the basis of the argument. Treating the social contract not as historical fact but as a thought experiment, they posited the social contract as a symbolic expression of the passage from natural state to civil order. With its virtual character acknowledged, power is not actually delegated from the people—the multitude—to their governors; the contract simply signifies the creation of the imaginative world of "the political." This is a political world in which we imagine ourselves as members of a collective association in which, as citizens, we are impressed with rights and responsibilities.

On this understanding, it is tenuous to assert that the "people is sovereign." If, as Schmitt believed, the sovereign refers to "the highest, legally independent, underived power,"[12] then in this constituted world of the political and the state, no "underived" power can exist. But although the existence of a sovereign might be contentious, the concept of sovereignty is not. Sovereignty comes into its own as a representation of the power and authority derived from the formation of this way of conceiving the world.

Sovereignty, then, vests neither in the ruler, nor in the office of government, nor in the people: it vests in the set of relationships established by these institutional actors. The trajectory of the idea of absolute authority moves from sovereign ruler, through the corporatization of the office, to a sense of sovereignty conceptually quite different from the actual institutional arrangements of government. Sovereignty expresses the autonomy and authority of this distinctively political way of viewing the world.

The Constitution of the State

Constitutionalism was originally designed as a method of establishing a regime of limited government that could protect the basic liberties of the subject. But once the concepts of state and sovereignty are brought into the frame, maintaining such a constitutional order is seen to involve more intricate considerations.

When Dieter Grimm explained that not all states have a constitution, but every state is constituted, he was drawing attention to the significant shift involved in drafting documentary constitutions.[13] His point is well taken, but our orientation is different. Constitutionalism concerns the appropriate form of the written constitution, but when we attend to the constitution of the state, we are directed to consider more precisely the way the state performs the integrative function of maintaining the political unity of a people. We are obliged to consider those factors that govern the traditional idea of the constitution, those that shape and reshape collective political identity. And it is from this perspective that constitutionalism is most clearly an ideology: already assuming the legitimacy of the established social order, it takes as its purpose the maintenance of the liberties enshrined in that order.

These different orientations were rigorously appraised by constitutional lawyers in the Weimar republic. Unexpectedly thrown into a new world of social democracy bolstered by a written constitution, they engaged in a rich methodological debate. At its core, their debates over methods and direction (*Methoden und Richtungsstreit*) involved a dispute about the status of the Weimar Constitution. Of particular significance are the challenges jurists posed to a prevailing legal positivism that claimed its authority derives from the norms of positive law enunciated in the text of that Constitution.

The distinction between the written constitution and the constitution of the state was most explicitly drawn by Rudolf Smend. Viewing the state as the cultural expression of the collective life of a people, in *Verfassung und Verfassungsrecht* (*Constitution and Constitutional Law*), Smend argued that the state's main purpose is to promote the integration of a people as a political unity through a continuous exercise of nation-building. The state's constitution acquires meaning through the immanent values of this integration rather than through legal interpretation of the formal rules of the written constitution.[14]

Schmitt's *Constitutional Theory* makes a similar claim, but he sets it in a more comprehensive analytical scheme. Distinguishing between absolute and relative conceptions of the constitution, Schmitt argues that the relative is more prominent due to a modern tendency to view the constitution as a formal document that takes effect as fundamental law. He calls this a relative conception because many provisions in constitutional texts do not concern fundamental matters. They are treated as "fundamental" only within an "approach to law that is indiscriminately formalistic and relativistic" and which distorts understanding of the constitutional order of the state.[15] It is only with reference to an absolute conception that a coherent constitutional theory can be generated.

Constitutional Theory presents a complex typology of six meanings of the absolute conception of the constitution but, replicating Jellinek's two aspects of the state, they divide into two basic groups: the ideal and the existential. Schmitt's objective is to expose the limitations of the ideal and accentuate the importance of the existential, but it is not necessary to accept his argument to recognize its utility.

The ideal sense presents the constitution as "a closed system of norms." It sketches an idealized account of the normative legal framework of the office of government as "a unified, closed *system* of higher and ultimate *norms*" having the status of fundamental law. Schmitt argues that this normativist scheme conflates state, constitution, and law: rejecting Jellinek's two aspects, the state is equated to the constitution and the constitution is equated to the legal order. The written constitution is assumed to embrace the constitution of the state. Presented as the "norm of norms," it mirrors the legal order's hierarchy of norms.[16]

In assuming the authority of the constitution as a self-positing and self-sustaining system of norms and equating it to state and law, this normativist account expresses the ideology of classical constitutionalism. Schmitt criticizes it on the ground that it must ultimately rest its claims on an existing political will and specifically from an act of the "constitution-making power" that sustains its authority. He contrasts it unfavorably with the existential sense of the constitution as "the concrete, collective condition of political unity and social order of a particular state." In this conception, the state "does not *have* a constitution . . . rather, the state *is* constitution." So Schmitt also equates state and constitution. But in his understanding, it is the constitution of the state that determines the meaning of the formal constitution. And since the state is in constant flux, that formal constitution must similarly express "the principle of the *dynamic emergence* of political unity, the process of constantly renewed *formation* and *emergence* of this *unity* from a fundamental or ultimately effective *power* and *energy*."[17]

Schmitt argued that the true meaning of constitution is revealed only through existential method. Prior to the enactment of a constitution there is an existing order, a sociopolitical reality that expresses the organization of a group's collective existence without which no constitution could be drafted. Schmitt's sociological realism stands in direct opposition to classical constitutionalism; in place of the normative scheme of the state, he asserts the primacy of material forces.

Yet, neither the normativism of classical constitutionalism nor Schmitt's materialist method fully engages with the dialectical aspects of the constitution of the state implied by Jellinek's two-sided theory. The jurist who does is Hermann Heller. Heller recognizes that the state, a more fundamental unit than the constitution, is nevertheless a "legally organized, political power." He argues that the state must adhere to legality both because of its essential integrative social function and also because it is needed to ensure its legitimacy. This double aspect is overlooked: "All the ideologists of force fail to recognize this power formation by law, while conversely all the pacifist ideologists do not want to recognize law formation by power."[18] Bringing the two elements into alignment, he offers a renovated account of the "normative power of reality."

Heller maintains that the brute fact of power can only sustain itself by winning belief in its justification. In this way, normality is transformed into normativity. But "alongside this normative force of the factually normal" is "the normalizing force of the normative." By this he means that the constitution formed by norms is able to establish its authority only on the foundation of the material constitution. The relationship between normativity and reality is dialectical: "the content and validity of a norm are never determined merely by its text, and never solely by the standpoints and characteristics of its legislators, but above all by the characteristics of the norm addressees who observe them."[19]

Heller's state theory comprehends the tension between the formal and the material, between the written constitution and the constitution of the state, highlighting its juridical significance by distinguishing between positive law and "political right." Schmitt recognized a similar distinction but maintained that the absolute constitution rested ultimately on an existential entity, the political unity of the people. For Heller, this material constitution is not simply a fact. "Every theory that begins with the alternatives, law or power, norm or will, objectivity or subjectivity," he argues, "fails to recognize the dialectical construction of the reality of the state and it goes wrong in its very starting point." Once the power-forming quality of law is appreciated, the constitution cannot be treated "as the decision of a norm-less power."[20]

Against the normativism of classical constitutionalism, Heller maintains that, although the constitution's validity and efficacy can be logically distinguished, "they nevertheless apply to the same constitutional reality, in which the assertion of one [validity] always supposes the other [efficacy] at the same time." Against the materialist account he argues that, although the state exists as an expression of collective political will, "without a normative act, a collection of people has neither a will capable of decision nor power capable of action, and at the very least it has no authority whatsoever."[21] The normative and material facets of constitutional order are mutually dependent.

These intense Weimar debates throw into relief the limitations of assuming the authority of the written constitution and the reasons why classical constitutionalism is inadequate. Every text has a context and behind the constitution is a rich history of the constitutional ordering of the state that illustrates how territory, people, and ruling apparatus have been drawn into alignment. Whatever authority the written constitution acquires must rest on the power of that narrative.

Chapter 4

THE PATH TO ORDO-CONSTITUTIONALISM

WHEN George Washington was elected the first president of the United States in 1789, what were his powers? Article II of the 1787 Constitution vests executive power in the president but neither defines it nor the organizational form of executive government. It states only that the president shall be "Commander in Chief of the Army and Navy," has the power to nominate and, with the advice and consent of the Senate, appoint ministers and other officers, and that Congress can vest the power to appoint inferior officers in the president alone.

Three executive departments, headed by the secretary of state, the secretary of war, and the secretary of the treasury, were immediately established. Alexander Hamilton, as treasury secretary, supervised the largest department, of thirty-nine clerks, as compared with Thomas Jefferson's five employees at the State Department. Excluding the military, Washington presided over a much smaller total staff in the federal government than the one hundred slaves who served him at his estate at Mount Vernon.[1] This was a world in which "the government" could truly be defined as an "executive" and the doctrine of the separation of powers, the idea of balanced government, and the classical theory of constitutionalism all made sense.

Today, the federal government is organized into fifteen departments, supplemented by a broad range of organizations, including the National Security Council and the Office of Management and Budget, grouped within the Executive Office of the President. The federal government employs over nine million people, has a budget of over $4 trillion, amounting to more than 20 percent of GNP, and assumes responsibility for a wide range of public services, including defense, homeland security, social security, health, education, energy, agriculture, urban development, and environment. The range and nature of the government's powers have been completely transformed since the era in which the role of the executive was determined according to a three-branch theory of constitutionalism.

Such changes in the nature, scale, and organizational arrangements of government in the United States have been replicated across the world. Under these dramatically altered conditions, it is widely recognized that the three-branch metaphor no longer offers an adequate account of the allocation of governmental tasks, and some have argued that the entire scheme of classical constitutionalism erects a barrier to understanding.[2] What are the implications for contemporary understandings of constitutionalism?

I address this question first by considering how government growth alters the character of the state and then by showing how, once it was realized that classical liberal ideals could not be met in an era of big government, neoliberals revised some of the basic assumptions of classical constitutionalism and devised a project appropriate to the times. Recognizing that free markets and individual liberty could be preserved only by vigilant governmental action, they advocated a new role for the constitution, that of establishing an institutional order that could guarantee the maintenance of a well-functioning market system. This new role for the constitution modifies the claims of classical constitutionalism and advances the philosophy of Ordo-constitutionalism.

The Character of the State

Jellinek's grand synthesis of nineteenth-century German state theory concluded that the state could be explained only by acknowledging its two essential aspects—the normative and the actual, *Recht* and *Macht,* the formal and the material. How do these two dimensions of the state function in the era of big government? This was the question that remained just below the surface of the Weimar jurists' debates over method. These debates, driven by the rise of what Sartori called "intense politics"—the coming of democracy, the adoption of legislation as the primary vehicle of law-making, and the rise of governing in an administrative mode—were replicated across the Western world during the early decades of the twentieth century.

These developments generated a series of related crises in conceptions of law, constitution, and state. Law came to be understood simply as a set of rules enacted by the legislature and mainly expressing the political will of government rather than parliamentary deliberation. Parliamentary deliberation was further etiolated by virtue of primary legislation being increasingly supplemented by executive law-making through regulations, directives, and decrees. Variously referred to as the "statutorification of law" and "motorization of legislation," these changes provoked wide-ranging debate about the nature of law in modernity.[3]

These changing forms of law gave rise to constitutional questions, especially as notions of the separation of powers and balanced government waned and governments responded to interwar crises with increased resort to emergency provisions within the constitution. And these legal and constitutional developments in turn exposed even more basic dilemmas concerning the character of the modern state. Over many centuries, argues Schmitt, "the sweeping horizons of European jurisprudence" have been determined by two competing movements: "on the one side, to theology, metaphysics and philosophy; on the other, to mere technical craft." But in the twentieth century, threats no longer came from theology and only occasionally from metaphysics; instead, they came from "an untrammeled technicism which uses state law as a tool."[4]

The implications for the state were exposed most dramatically in 1933 by the overthrow of the Weimar Constitution by the Nazi dictatorship. In *Behemoth,* Franz Neumann advanced a materialist account of National Socialism, arguing that it amounted to a totalitarian version of monopoly capitalism. Its workings had destroyed any authentic sense of the state and, by reducing law to a mere instrument of domination, it had established a regime of lawlessness and anarchy.[5] But his erstwhile law partner, Ernst Fraenkel, presented a more nuanced analysis. Far from overthrowing the state, argues Fraenkel, the Nazi dictatorship exploited the distinction between its two aspects. Under the Nazi regime, the state divided into two coexisting aspects: the normative state (*Normenstaat*), a system structured by statutes and court orders, and the prerogative state (*Maßnahmenstaat*), a set of measures established in accordance with the exigencies of party rule.

Fraenkel argues that the emergence of this "dual state" enabled Hitler, after grasping power, "to transform the constitutional and temporary dictatorship (intended to restore public order) into an unconstitutional and permanent dictatorship." By eliminating restraints on police powers, abolishing judicial review, and elevating the Nazi party into its primary decision-making body, the prerogative state became a regime of institutionalized lawlessness. Since its limits were not externally determined but "imposed by the Prerogative State itself," its chief characteristic was "the complete abolition of the inviolability of law." But, critically, the normative state was still a necessary—though dependent—complement, making the two parts "constitute an interdependent whole."[6]

The main function of the normative state was to lend an edifice of formal rationality to the regime. It functioned as the legal framework for market activities and other kinds of contractual relations and for regulating relations between government and business. Even though the governing powers could unilaterally change the rules of the game, some rules were indispensable for securing a predictable basis for economic activity. Driven by a perverse and irrational ideology, the Nazi regime still needed the edifice of a normative order to supply the stability that enabled capitalism to flourish.

Fraenkel's thesis about the dual state (*der Doppelstaat*) recognizes that the Nazi regime totally supplanted the *Rechtsstaat*. In the *Rechtsstaat* "the courts control the executive branch of the government in the interests of legality," whereas in the *Doppelstaat* "the police power controls the courts in the interest of political expediency."[7] But the regime was more than a lawless dictatorship: the substantive irrationality of the prerogative state was bolstered—and in certain respects legitimated—by the formal rationality of the normative state.

The Nazi dictatorship, though a deviant case, can still be situated within the framework of the two-sided theory of the state. In less extreme circumstances, the dialectic by which the modern state functions is not, as in the Nazi regime, between formal rationality and substantive irrationality but between the right and the good—that is, between formal and substantive rationality. The value of such a framework is highlighted in Michael Oakeshott's study of the character of the modern European state. For Oakeshott, the modern state expresses "an unresolved tension between the two irreconcilable dispositions," between the state as a set of rules of conduct and the state as a corporation established to further certain designated purposes. Labeling these two dispositions *societas* and *universitas,* he emphasizes that they are not alternative accounts of the nature of the state but rather the "specification of the self-division of this ambiguous character."[8]

Oakeshott explains that many theorists have commonly identified the state as *societas*—that is, as a formal rule-based relationship in which the conditions of association are specified by a system of law. But while the rule of law flourishes in theory, this disposition has not prevailed in practice. What he calls the "unpurged relic of 'lordship' hidden in the office of modern monarchs" has been so exploited by their successors that the modern state is now recognized as a corporation, its territory an estate, its government a form of estate-management, and its laws a set of rules for advancing the enterprise. Oakeshott attributes this development mainly to governmental responses to the question of social justice. In their attempts to resolve this question, governments have commanded resources, modified laws by making provisions for substantive benefits, promoted administrative regulation at the expense of judicial control, and overlaid civil rule with a notion of teleocratic rule.[9]

Oakeshott's account of the modern state as an amalgam of two antagonistic ideal types replicates Jellinek's two-sided theory of the state. Just as Jellinek had argued that the state was not a purely normative construct of *Recht* nor a social-historical phenomenon of *Macht,* so Oakeshott contends that the state exists by virtue of "a political imagination which is itself constituted in a tension" between a rule-based and purposive order. Both would recognize Fraenkel's conceptual framework of the Nazi regime as a "dual state" comprising a division between a normative order functioning alongside a state of measures. In Fraenkel's study it is easy to conceive the "prerogative state" as a corrupt and debased form. But Oakeshott's important point is that the conjunction of these divergent modes remains "the most effective apparatus for understanding the actual complexity of the state."[10]

Too many jurists assume that the state is a rule-based order, and this leads them unreflectively to adopt the nostrums of classical constitutionalism. A less ideologically inflected analysis is needed. For assistance, we might invoke Paul Kahn's study of the evolution of the American constitutional regime. In *The Origins of Order,* Kahn argues that when imagining constitutional order we are held captive by models, two of which—project and system—have been particularly influential.

For Kahn, modernity is signified by our aspiration for autonomy, an aspiration that finds expression in political imagination. "Revolution in practice and social contract in theory are both political responses to this need for autonomy." But alongside this is the desire for belonging, for being part of something more like an inherited *system* than a self-created *project*. And the overriding characteristic of modernity is that it is "a condition under which no matter which perspective we choose, we will be subject to criticism from the other perspective." Project and system, the aspiration for freedom, and the desire for belonging "can never be brought into a stable alignment."[11]

Kahn presents his thesis through a study of US constitutional development. The constitutional project is to establish a system that endures, yet at the same time, a constitution too strictly constrained by past decisions "would become our prison, rather than an expression of our capacity for self-government." Politics begins with the design of a constitutional order, that is, as a project made by "the people." Having faith in the project demands integrity with the intentions of the author: "Project is the language of the first-person plural: We the people declare and we act."[12] Classical constitutionalism, then, is a project in which the ends are the maintenance of the basic rights of the citizen, and the means are provided by constitutional design.

For most of the nineteenth century, the Constitution as project was dominant. Lincoln's Gettysburg Address, opening with the claim that "four score and seven years ago our fathers brought forth on this continent, a new nation, conceived in Liberty, and dedicated to the proposition that all men are created equal," is exemplary. But in the period after the Civil War the idea of "the living constitution" gained influence: project was increasingly challenged by system. By the end of the century, the notion of a fixed, written constitution was an anachronism, not least because the idea of a project is limited by the imagination of its author, whereas system knows no such bounds. The narrative of the constitutional project had a precise beginning in the American Revolution. But from the perspective of system, "the very idea of a beginning is an error," one that "confuses the appearance of deliberate intentions with the reality of immanent order."[13]

When conceived as system, "the *real* Constitution is not the written text, but written customs and practice and belief." Rather than "a project put in place through deliberate intentional action in 1789," it is "an immanent order of reason—a system—that has no definite beginning and operates quite independently of the deliberate efforts of the Founders." Constitutional order is seen as a product of experience and growth. Consequently, legal science "can no more make political order than biology can make organic order." The role of legal science is merely to reveal "the systemic character realized in and through natural growth."[14]

There are many ramifications of Kahn's study, but its value at this stage of our inquiry is to highlight parallels between Jellinek and Oakeshott's two-sided theories of the state and Kahn's divergent conceptions of constitutional order. The constitution as an immanent normative scheme has affinities with the idea of the state as a rule system (*Recht / societas*), while the narrative of project, especially with respect to its means-end rationality and the constitution as the expression of political will, is analogous to the idea of the state as a purposive entity (*Macht / universitas*). Classical constitutionalism accentuates the former and neglects the latter. By bringing these into closer alignment, the challenges of reviving constitutionalism in a world of big government are clear.

The Constitution of Liberty

In the narrative of the constitution as project, the social is subordinate to the political: the political consists of a collective will that adopts the constitution to advance social change. But in the narrative of system, the political is subordinate to the social. There is no concept of the sovereign will in a social system that evolves historically, only a prevailing sense of right generated by the configuration of social forces. Kahn argues that the tension between these two narratives is an intrinsic feature of modernity, and it would therefore be wrong to think of them "as a problem to be resolved."[15]

Contrary to such jurists as Jellinek, Oakeshott, and Kahn, who treat these irreconcilable dimensions of state and constitution as fixed features of modernity, classical liberals maintain that the two dimensions represent true and debased conceptions. No one has done more to advance this argument than Friedrich Hayek. Drawing on a long lineage of liberal thought, Hayek claims that such two-sided doctrines are unfortunate by-products of the ideas of the Enlightenment. The entire narrative of project is a form of Cartesian rationalism he calls "constructivist rationalism"—the belief that society can be constructed anew through an exercise of human reason. For Hayek, this erroneous belief has fueled the tremendous growth of modern government and is the source of socialist ideas that are destroying freedom and ushering in a new era of servitude.

The case was first presented in 1944 in his short book *The Road to Serfdom*. Arguing that we have been progressively moving away from "the basic ideas on which Western civilization has been built," Hayek maintains that we are creating modern regimes of governmental planning that institute "arbitrary rule" and erode "the great principles known as the Rule of Law." National Socialism, then, was not "an irrationalist movement without intellectual background" but "the culmination of a long evolution of thought." It was a "lamentable fact" that Western democracies, in their dealings with dictators, had revealed "confusion about their own ideals and the nature of the differences which separated them from the enemy." So many features of Hitler's system, he argues, are integral parts of our own contemporary systems of government. If freedom is to be restored, we must start by reevaluating the liberal ideals of the Enlightenment era.[16]

Hayek's reevaluation takes the form of two major works, *The Constitution of Liberty* (1960) and his three-volume study, *Law, Legislation and Liberty* (1973–1979). In the former, he emphasizes that "the great aim of the struggle for liberty has been equality before the law," a principle leading inexorably to the demand for everyone to share in the making of law. This is the point at which classical liberalism and democracy not only meet but also where views diverge. This is because liberalism "is concerned mainly with limiting the coercive powers of all government," whereas the democrat "knows only one limit to government—current majority opinion." Herein lies the confusion: whereas the liberal holds to the idea of law as a set of general rules of conduct, the democrat is liable to call a specific command "law" merely because it emanates from the legislative authority, a belief that leads to legislation becoming "the chief instrument of oppression."[17]

Hayek argues that the only solution is the reinvigoration of classical constitutionalism. This requires that all power "be exercised according to commonly accepted principles" and all persons on whom power is conferred being "selected because it is thought that they are most likely to do what is right." A free society, he emphasizes, "needs permanent means of restricting the powers of government." This can only be realized within a constitutional system founded on the separation of powers and that establishes the rule of law as a metalegal doctrine requiring that all laws conform to certain principles and all governmental powers be subject to its ideals.[18]

It is, however, only in *Law, Legislation and Liberty* that the full implications of Hayek's arguments are made explicit. Only after restating the classical doctrine of constitutionalism in the 1960 volume did he come to realize why constitutionalism had not gained enough support in the modern era. He gradually became conscious of "three fundamental insights which have never been adequately expanded," and therefore devotes this three-volume study to each of them.[19] The first is that there are fundamental differences between a spontaneous order and an organization—between what Kahn calls system and project—differences inherent in the two kinds of "laws" that prevail in each. The second insight is that the modern principle of social justice only has meaning within a purposive organization. The third is that a system of government in which the representative body of the legislature both enacts the rules of just conduct and directs governmental action necessarily leads to the gradual transformation of the spontaneous order of a free society into a totalitarian regime.

Of particular importance is his critique of what he calls the constructivist rationalist fallacy, the assumption that all social institutions are the product of deliberate design. Attributable to our unbounded confidence in science, this rests on a fiction of the "synoptic delusion," the belief that "all the relevant facts are known to some one mind, and that it is possible to construct from this knowledge of the particulars a desirable social order."[20] He then founds his central argument on a distinction between two kinds of order, those that are made and those that have grown. The former, which he calls *taxis,* is constructed, the type of order implied by organization. The latter, called *cosmos,* is spontaneous order, the type of order implied by organism. While the former is the product of rational design, the complexity of the latter is not limited to what the human mind can grasp.

This distinction between types of order is then extended first to embrace government and society, with government being an organizational mechanism and society a consequence of organic evolution, and then between legislation and law. Arguing that law is much older than legislation, Hayek distinguishes between "made law," or *thesis,* and "grown law," or *nomos.* Understood as a set of rules of conduct, *nomos* is the product of spontaneous growth. It may require the deliberate efforts of judges and jurists to improve the existing system of law by incrementally laying down new rules, but this law is both the outcome of a process of evolution and depends on lawyers striving to make the system coherent. By contrast, "the law of organization of government" consists either of directions to particular officers or agencies, which are more appropriately described as "the regulations or by-laws of government," or, in the case of constitutional law, is better understood as "a superstructure erected to secure the maintenance of *the law,* rather than . . . the source of all other law."[21]

Hayek's critique of constructivism indicates why the attempt of modern governments to realize "social justice" through the use of legislation is a "mirage." In his second volume he goes on to argue that social justice is a "vacuous concept," an "incubus which today makes fine sentiments the instruments for the destruction of all values of a free civilization."[22] His third volume is of particular interest because it outlines "a model constitution."[23]

The basic purpose of the constitution, he explains, must be to prevent all authorities, including the legislature, from imposing arbitrary restraints on liberty. It must therefore include a clause stating that any restriction on liberty could be imposed "only in accordance with the recognised rules of just conduct," which should also contain "a definition of what can be law in this narrow sense of *nomos*." Such a clause, he suggests, would achieve more than bills of rights were meant to secure, and "it would make any separate enumeration of a list of special protected fundamental rights unnecessary."[24] With respect to constitutional design, he argues that since legislation should be enacted in accordance with opinion rather than interests, only those above the age of forty-five can select representatives to the Legislative Assembly. That assembly, in turn, would elect members of the Government Assembly. Adherence to the "rules of just conduct" would then be policed by a constitutional court.[25]

Hayek's trilogy slowly reveals the radical nature of his original proposal to reinvigorate classical constitutionalism. He resolves the tension implied by all dualistic theories of state and constitution—between *Recht* and *Macht*, *Normenstaat* and *Maßnahmenstaat*, *societas* and *universitas*, system and project—by rejecting entirely the legitimacy of all governmental activities that use power, measures, and enterprise for the purpose of delivering "the good." But he goes even further. He begins in *The Constitution of Liberty* by committing to the idea of limited government, the values of the *Rechtsstaat*, and the precepts of classical constitutionalism. He eventually comes to realize, though, that even this regime is founded on an acceptance of the legitimacy of the state as a bounded political community. It is, after all, the idea of boundedness at the root of a sense of solidarity that drives notions of social justice. Consequently, he ends up repudiating the entire political worldview on which concepts of state, sovereignty, authority, and constitution—and, ultimately, classical constitutionalism—have been founded.

Freedom, it would appear, can only exist in the evolving order of society. For Hayek, liberalism "is no longer a state ideology but a theory of the free

society that transcends political boundaries."[26] Institutional mechanisms to
limit the power of the state, he comes to realize, will never achieve their os-
tensible objectives. To protect liberty, the social must be reconceived in terms
that renounce the entire political worldview. The constitution of liberty demands the transcendence of classical constitutionalism's precepts.

Ordo-constitutionalism

Hayek argues that freedom depends on the flourishing of spontaneous orders
of society, especially those of markets and law. To realize this aim, any sense
of a state teleology or of a constitutional project must be abandoned. Given
the world as we know it, these are patently unrealistic ideals. In the mid-
twentieth century, however, a group of German scholars came together who
shared Hayek's liberal values but disagreed over his method. They agreed that
the preservation of markets and law was vital to the maintenance of liberty
but realized that such systems do not develop spontaneously. For such systems to flourish, an order must be imposed. Drawing on Aquinas's scholastic
philosophy of ordered existence,[27] the school of Ordo-liberalism argued the
need for a robust institutional framework to maintain a well-functioning
market system.[28] This was the state's essential task. Classical constitutionalism, they maintained, could only be realized through a state project. The
state's purpose must be to establish an "economic constitution," a framework
for a market order and a set of duties imposed on public authorities to preserve it.

The claim of their "Ordo Manifesto" of 1936 was "to bring scientific reasoning, as displayed in jurisprudence and political economy, into effect for
the purpose of constructing and reorganizing the economic system." And
because the various sectors of the economy are interconnected, "the treatment of all practical politico-legal and politico-economic questions must be
keyed to the idea of the economic constitution."[29] This order-based method
reconciled the values of economic efficiency and individual freedom. It also
restored the political to a central role but placed it firmly in the service of
market freedoms.

Driving the German Ordo-liberal project was the experience and cata-
strophic collapse of the Weimar Republic. Contrary to classical liberals,
Ordo-liberals recognized that the laissez-faire policies of the Weimar era had

led directly to the emergence of monopoly or cartel-dominated capitalism. Despite its social-democratic credentials, the Weimar Constitution lacked a strong legal framework to prevent this misuse of economic power.

Walter Eucken, one of the leaders of the Freiburg school of Ordo-liberalism, argued that the two economic orders—a centrally planned economy determined by the state and an exchange-based economy dependent on individual interactions—both lead to destructive outcomes. A planned economy was incompatible with the rule of law, and an exchange-based order, though formally compatible with the rule of law, produced an accumulation of private power that eroded the freedoms ostensibly protected by the rule of law.[30] If economics and politics, market and state, could not work in harmony, they would destroy each other. The solution, Ordo-liberals argued, was a constitutional order that would outlaw monopoly power and impose an obligation on the state to preserve competitive free markets. This thesis gave birth to the principle of *Ordo-constitutionalism*.

Ordo-constitutionalism postulates the establishment of a constitution that imposes duties on public authorities to safeguard the operation of the private market system. Its mantra is "the free economy and the strong state." The constitution must guarantee a market-based economic order and prohibit government from becoming an active agent in economic activity. Just as the liberal democratic constitution ensures a properly operating system of representative democracy, a constitution structured on Ordo-liberal lines must perform the similarly important function of guaranteeing a properly operating market system. This requires a strong but constitutionally restrained state.

This argument was advanced by Franz Böhm in his paper on "the rule of law in a market economy." For Böhm, classical liberals misunderstand modern society if they see it in terms of the individual and the state. Classical liberalism overlooks the fact that the connection of the individual to the state is refracted through the medium of what he calls "the private law society," the clubs, associations, and competitive mechanisms that private law supports but "are not constituents of the political constitution." This private law society—more commonly known as "civil society"—should be controlled by "an automatically functioning coordination system" that would "relieve the state of the task of maintaining central economic controls." In this type of regime, the "constitutionally determined mandate to legislator and government is to create, preserve and manage that regulative framework which guarantees the functioning of the free market as an allocation device."[31]

These Ordo-liberal ideas helped shape the Federal Republic of Germany's postwar constitutional settlement. Monetary policy and the maintenance of price stability enforced by a central bank independent of all political influence came to symbolize the so-called German economic miracle (*Wirtschaftswunder*). It was rarely made explicit, but the "social market economy" was established on the foundation of a comprehensive constitutional order. This included an "eternity clause" to ensure that certain arrangements and rights could never be the subject of constitutional amendment, making it possible for the German Federal Constitutional Court to reject the classical liberal distinction between public and private and assert that the Basic Law erects "an order of objective values" that permeates the entire regime.[32]

Ordo-constitutionalism has now become an influential constitutional model.[33] Based on the principle of "militant"—meaning "constrained"—democracy, it promotes a regime that rejects the classical liberal stance of maintaining neutrality over ends in favor of explicit protection of the liberal order.[34] Its characteristic feature is a range of counterdemocratic mechanisms that ensure that electoral majorities are prohibited from undermining the liberal order instituted by the exercise of the people's constitutive power.[35] An independent judiciary acting as guardian of the constitution and the protector of basic rights is absolutely necessary, as is an independent central bank needed to protect monetary policy from political influence. Ordo-constitutionalism moves beyond the classical liberal distinction between state and society, public and private, according to which the constitution constrains government to allow private freedoms to prosper. Coming into its own in the age of constitutionalism, Ordo-constitutionalism acknowledges the idea of the total constitution, imposes major restrictions on democratic decision-making, and advances a powerful project designed to protect a specific system.

PART II

Elements of Constitutional Democracy

Chapter 5

CONSTITUENT POWER

THE authority of the constitution rests on it having been drafted in the name of "the people." Through an exercise of their constitution-making power, the people engage in an act of collective self-government. This acknowledges the principle of democracy in constitutional thought. First formulated with precision during the American and French revolutions, the origins of this constituent power can be traced to seventeenth-century revisions to Bodin's concept of sovereignty. Particularly influential was the work of Calvinist jurists who asserted that the state is founded on a double sovereignty: "personal" sovereignty (*majestas personalis*) might be held by the prince, but "real" sovereignty (*majestas realis*) lies with the people.[1] This exposed the kernel of a distinction between the constituted power that vests in the office of government and the constituent power of the people that authorizes the establishment of the office of government.

These revisions are found in John Locke's *Second Treatise of Government*. Locke explains that political society is an original compact entered into by a freely consenting people to establish a fixed system of government that could guarantee the protection of their property. If the government ever breaches the terms of this compact, they are placed in "a state of War with the People," who have "a Right to resume their original Liberty, and, by the Establishment of a new Legislative (such as they shall think fit) provide for their own Safety and Security."[2] Locke may not use the term "constituent power," but it is the basis of his scheme of government. By recognizing that the people have the right to overthrow the regime if the terms of the governing trust are breached, he resolves the issue of resistance to authority that had always been ambiguous in the practices of medieval constitutionalism.[3]

In 1776, when the American colonists broke away from the British Crown, their Declaration of Independence closely followed the logic of Locke's argument. The preamble states that "to secure these [unalienable] rights [of Life, Liberty and the pursuit of Happiness] Governments are instituted among men, deriving their just powers from the consent of the governed." It continues that "whenever any Form of Government becomes destructive to these ends, it is the Right of the People to alter or to abolish it, and to institute new Government, laying its foundation on such principles and organizing its powers in such form, as to them shall seem most likely to effect their Safety and Happiness."[4] Through an exercise of constituent power, the American colonists asserted their right to break from the original compact with the British Crown and to establish a new type of government. The new regime was established in the federal Constitution of 1787, the world's first modern constitution.

Sieyes and the French Revolution

The French Revolution soon followed. It began on 17 June 1789, when the meeting of the Third Estate declared itself to be the National Assembly. That momentous declaration had been drafted by Emmanuel-Joseph Sieyes, who explained its significance in his pamphlet *What Is the Third Estate?*[5] Faced with the imminent bankruptcy of the state, the king had convened a meeting of the Estates-General as a grand advisory assembly. Claiming that France was experiencing a much deeper bankruptcy of the entire political order, Sieyes called instead for a constituent assembly that might address the case for fundamental constitutional reform. The ancien régime had lost its authority, he argued, and prime responsibility lay with the nobility. Far from being producers of the nation's resources, they had become its most avaricious consumers. No longer an aristocracy charged with the task of governing, they had become a caste with privileges but no corresponding duties, in effect seceding from the nation and becoming its enemies.

Sieyes's pamphlet proclaimed the Third Estate the nation itself. Reconstituting the meeting as the National Assembly, they demanded that sovereign authority be transferred from the king to that body, initiating both a political and a legal revolution. On 4 August 1789, the newly established National (Constituent) Assembly removed the privileges of nobles and clergy, thereby abolishing feudalism and establishing the principle of equality before the law. The assembly then established a committee to prepare a draft constitution, and on 26 August adopted the *Declaration of the Rights of Man and the Citizen* as its preamble. This proclaimed that "men are born and remain free and equal in rights" (Art. 1), that the aim of "political association is the preservation of the natural and imprescriptible rights of man" (Art. 2), that "sovereignty resides essentially in the nation" (Art. 3), that law is "the expression of the general will" (Art. 6), and that, without a defined separation of powers, a society "has no constitution at all" (Art. 16).

For Sieyes, the nation is created by a social contract that transforms an aggregate of individuals into a unified body politic with a common will. The nation, he explains, "exists prior to everything; it is the origin of everything. Its will is always legal. It is the law itself." It follows that the nation, which "cannot alienate or prohibit its right to will," is not bound by any prior constitution. As the bearer of constituent power, the nation determines the constitutional form of the state.[6]

Today it is accepted that constitutional law is fundamental law. The point Sieyes makes is that while the law of the constitution may take effect as fundamental law with respect to the institutions of government, the constitution itself is established by the higher authority of the nation. In this, Sieyes is following Rousseau, though he disagrees with him on the manner of forming a national will. Rousseau had claimed that sovereignty could not be represented because the moment a people give themselves representatives, it is no longer free.[7] Sieyes, by contrast, maintains that a constitution can only be made by representatives. Rousseau had extolled the constitutions of the ancient republics, but in the modern state some political division of labor is necessary. The basic law, Sieyes explains, is not an idealized "general will" but rather a "common will" that, though formulated by a representative body, is as valid as that of the nation itself.

Lucia Rubinelli has argued that in Sieyes's account, the power of the people is limited exclusively to authorizing the constitution, which means that, once adopted, "the people's constituent power is present only indirectly."[8] She therefore claims that Sieyes devised the concept not as an expression of popular sovereignty but as a replacement for it.[9] Concerned that sovereignty implied too much absolute power, which if transferred from the king to the people could lead to its despotic abuse, he posited the people's constituent power as an extraordinary power, to be exercised only at certain founding moments.

Rubinelli's claim is reinforced by Sieyes's treatment of representation. Acknowledging the nation as the bearer of constituent power, he argues that since the nation cannot in reality assemble whenever conditions require, it is obliged to entrust this power to a representative body. This body of extraordinary representatives acts as "a surrogate for an assembly of that nation" and is distinguished from the ordinary representatives who are entrusted only with "that portion of the common will that is necessary for good social administration." And yet these two groups could comprise the self-same individuals, albeit with distinct powers—one acting as an ordinary legislature whereas the other, exercising constituent power, deliberating "as would the nation itself" to establish the Constitution.[10]

Sieyes's account was explicitly designed to appeal to the bourgeoisie, who anticipated becoming the governing class of an emerging commercial society. Since this commercial society is founded on productive work and the division of labor, we see why Sieyes would extend a similar division of labor to the political domain.[11] His account of constituent power underpins the formation of a bourgeois expression of constitutional democracy.

Having excluded the nobility from the political nation, Sieyes goes on to exclude women, beggars, vagabonds, domestic servants, and anyone dependent on a master. The nation's representatives must be limited to that class within the Third Estate "with the kind of ease that enables a man to be given a liberal education, to cultivate his reason, and to take an interest in public affairs."[12] Sieyes therefore argues first "that the Third Estate is the entire nation because its members do all the useful work of society and that the nobility is alien to the nation because of its idleness" and second that the legitimate representatives of the people are "those classes of the Third Estate whose wealth frees them from the daily press of labor and gives them sufficient leisure to concern themselves with public affairs."[13] His account legitimates the transfer of political power from the aristocracy to the bourgeoisie.

Constituent Power and Constitutionalism

Following these revolutionary movements of the late eighteenth century, many nation-states facing existential crises adopted a constitution as a sign of refounding. Such moments brought into clearer focus the hierarchical relationship between ordinary law, constitutional law, and constituent power. But once the new regime had stabilized its rule and the constitution established its authority, constituent power seemed destined to become a marginal, if not redundant, concept. Since the constitution makes a provision for change through the power of amendment, there is no reason to fall back on the potentially unruly notion that governmental authority depended on the will of the multitude.[14]

The concept of constituent power was retained, but its meaning gradually altered. Specifically, constitutional lawyers devised a doctrine of "derived constituent power," a power that vested in special assemblies charged with the task of constitutional amendment or revision. As the French jurist Raymond Carré de Malberg explained, "Constituent power can be conceived as an essentially legal power only so long as it has its origin in an anterior statutory order and is exercised in accordance with that pre-existing order."[15] The effect was to absorb constituent power into constituted power, which meant that it could be reinterpreted as a principle of constitutionalism, reinforcing the permanence of the constitution itself.

In practice, however, the ambition to transform constituent power into a special category of constituted power was not so easily realized. The French experience was evidence of their serious difficulty in establishing a constitution that could bring a halt to the revolution.[16] Contrary to the orthodox interpretation of constitutional lawyers, it became clear that constituent power was not available for purely liberal purposes.[17] Ernst-Wolfgang Böckenförde maintained that constituent power "was not transferrable to the monarch, because his position of power . . . stood within an entirely different legitimatory context."[18] But other jurists have argued that constituent power is simply the political will that establishes a constitution, and it was in this sense that Napoleon could assert "I am the constituent power."[19] Consequently, in the period after 1815, French constitutional development was driven by "the clash between monarchy and popular sovereignty as two formative political principles," and in this dispute "the monarch also laid claim to the constituent power."[20]

The most significant reason why constituent power could not be absorbed into constitutionalism is because of ambiguities in Sieyes's account. It is axiomatic that constituent power vests in "the nation," but Sieyes used that term in two distinct senses. Its idealized meaning was "a body of associates living under a common law," in which sense the nation is "the origin of everything."[21] But Sieyes also gave the term the more concrete meaning as a power located in the governing class. Constitutional scholars have since used the difference between abstract and concrete meanings—between norm and fact, formal and material—to advance conflicting accounts. This explains why his claim that constituent power could replace sovereignty in modern constitutional thought proved ill-founded. The meaning of constituent power remains contested because it is inextricably bound up with competing conceptions of sovereignty.

Constituent Power as Sovereign Power

In the early twentieth century, the controversy over constituent power that had shaped nineteenth-century French debates acquired wider import. The toppling of European monarchies and their replacement by constitutional democracies forced a return to first principles. Nowhere were constitutional debates more intense than in Germany. The German Revolution of 1918 transferred authority from the kaiser to the people, a shift symbolized by the declaration in Article I of the 1919 Constitution that "the power of rule (*die Staatsgewalt*) derives from the people." But many issues concerning the legitimacy of the new constitutional order remained unresolved, for guidance on which jurists often returned to the French revolutionary debates.[22]

As an explanation of the meaning and status of constituent power, Carl Schmitt provides the most forthright answer: the constitution is established by an exercise of sovereign will, a specific political decision given jural form as constituent power. This was rejected by those such as Hans Kelsen who, asserting the autonomy of law, equates the state with the legal order, treats the state's authority as a presupposition of legal thought, and eliminates constituent power as a category of legal thought.[23] Schmitt, however, maintains that the attempt to sever legal norms from political facts distorts both legal knowledge and the nature of constitutional arrangements.

For Schmitt, the state is no abstract idea. It is the product of an actual historical process that yields the relative homogeneity of a people. As the concrete condition of political unity, the state precedes the written constitution. He argues that to counter competing interests within the state, a sovereign power able to impose its will in response to any threats to political unity is needed. In normal times, this sovereign remains hidden, and formal constitutional norms are sufficient to resolve disputes. But the sovereign is always necessary because issues that threaten unity can never be predicted. For Schmitt, the sovereign is the agent that identifies that threat and resolves it, in which situation the law—including constitutional law—recedes, but the state, the condition of political unity, remains.[24] This is the sovereign presuming to exercise constituent power.

For Schmitt, then, constituent power is the political will that determines the institutional form of the state. It establishes the constitution but, contrary to Sieyes, it is a power that continues to uphold the authority of the constitution. The question of who bears constituent power is circumstantial. Constituent power is exercised in the name of the people, but since "the people" do so only through representatives, who then is best able to represent the people? In Weimar Germany, Schmitt argued that the president, directly elected by the people as the republican version of the monarch, holds the constituent power. Schmitt presents a legal analysis of presidential power, but his basic point is that the president is more than a mere creature of the constitution. The president is the agent who can maintain unity and safeguard the "substance" of the constitution.[25]

This concrete conception of constituent power not only expresses the political will that makes the formal constitution but also maintains the constitutional order of the state. Constituent power is commonly thought of as the will of the people in whose name the constitution is adopted. But this abstraction does not answer the question of who is authorized to speak in the name of the people. Schmitt's answer is that "whoever decides on the exception is sovereign." Sovereignty is simply "the highest, legally independent, underived power."[26] Collapsing the abstract into the concrete, it follows that constituent power is an expression of the "highest, legally independent" political will. It is the essential foundation of legal normativity, the product of "actual interests," and it both establishes the constitution and maintains a sense of continuing unity. Making use of Sieyes's analysis, Schmitt nonetheless goes far beyond the limits Sieyes imposed.

Sovereignty and Constituent Power

During the Weimar debates Heller had sided with Schmitt against Kelsen. Accepting the distinction between the formal constitution and the substantive constitution of the state, he nevertheless could not agree with Schmitt's explanation for it. The normative scheme of the constitution must be distinguished from the political reality through which it acquires authority, but because law has a "power-forming quality" the constitution could not be the decision of a normless power. Whether the bearer of constituent power is the prince or the people, Heller argues that that power is not acquired existentially; it must be generated through the normative order of the state.[27]

Heller's critique presents an alternative conception of constituent power that derives from Schmitt's determined refusal to accept any abstract conception of sovereignty. He accepts Schmitt's account of the role of the sovereign. But he cannot accept Schmitt's rejection of the political worldview wherein we imagine ourselves as citizens with powers and rights, able to reflect on the terms by which the collective association—the state—is organized. In Heller's view, no entity, whether the people or the prince, has "legally independent, underived power." The standing of the sovereign remains unsettled, but sovereignty, the symbol of power and authority created in that worldview, is not.

If sovereignty represents the set of relations generated through the establishment of a political worldview, what is the role of constituent power? In Locke's account, the concept conferred the right of rebellion: if the constituted authority breaches the terms of trust, power reverts to the people. But constituent power in this case means more than a de facto power relationship: it rests on the distinction between the right of the constituted authority to make law and the right by which this power to make law is conferred, the latter being the kind of political right Rousseau refers to in *The Social Contract*. Constituent power can then be more precisely called "constituent right," what Heller called *Rechtsgrundsätze*. Constituent right expresses not so much the founding ideals of the constitution but rather the political dynamic through which those ideals strive to be realized.

Constituent power, then, expresses the way in which the normative scheme of the constitution changes in response to new material circumstances. It expresses a dialectic of political right (*droit politique*), a power-generating quality that constantly irritates the institutionalized form of constituted authority. Contrary to Schmitt's materialist account, constituent power is not the same as the will of a multitude or of an entity that enforces unity. Reducing power to a particular will ignores the symbolic dimension of the political. Constituent power is generated when the multitude can be represented not just as the will of a majority but—in some senses at least—of everyone. But contrary to Kelsen's normativist account, the concept cannot be entirely absorbed into the normative scheme of the constitution.[28] This would simply eliminate the tension that gives the political worldview its open and provisional quality. This is the normativist fallacy, the realization of which would lead not to "the rule of law"—an impossible dream—but to the destruction of political freedom.

Constituent Power Defined

The concept of constituent power was formulated in the late eighteenth century as part of a movement to jettison the absolutist connotations of sovereignty. In its stead would be the power of representatives of the people to draft a constitution to define the legitimate powers and duties of governing institutions. It was a key component of a liberal progressive movement from traditional to modern in thought, from feudalism to capitalism in society, from aristocracy to bourgeoisie as the ruling power, and from traditional to legal-rational claims to authority. Its endpoint was the establishment of constitutional democracy.

But the constitution is not a self-enforcing document whose authority can simply be assumed, and in this important respect the issue of sovereignty persists. Because of this, it is unconvincing to claim that constituent power is invoked only at the enactment of the constitution and thereafter converts into a type of constituted power. Sieyes may have invoked constituent power to replace a notion of sovereignty, but the two concepts remain bound together.

Sovereignty has nevertheless been evolving in two different ways, the concrete and the abstract, each of which identifies constituent power as not just the power that makes the constitution but also that which, through constitutional development, maintains governmental authority. The way it has evolved reflects differing understandings of sovereignty that, in turn, yield different conceptions of law. The concrete, in which sovereignty is simply the power of a sovereign, presents law as *voluntas* (will). The abstract, in which sovereignty is a set of politicolegal relations, conceives law as *ratio* and specifically as *ratio status,* political reason.

From this account, we discern, first, that a constitution cannot be assumed to have eliminated sovereign power such that all politicolegal relations are refracted through its formal structures. That is, it cannot be assumed that the constitution expresses the way the state is constituted, this being the type of normativist method promoted by constitutionalism, which seeks to eliminate constituent power as a category of constitutional thought. We see, second, that the issue of sovereignty remains and that it evolves along two tracks. The concrete treats the sovereign as the constituent power that works to preserve the political unity of the state, occasionally by having to displace certain provisions of the constitution.[29] The abstract treats sovereignty as an expression of a dialectic of constituent right, an evolving relation of norm (the constitution) and fact (the political reality) that operates to give the constitution its open and provisional quality.[30]

Chapter 6

CONSTITUTIONAL RIGHTS

THE modern constitution is the product of a revolutionary shift in the foundation of governmental authority. Once based on superstition or conquest, the constitution now calls upon reason and "the common rights of man." The American Revolution, argued Paine, marked the beginning of the end of regimes of monarchical government and their replacement by governments "founded on a moral theory, on a system of universal peace, on the indefeasible hereditary Rights of Man." This was the moment and place when "the principles of universal reformation" were instituted. Government that had been legitimated by divine will or sacred custom was now opposed by a modern principle which authorized government by the consent of free and equal citizens.[1]

In this new order, governmental authority rests on its capacity to protect the interests of the rights-bearing individual, the primary means of such protection being the constitution. Drafted in the name of the people, it becomes the mechanism of "universal transformation." In the Declaration of Independence, Americans claimed as "self-evident truths" that "all men are created equal" and "are endowed by their Creator with certain unalienable Rights." But are "unalienable" rights indeed "self-evident"? Do they derive from God? How precisely does the constitution work to ensure their protection?

Such rights went unrecognized in the medieval world, the word "right" then meaning simply "that which is right" and "right ordering" being determined according to strict principles of hierarchy. The American colonists broke entirely from this medieval worldview. Rights became vested in the individual, allocated equally and, being ascribed by nature, could not be transgressed by government. This modern world of equality rejected the medieval laws of hierarchy in favor of the "true," natural order of things.

The question remained: How are such natural rights identified? Divine revelation was hardly robust, not least because it required faith in some prophet
to reveal the truth. And how to judge and rank the wide range of moral practices that exist in the world? The only sure route to knowledge of God's will,
argued Enlightenment radicals, was to discover the laws of nature that, asserted Jefferson, constituted "the laws of 'nature's God.'"[2] Right conduct
would be revealed by explicating these laws of nature and from which those
"unalienable rights" could be derived. This was a practical challenge for those
charged with drafting the American Constitution. But it was also a critical
weapon in the general liberal struggle of the period.

The individual's claim to unalienable natural rights was invoked as a
powerful instrument to erode the authority of traditional hierarchies, establish checks on arbitrary power, and promote equality of respect. It was also
a drive to change power relations permanently. Natural rights, presented
as "things" to be "discovered," like laws of nature, were in reality created
by political movements. Advancing new capacities and freedoms, they also
worked in the service of emerging powers.

This much was recognized by leading jurists of the period. "It affords a cu-
rious spectacle to observe," noted John Millar, "that the same people who
talk in a high strain of political liberty, and who consider the privilege of imposing their own taxes as one of the unalienable rights of mankind, should
make no scruple of reducing a great proportion of their fellow creatures into
circumstances by which they are not only deprived of property but almost
of every species of right." How Americans claimed their natural rights at the
same time as denying them to slaves, he elaborated, could not be "more cal-
culated to ridicule a liberal hypothesis, or to show how little the conduct of
men is at the bottom directed by any philosophical principles."[3]

Millar's point was that even if used to promote liberal reforms, these claims
were far from "natural," "unalienable," or "universal." Invoked by American
colonists to establish the new order of the ages, this same discourse was also
used to legitimize the regime of a slave-holding republic. Far from being "self-
evident," the rights proclaimed by the Declaration of Independence justified
a very particular distribution of freedom and authority. Rights claims can
be used to inspire a variety of political movements—those that promote social equality or bolster existing property relations, strengthen social solidarity

around common principles or promote an atomistic individualism that erodes common feeling. Is it therefore conceivable that they could ever be used to establish objective standards against which governments might be measured?

Jeremy Bentham emerged as the most vehement critic of natural rights. His critique of the French *Declaration of the Rights of Man and the Citizen* of 1791 maintained that rights cannot exist before government is established. A right can be understood only as the product of law: "natural rights is simple nonsense: natural and imprescriptible rights, rhetorical nonsense,—nonsense upon stilts."[4] But many modern legal philosophers now assert that rights do indeed exist prior to formal legal enactment and that such rights hold the key to the interpretation of the fundamental law of the constitution.[5] The early proclamations, such as those of the Declarations of the American and French Revolutions, were essentially statements of political ideals intended to inspire the cause rather than impose a legal obligation.[6] Rights-based readings of the constitution are twentieth-century creations. But now that inclusion of a charter of rights in a constitution is commonplace, their formal legal standing becomes a more pressing question.

To make headway with this task we should review the frameworks of early modern social contract theorists. Paine had argued that natural rights are the foundation of civil rights, that natural rights are the foundation of constitutional rights.[7] Yet even those social contact theorists who accept the existence of natural rights greatly differ about the status of those rights within civil order. Their divergence demonstrates precisely why constitutional rights possess such an ambiguous character.

Natural Rights in the Construction of the State

I begin with Thomas Hobbes who, as the foundational theorist of the modern state, overthrew the entire edifice of medieval constitutionalism and proceeded to construct an account of the state based on the natural rights of the individual. But he drew radical implications from the modern assumptions that humans are bearers of natural rights and, by nature, free and equal. If we are left free to exercise our inherent natural rights, he argued, we end up simply destroying ourselves. With a powerful narrative account of life without government, life in a state of nature, Hobbes shows why we must relinquish these rights in order to preserve them and, through the device of a social contract, bind ourselves to the authority of a coercive power.

Hobbes argues that the fundamental natural right of the individual is that of self-preservation. This is hardwired into our nature such that "we cannot be blamed for looking out for ourselves, for we cannot will to do otherwise." This gives us the right to do anything to anybody and to use and enjoy whatever we can get. And it is precisely because we are equal that this fundamental right to preserve our existence inevitably leads to perpetual conflict, to "a war of every man against every man."[8] He acknowledges the existence of certain laws of nature, such as those of mutual respect and fair treatment, but in a state of nature they bind us only *in foro interno;* they cannot become true laws until a superior power exists to enforce them.[9] His logical conclusion is that "the effect of this *right* [of self-preservation] is almost the same as if there were no *right* at all."[10]

Rejecting the Aristotelian claim that man is a social animal, Hobbes maintains that humans, despite their powers of reason, are essentially self-centered, competitive creatures driven by their passions and fears. It follows, paradoxically, that in order to preserve their rights of liberty and equality, humans must relinquish them and entrust their care to an all-powerful sovereign.[11] The covenant through which this is effected transforms the multitude into a single people.[12] It therefore makes both a state and, by creating the sovereign as the representative person of the state, its office of government. Entrusted with an unlimited power of law-making, the sovereign is the sole source of right and wrong, of justice and injustice.

Hobbes's image of the state and its law is evidently authoritarian. Law is simply the command of the sovereign; it is sovereign authority, not wisdom or truth, that makes law. The multitude may have formed itself into a people by virtue of a contract, but because the sovereign created by this contract is the sole representative of the state, the state is an autonomous entity. So although the social contract is engendered by the moral imperative of avoiding perpetual conflict, sovereign will overrides any individual moral claim. There is therefore no such thing as an unjust law, nor can there be rights vested in the people against the sovereign.

Since Hobbes's sovereign exists to make rules for the maintenance of civil peace, citizens have the right to pursue their own ends in spheres of life not regulated by the sovereign's commands. But right and law are distinct: right is a liberty, whereas law is an obligation. Much human activity is beyond the scope of the law, and in these spheres citizens retain their liberties, "that part of natural right which is allowed and left to the citizens by the civil laws." Laws, Hobbes explains, are enacted "not to extinguish human actions but to direct them; just as nature ordained banks not to stop the flow of the river but to direct it." The sovereign's laws ensure the maintenance of "the good of the citizens and of the commonwealth."[13] The Hobbesian state may be authoritarian, but it is not absolute.

Hobbes does not say much about the constitution of government. Since all power vests in the sovereign, a system of government is established simply by the sovereign act of delegating competencies to subordinate magistrates and judges.[14] The state is built on authoritarian foundations, and the constitution of its government will only be the product of a set of circumstantial arrangements designed to promote the common good. These governmental arrangements do not depend on divine revelation, natural law, or claims of natural rights. They are worked out according to the precepts of "civil science," a new field of knowledge that Hobbes claims to have invented.[15]

Natural Rights in the Construction of the Constitution

An early attempt at establishing constitutional orders was undertaken in 1672 by Samuel Pufendorf. Claiming that the Hobbesian contract was too truncated, *On the Law of Nature and Nations* shows how the absolute sovereignty of the state can be compatible with limited powers vested in governing bodies. The founding of the state, he argues, is marked not by a single pact but by two covenants and a decree. The first covenant creates the political unity of the state and expresses its constitutional order; the second constitutes the office of government; and the decree proclaims the constitution of government as a special type of positive law.[16] Pufendorf argues that although sovereignty is absolute and indivisible, the powers of government can be—and, in order to maintain authority, must be—limited and divided. The institutionalization of sovereign power, he suggests, is not incompatible with the state's sovereignty or the allocation of the powers of government in a formal constitution.

This provides the point of departure for Locke. In his *Second Treatise of Government*, he follows Hobbes and Pufendorf in presenting a fable of life in a state of nature, but his purpose is to offer a radically different justification for civil government. Whereas for Hobbes the main threat in the state of nature is physical harm, for Locke it is the inability to acquire the basic means of subsistence. People sustain themselves by appropriating the fruits of the earth and, having a natural right to do so, they acquire ownership of things. Through these actions, the concept of property emerges and with it we recognize the benefits of commodity exchange. A rudimentary form of society therefore evolves long before a system of government is established.

So why, Locke asks, do we part with our natural freedoms and subject ourselves to "the Dominion and Control of any other Power"? His answer is that we enter into the social contract to ensure the more effective enforcement of natural law and the better protection of our natural rights. The problem in a state of nature is that since natural law exists only "in the minds of Men," they may "mis-cite, or mis-apply it." We adopt the social contract and establish a system of civil government to provide clarity on the meaning of law, to provide for an impartial judge to resolve disputes, and to establish executive officers to ensure effective law enforcement. But the overriding purpose of establishing a system of government is to legitimate the established social system: "The chief end . . . of men's uniting into Commonwealths, and putting themselves under Government, is the preservation of their property."[17]

The Lockean social contract does not extinguish natural rights. It is a covenant of delegation by which only those natural rights that must be pooled in furtherance of the public good are relinquished. This covenant is made between rights-bearing individuals to preserve and strengthen those rights, to which end the Lockean social contract takes the form of a written constitution of government. Governmental powers are both defined and limited; government is not a matter of *will* but an institutional matter, a matter of *law*. This is a theory of limited, law-bound, rights-protecting constitutional government.

Locke allocates governmental tasks between the legislature and executive but, being more concerned with the legitimacy of governmental power, he does not provide a modern theory of separated powers. Government is a fiduciary responsibility, and governors are trustees with powers limited to those ends. Without specifying the basic rights of the individual, he does explain what happens if governors act in breach of that trust. His stark answer is that "the community perpetually retains a supreme power of saving themselves" from the foolish or wicked actions of their governors. If governors are not loyal to their fiduciary responsibilities, the bond of obligation is forfeited, and power reverts to the people. But will this not "lay a ferment for frequent rebellion" and, as Hobbes suggests, destabilize the regime? To this Locke responds that "rebellions happen not upon every little mismanagement in public affairs," and the very threat of legitimate rebellion dissuades those in power from abusing it.[18]

Locke's theory evidently inspired the American colonists in their struggle against the British Crown. The Declaration of Independence was mainly drafted by Jefferson but the ideas, and many of the actual words, are Locke's, as are key features of the constitutional settlement of 1787–1791.[19] Most significant is Locke's assertion that the social contract requires only the delegation of some of the individual's natural rights. By formally enumerating them, the Constitution transforms many of these retained natural rights—freedom of speech, freedom of the exercise of religion, and protection of life, liberty, and property—into constitutional rights. But whether formally specified or not, these natural rights become the guiding principles for the legitimacy of modern government.

Locke's ideas about natural rights shape the contours of constitutionalism in more fundamental ways. There is no place in Locke's scheme for the concepts of state and sovereignty, which are replaced by society and government. Neither is there a place for the concept of absolute authority; Locke's scheme establishes a system of government not just according to law but also subject to law. And the natural rights implicitly retained are formalized as constitutional rights imposed by society on government. The constitutional rights at the very core of Locke's scheme are, in fact, negative freedoms, which protect the freedom of the individual, including the freedom to own property and freedom from any form of government interference.[20] These are the basic elements of what Sartori calls a *garantiste* constitution, an expression of negative or classical constitutionalism.

Constitutional Rights in the Construction of Aspirational Constitutionalism

Locke's influence prevailed until well into the twentieth century, which is why progressive political movements often saw the modern constitution as a device to bolster bourgeois interests. Reformers in the era of what Sartori called "intense politics" placed more faith in winning a legislative majority than in drafting a new constitution.[21] But in the late twentieth century, an alternative conception emerged as newly drafted constitutions regularly included a series of social and economic rights designed to enable the citizen to realize positive freedom. This is aspirational constitutionalism, the origins of which can be traced to Rousseau's social contract.

Rejecting the accounts of Hobbes and Locke, for Rousseau, the social contract is an imaginative device for human renewal. Hobbes's man in a state of nature is just bourgeois man, corrupted by property, competition, and social striving. Locke fares no better: if a right is a relation between citizens, no *right* to property can exist in a state of nature. Locke's concept of property acquired through labor is merely an act of appropriation achieved through force or fraud. His social contract is an elaborate trick devised by property holders to protect their interests: claiming that a law-governed regime provides security and liberty, "all ran towards their chains in the belief that they were securing their freedom." For Rousseau, Locke's scheme imposes new fetters on the poor to confer new powers on the rich, transforming "a skillful usurpation into an irrevocable right."[22]

In *The Social Contract,* Rousseau outlines the conditions to reconcile liberty and law and to establish the basis for legitimate constitutional order.[23] First, contra Hobbes, he argues that the sovereign cannot be a single person or a representative office; it must be the people themselves who, by an act of association, form a collective body. The sovereign is not the office of the representative of the state but the public person formed by the union of all; that is, the state is the sovereign. This is the principle of solidarity. Second, Rousseau argues that the social contract replaces *natural inequality* with *political equality.* This is the principle of equality. Third, political equality is the precondition for the formation of a single will. Everyone has the same rights over others as they have themselves. Therefore, all must be acknowledged as equals, leading to the greatest good of all. This is the principle of equal liberty, otherwise known as the "general will" or the will of the sovereign.

The general will is the fundamental law of the political domain and the source of all constitutional rights. In contrast to Locke's negative freedom, Rousseau gives an account of positive freedom.[24] The purpose of Rousseau's social contract is not to protect bourgeois property rights but to elevate humans from "stupid and bounded animals" into "intelligent beings." This can only be achieved in accordance with the fundamental law. Whoever refuses to obey it must be constrained to do so; that is, they "shall be forced to be free."[25]

These are the essential elements of *aspirational constitutionalism*. Whereas Hobbes describes the authority of positive law-making in the modern state and Locke protects natural rights within the constitution, Rousseau offers an account of the principle of equal liberty from which all rights contained in the constitution must be derived, thereby transforming subjective rights into objective law. Contrary to Locke, for whom society is a prepolitical category, Rousseau's social contract establishes a constitution not just of government but also of political society, that is, the state. Consequently, Rousseau's catalog of rights does not just protect the existing social order from government; it establishes the legitimacy of the regime. Rousseau's aspirational scheme has such an emancipatory dynamic that, ever since it was first embraced by French revolutionaries,[26] it has politicized all subsequent attempts to institute a stable constitutional settlement.

∼

This sketch of the evolution of constitutional rights discourse throws into relief the tension between rights and law. Hobbes jettisoned medieval constitutionalism to replace it with the idea of law as the will of the sovereign; the constitution simply describes the established arrangement of government. Locke then outlined a system of limited government based on respect for individual rights; the constitution is created as an articulation of classical constitutionalism. Rousseau radicalized each of these claims, arguing first, that the will of the sovereign is the will of the people and secondly, that the state must replace established rights with the right of everyone to equal liberty. The regime he devised was created in the image of aspirational constitutionalism. Hobbes believed that natural rights must be extinguished in order to establish civil order. Locke promoted natural rights as a measure of the legitimacy of civil order. And Rousseau converted the principle of subjective right into objective law.

The modern constitution transforms these competing claims into positive law, changing the character of law in important ways. As Part I showed, in its origins constitutionalism reflects Locke's ideas and seeks to protect negative rights. But as the modern practice evolves in accordance with Rousseau's ideas, rights are elevated into architectonic principles of the entire regime. This is the dominant rhetoric of recent developments in "the age of constitutionalism," the subject of Part III of this book. As we have already seen, constituent power involves a discourse of right as much as of power. Similarly, the nature of constitutional rights reflects a discourse of power as much as right. Power and right, the conditions of public and private autonomy, remain intertwined, an issue that the concept of constitutional democracy must address.

Chapter 7

CONSTITUTIONAL DEMOCRACY

MODERN government acquires legitimacy from adherence to a constitution that "we the people" have authorized. This is the principle of public autonomy that, reflecting the ostensibly democratic founding of the modern state, assumes juridical form as constituent power. Government also acquires legitimacy by virtue of particular conditions imposed on the way it can use its powers. This is the principle of private autonomy that, reflecting respect for individual liberty, acquires juridical form as constitutional rights. Which of these principles has primacy? This is one of the most perplexing questions of modern politics.

Civic republicans prioritize the former, the democratic principle of equal citizen participation in the processes by which they are governed. Liberals prioritize the latter, the principle that upholds the primacy of protecting the citizen's basic rights. By upholding the value of both principles, a regime of constitutional democracy is assumed to be able to resolve conflicts between them and to determine the circumstances under which either the will of the people must be circumscribed to guarantee the rights of the subject or basic rights must be qualified in pursuit of the common good.

The tension between these principles nonetheless continues to torment constitutional discourse. If the constitution merely establishes a framework of government for a single generation, that tension can be negotiated through political deliberation. But if, according to the precepts of constitutionalism, the constitution is intended to be permanent, the question of the relative priorities of these competing principles becomes much more pressing. Without a clear steer, the question is most likely resolved quietly on a case-by-case basis by unelected judges. This likelihood led republicans like Jefferson, convinced that one generation had no right to bind another, to fear that the establishment of a permanent constitution subverts democracy.

Some theorists argue that there is no need to trade between the principles of democracy and rights. They question whether republican values demand acquiescence to the unrestrained will of the people and whether liberal values rule out a reciprocal acknowledgment of the limits on individual rights, suggesting that the two values can be reconciled because they are interdependent. This is the critical issue around which the distinction between a regime of constitutional democracy and one founded on the philosophy of constitutionalism revolves.

The Liberty of the Ancients and the Liberty of the Moderns

The tension between democracy and rights played out differently in the politics of the American and French Revolutions. From the outset, the framers of the US Constitution were concerned about the impact of democracy on their regime. Advocating the establishment of a modern republic that included powerful institutional mechanisms to mitigate what Madison in *Federalist* 10 calls the deficiencies of a "pure democracy," they implicitly upheld the primacy of individual rights. French revolutionaries, by contrast, modeled their regime on the republican virtues of ancient Greece and Rome, a quest that drove them to pursue a revolutionary cause without limitation. Into this febrile environment stepped Benjamin Constant. Following his arrival in Paris in 1795, he offered guidance on how the new French republic might direct its revolutionary fervor toward more stable institutional arrangements.

Reflecting on those developments twenty years later, Constant observes that the intensity of deliberation over constitutional forms that had engaged French writers since the Revolution was now out of favor. In the decade following the Revolution, the French "tried some five or six constitutions and found ourselves the worse for it." Instead, "in the name of freedom . . . we got prisons, scaffolds, and endless multiplied persecution." Far from liberating the people, the descent of the Revolution into the Terror had simply made them fearful, insecure, and ripe for servitude.[1]

His explanation is instructive. The great failure of the revolutionaries was in trying to build their regime by "grinding and reducing to dust the [inherited] materials that they were to employ." Having removed this "natural source of patriotism," they sought to replace it with "a factitious passion for an abstract being, a general idea stripped of all that can engage the imagination and speak to the memory."[2] Authority could only be restored and political power generated by strengthening institutional arrangements that command respect. The only hope of reconciling competing principles of democracy and rights, he concludes, was by devising a constitution that accorded with the customs of the people.

Constant's argument synthesizes the principles of Rousseau and Montesquieu. From Rousseau, he derives the principle that a regime gains legitimacy from popular sovereignty, and from Montesquieu, the principle that the ruling power gains authority not only from popular will but also from how power is exercised. Modern governments must be able to claim a democratic mandate but, to strengthen their authority, they must act within accepted constitutional forms.[3]

The Revolution took a wrong turn, Constant maintains, because it conflated two rather different concepts of liberty. Modern liberty, founded on individual subjective rights, protects a zone of privacy and independence from the exercise of arbitrary power. The ancient idea of liberty, by contrast, expressed independence from rule by foreigners and required the participation of citizens in collective self-government. This was the type of liberty that could only be realized in a small, culturally homogeneous city-state pursuing a politics of virtue founded on martial spirit, a type of state that was invariably a slaveholding, warrior republic of male citizens. It was also the type of liberty that could not be enjoyed equally. For some to be free, others had to be slaves.[4]

Acknowledging the value of each kind of liberty, Constant argues that the task is to find a balance between the two. The prevalence of the modern concept is as distortive as the dominance of the ancient: the atrophy of politics by retreat to a private sphere could be as dangerous as a total politicization of society. Liberty in the modern world involves a novel challenge: it must accept the distinctions between public and private, political and social, and participation and independence. Political liberty presupposes civil liberty, and the primary aim of the constitution must be to establish an interlocking arrangement in which these two forms of freedom reinforce one another.

How can this be realized? Constant argues that the emergence of a civil society founded on subjective rights need not diminish the domain of the political founded on objective law. Indeed, the autonomy of the political and the autonomy of the social presuppose one another. His profound point is that democratization releases social power at the same time as it extends the nature, scale, and range of governmental power. Under a modern constitution, hierarchical ordering, a characteristic feature of regal authority, diminishes, but "the political" continues to operate as "society's symbolic underpinning, the source of its collective identity and cohesiveness."[5]

This "symbolic underpinning" must be reflected in a constitution drafted not in terms of command and obedience but on the principle of highly differentiated modes of association. To maintain the government's authority and legitimacy, the modern constitution must assume the crucial function of representing society, to which end it must somehow establish its authority as a neutral power. It must be able to bolster the authority of the office of government against the forces of division.

Maintaining Political Freedom in Modern Democracy

Writing in the mid-nineteenth century as a member of the first postrevolutionary generation, Alexis de Tocqueville was driven to understand the significance of the two great political revolutions of the late eighteenth century. His task was to explain the profound implications for government and society of the decline of monarchy and aristocracy and the emergence of democracy.

Tocqueville produced two major studies, each of which became a classic of modern political thought. *Democracy in America,* published in two volumes in 1835 and 1840, and *The Ancien Régime and the French Revolution* in 1856 analyze the crisis of European regimes. How, he asks, might political freedom be realized in these emerging democracies? These societies cannot prevent these modernizing developments, he concludes, but "it depends upon themselves whether the principle of equality is to lead them to servitude or freedom, to knowledge or barbarism, to prosperity or to wretchedness."[6] The freedom he upholds as a cardinal virtue is not individual freedom from political engagement but the maintenance of the conditions of freedom as collective self-government.

Tocqueville recognized that the relentless force destroying monarchy and aristocracy and driving toward democracy was "the gradual development of the principle of equality." Whereas his contemporary, Karl Marx, had once rhetorically declared that democracy "is the resolved mystery of all constitutions," Tocqueville set himself the task of unpacking that solution. His lasting reputation derives from his total commitment to the political as a distinct domain of human interaction, a commitment that leads him to make a powerful contribution to a "new science of politics . . . for a new world."[7]

The new regime he foresaw sweeping the world was not simply democracy in the broad sense of moving toward an equality of conditions.[8] He saw that the only regime that could truly legitimize a modern government was a constitutional democracy. The primary aim of *Democracy in America* was to reveal the basic principles and working practices of such a democracy. Revolutionary movements destroy traditions and create new opportunities, but the paradoxical threat he identifies is that the liberty generated in this upheaval can also lead to an equality that, enforcing conformity, destroys liberty. Tocqueville follows Constant in arguing that any new basis of authority must find its expression in the constitution.

Constitutional democracy, he argues, can be understood by reference to changes in three basic phenomena: power, constitution, and law. Political power is transformed in modernity; no longer emanating from the ruler, it assumes the amorphous form of social power. Democracy must therefore be conceived not as a system of government but as a form of society in which power is generated from the growth of equality. This power "appears to belong to no one, except to the people in the abstract, and which threatens to become unlimited, omnipotent, to acquire an ambition to take charge of every aspect of social life."[9] The key challenge is to establish a constitution that channels this social power and, through institutionalization, harnesses it and converts it into political power.

Symbolically, power rests with "the people," but it is only through the constitution that it is channeled into a political form that enables people to conceive of themselves as a unity. Beyond this, it is unclear whether the constitution merely establishes the office of government or is able to determine the constitutional order of the state. Tocqueville was sensitive to this ambiguity. He emphasizes that to be effective, the constitution's formal written principles and procedures must work with the grain of society. "Without ideas held in common," he notes, "there is no common action, and without common action, there may still be men, but there is no social body."[10]

The third innovation concerns a transformation in the role of law. The democratic impetus leading to a documentary constitution converts it into a kind of higher-order law with, at least in the American model, the judiciary acting as its guardian. This is an important aspect of constitutional democracy. If the danger to democracy is a sense of equality that jeopardizes liberty, the bulwarks against this threat are lawyers. The influence of lawyers on governmental power, argues Tocqueville, is "the most powerful existing security against the excesses of democracy." This is because their professional training endows them with certain orderly habits that "render them very hostile to the revolutionary spirit and the unreflecting passions of the multitude." They neutralize the vices inherent in popular government because, however much they value liberty, they "are attached to public order beyond every other consideration." And they "secretly oppose their aristocratic propensities to its democratic instincts, their superstitious attachment to what is antique to its love of novelty, their narrow views to its immense designs, and their habitual procrastination to its ardent impatience."[11]

Once equipped with the power to declare laws unconstitutional, the American judge "perpetually interferes in political affairs." And since there are so few political questions that do not eventually come before the judiciary, organized political movements soon begin to express themselves in the language of constitutional law, and "the spirit of the law" gradually extends beyond the courtroom to "the bosom of society." "Without this admixture of lawyer-like sobriety with the democratic principle," Tocqueville concludes, "I question whether democratic institutions could long be maintained."[12]

Tocqueville identifies constitutional democracy, born of the combined transformation of power, constitution, and law, as the legitimating principle of modern regimes. His purpose was to persuade European politicians of its value and so avoid the threat of an emerging "democratic despotism." That threat was most real in his own country. In the four decades before he set off on his American voyage, France had experienced revolution, constitutional monarchy, regicide, the Terror, war, republican government, empire, monarchical restoration, and in 1830 revolutionary overthrow. But he is careful not to project an idealized image of constitutional democracy. Democracy releases new energies and confers new rights, but it also creates new possibilities for servitude born of standardization and normalization. Noting that "every man allows himself to be put in leading-strings, because he sees that it is not a person or a class of persons, but the people at large who hold the end of his chain,"[13] he expresses a profound paradox of constitutional democracy.

The Internal Relation between Rights and Democracy

Tocqueville's ideas about power, constitution, and law have also shaped the thought of the most influential European social philosopher of the late twentieth century. Jürgen Habermas's major work of the 1990s is a powerful analysis of the legitimacy of contemporary constitutional democracy. *Between Facts and Norms: Contributions to a Discourse Theory of Law and Democracy* ostensibly advances the thesis that "in the age of a completely secularized politics, the rule of law cannot be had or maintained without radical democracy."[14]

Habermas's study of constitutional democracy must be situated within his general social theory. In earlier work, he argues that modernity is signified by a growing systematization of ordinary life, leading to social relations being formally organized by law. He identifies four stages in this increasing juridification of social relations: the *bourgeois state* developed during the period of absolutism, the construct of which we saw in the work of Hobbes; the *constitutional state* associated with nineteenth-century jurists of the *Rechtsstaat* and exemplified earlier in the work of Locke; the *democratic constitutional state* identified as having "spread in Europe and in North America in the wake of the French Revolution" examined by Tocqueville; and finally the *democratic welfare state,* a twentieth-century product of the struggles of workers' movements to provide social welfare that Habermas, following Tocqueville, recognizes is now being undermined by "the ambivalence of guaranteeing freedom and taking it away."[15]

During the 1970s, Habermas argued that this last stage was leading to a "legitimation crisis" in which the political system was not generating sufficient problem-solving capacity to guarantee its own continued existence.[16] *Between Facts and Norms* examines the crises that fiscal strains, welfare burdens, bureaucratization, and growing social complexity are imposing on contemporary constitutional frameworks. He acknowledges that functionally differentiated, decentered modern societies cannot easily be politically constituted; they may be integrated systemically but cannot be integrated socially through shared meanings. The critical issue is whether this political relationship can be reconstructed within a constitutional arrangement that respects both individual rights as normative ideals and democratic will-formation through the governmental system.

To address this, Habermas first considers the strains between the two main schools of constitutional order: liberals who prioritize respect for individual rights and republicans who uphold the value of popular sovereignty. Redefining the differences between them, he suggests that the principles they advance are not antagonistic but reciprocal. Constitutional democracy is capable of fully acknowledging both private and public autonomy, reason and will, rights and democracy.

This internal relation between rights and democracy is explained by reconstructing the regime of constitutional democracy entirely in the language of rights. Five sets of rights needed to establish a constitutional democracy are specified. The first three establish a horizontal association of free and equal persons. These are rights to "the greatest possible measure of equal individual liberties," status rights acquired as a member of the association, and rights to due process of law. Such rights guarantee the private autonomy of the individual, recognizing the individual as a subject of the law. The next two sets of rights acknowledge the individual as a citizen. First is the right to equal participation in the processes of opinion-formation and will-formation, which expands private and public autonomy simultaneously. The final set establishes rights to the basic material conditions needed so that citizens can actually make use of their civil and political rights.[17]

This rights-based account is the core of Habermas's co-originality thesis: "The principle of popular sovereignty is expressed in rights of communication and participation that secure the public autonomy of citizens and the rule of law is expressed in those classical basic rights that guarantee the private autonomy of members of society." He acknowledges that his argument has the greatest plausibility with respect to rights that safeguard the exercise of public autonomy and seems less plausible with respect to classical individual rights that guarantee private autonomy. But he stresses the point that without basic rights securing private autonomy, there can be "no medium for legally institutionalizing the conditions under which these citizens . . . can make use of their public autonomy." Private autonomy rights, or negative liberties, which republicans might treat as constraints, are to be reinterpreted as enabling conditions.[18]

The key to Habermas's thesis is that "political power is not externally juxtaposed to law but is presupposed by law and is itself established in the form of law."[19] On this, he is following Heller, though surprisingly without citing him. Habermas presents democracy as an expression of rightful authority, and by "law" here, he must surely mean (again following Heller) an idealized expression of "political right." It is on this implicit understanding that Habermas maintains the mutual presupposition of public autonomy and private autonomy.

Habermas's sophisticated philosophical treatment has transformed the terms of the debate.[20] But it has not escaped criticism. Frank Michelman, for example, argues that once the actual processes of constitution-making are examined, the rudimentary tension between liberal and democratic presumptions persists, and Habermas's attempt to resolve this by postulating some hypothetical universal agreement is "pure abstraction, a transcendental-logical deduction necessitated by the prior determination of a thinker to think something."[21]

Habermas has responded by maintaining that the internal relation between will and reason evolves over time so that we should see constitutional ordering as "a self-correcting historical process." Michelman's argument that it leads to an infinite regress, he suggests, is "the understandable expression of the future-oriented character, or openness, of the democratic constitution." But constitution-making should be seen as "a tradition-building project" in that "later generations have the task of actualizing the still-untapped normative substance of the system of rights laid down in the original document of the constitution." It requires acceptance of a "dynamic understanding of the constitution," such that it can be conceived as "a self-correcting learning process," whereby "with the inclusion of marginalized groups and with the empowerment of deprived classes, the hitherto poorly satisfied presuppositions for the legitimacy of existing democratic procedures are better realized." Subsequent generations, Habermas concludes, "can learn from past mistakes only if they are 'in the same boat' as their forebears."[22]

This explanation clarifies, but does it resolve? One obvious limitation is that it offers a conceptual solution to a practical problem. But even on its own terms, it leaves doubts. Whereas Michelman argues that Habermas skews reciprocity towards liberalism,[23] Charles Larmore thinks the co-originality thesis privileges republican democracy. In Habermas's scheme, Larmore argues, individual rights do not limit the authority of popular sovereignty but "draw their rationale from their supposed ability to make democratic self-rule possible." Basic rights are therefore presented as devices that empower individuals to participate in the process of democratic self-rule. Rather than protecting us from collective will, rights are shaped in such a way as "to protect the means necessary for creating a collective will." In Habermas's version, Larmore concludes, democratic self-rule is "the sole normative foundation of the modern liberal-democratic state."[24]

Habermas's argument rests on the claim that in modern functionally differentiated and culturally heterogeneous societies, the legitimating principles of constitutional democracy cannot presuppose the validity of conceptions of the common good. Legitimating principles must be procedural: the right must be prior to the good. Unable to depend on the standard republican argument about civic virtue, he turns instead to a set of universal principles he calls "discourse ethics." This ambitious move nevertheless becomes less compelling in the context of change over time. Even if he solves the paradox between democracy and rights in the task faced by framers of the constitution, the argument fails if future generations who did not consent with one another are similarly bound by that constitution.

Habermas's attempt to resolve this by suggesting that successors should recognize they are "in the same boat" as their forebears is revealing. The "boat" must surely be something more fundamental than the enacted constitution. As Alessandro Ferrara notes, the metaphor requires that we "conceive of the political identity of the people as something that pre-exists the constitution,"[25] that is, there must be a broader sense of a political association that precedes the constitution. This is what I have been calling the state. "We the people" endowed with a historically derived cultural and political identity recognize that our forebears drafted these governing arrangements as a constitution. The problem for Habermas is that this brings him back to the question of the common good and the sense of patriotism as loyalty to a set of common values that make up a political tradition.

It is a problem for Habermas because he maintains that the only patriotism that can be coherently embraced today is what he calls "constitutional patriotism" *(Verfassungspatriotismus),* an allegiance to the principles inscribed in the constitution.[26] This surely underestimates the degree to which a common life that shapes the political identity of a people continues to provide the basis of political allegiance. In making this move, Habermas's thesis begins to look much less like an argument for "radical democracy" or even "constitutional democracy." In promoting allegiance to the principles in the constitution, it ends up as nothing less than a defense of constitutionalism.

Constitutional Democracy or Constitutionalism?

The concept of constitutional democracy contains apparently ineradicable tensions between democracy and rights, will and reason, power and right, and ultimately between facts and norms. In their different ways, social contract thinkers help us appreciate how these tensions might be negotiated. Habermas's study of constitutional democracy is the latest of this type. He clarifies the character and extends the ambition of constitutional democracy, not least in synthesizing the classical constitutionalism of Locke and the aspirational constitutionalism of Rousseau. But like those of his social contract predecessors, this seems ultimately to be an account in which the conclusions follow from built-in assumptions.

Contractual thought experiments illuminate the conditions of legitimate order, but they underestimate the role of power in the task of generating authority. The constitution does not acquire authority by virtue of its creation. Its authority is generated through social processes in real historical time, and that authority is always conditional. Contractual writers show how the tensions between democracy and rights can be reconciled in thought. In practice, though, constitutional democracy is ever an exercise in continuous upheaval generated by the indeterminacy of its founding principles. Habermas's "boat" needs to be filled with common historical experiences generated by memories of past conflicts over competing ideas of the common good. Abstract constitutional principles acquire determinate meaning only because of what has been learned, especially through historical instances of what happens when a people fail to uphold them.

The written constitution performs a critical role in providing a framework for institutionalizing such social conflicts. It is a medium through which people express their sense of the right, the good, and the just in ways that transcend particular interests. But the regime retains its democratic character only when, far from achieving reconciliation between basic principles, it holds them in a condition of indeterminacy. Democracy, notes Claude Lefort, is "instituted and sustained by the *dissolution of the markers of certainty*."[27]

Democracy persists through continuous and active political deliberation over the right and the good. Conflict and dissent are constitutive features that must be preserved, and they are preserved by ensuring that the meaning of these basic and contestable values remains the subject of continuous political negotiation through democratically constituted and democratically accountable processes.

This feature of democracy places structural limitations on the degree to which it can be sublimated into constitutionalism. Once a political regime is conceptualized in the language of rights, lawyers too readily assume that it contains an overarching framework to be attended to by the judiciary, with legislative and administration activity being reduced to mere regulative action that can be trumped by a claim of right.[28] This overvalues the ability of the judiciary to reach political judgments on intensely contestable rights claims and undervalues the importance of the implicit rights judgments that legislatures and other officials make.[29] The maintenance of institutional sites of democratic deliberation, decision-making, and accountability are essential markers of indeterminacy. They are essential preconditions for upholding Tocqueville's vision of political freedom.

Can modern societies maintain political unity while keeping open this theater of contestation, or is it inevitable that Tocqueville's conduits, the lawyers, will colonize constitutional discourse to such an extent that they stifle open deliberation and extinguish indeterminacy? To the extent that they have done so, we find ourselves in the grip of a pervasive ideology, an ideology of constitutionalism that blends the values of classical and aspirational constitutionalism so that the constitution is transformed into the authoritative medium through which all inherent tensions between power and right are resolved. This theme is taken up in Part III.

The Age of Constitutionalism

Chapter 8

THE CONSTITUTION
AS CIVIL RELIGION

ACCORDING to the precepts of classical constitutionalism, the main purpose of the constitution is to establish a comprehensive scheme of limited government. However, this innovation was assumed to have been brought about not by some social contract but by the workings of certain natural laws of social development that bound us to interests we hold in common. Consequently, the crucial distinction in constitutional thought was not between the state of nature and civil order but between society and government. Since it was society rather than government that elevated mankind, it was assumed that society would replace the state as the representation of unity. The constitution was therefore devised as a method that could protect the workings of the natural laws of an emerging commercial society from undue governmental interference. Public powers must be constrained so that private freedoms can flourish.

Were these assumptions well founded? G. W. F. Hegel maintains that the rise of civil society driven by the laws of political economy advanced a purely formal concept of freedom that would only fuel competition and conflict and reinforce existing inequalities. Concerned mainly with "the security and protection of property and personal freedom," civil society could not replace the state's rationale of achieving objective freedom. Once civil society is left to operate according to its own laws, he surmises, the need for public controls "to diminish the danger of upheavals arising from clashing interests" will become ever more urgent.[1]

Hegel's perception that the operation of the modern laws of political economy does not lead to a diminished role for government has proved sound. But with what constitutional implications? Once governmental responsibilities significantly expanded, it was evident that the constitution could not function according to the presuppositions of classical constitutionalism. The expansion of civil society together with the emergence of democracy combined to form a regime that releases social power at the same time as it extends the nature, scale, and range of governmental power. The critical challenge was whether the constitution could establish a framework that regulates not just government but also society.

As explained in Part I, this challenge has been obscured by ambiguity in the concept of the constitution. Alongside the modern constitution, which establishes the framework of government, the traditional idea of the constitution as an expression of a regime's customary practices and its people's identity remained influential. With continuing processes of individualization, pluralization, fragmentation, and increasing functional differentiation, however, the authority of many of these traditional networks of solidarity was being eroded. To maintain social integration, then, it became necessary to place ever greater reliance on more formal systems. And at this critical moment, the constitution acquired a new responsibility.

The constitution was required to extend beyond its original role of establishing a comprehensive scheme of limited government to provide a symbolic representation of collective unity. Once divided between the formal constitution of government and the material constitution of the state, in late modernity these legal and social functions became dedifferentiated. To maintain the authority of *government*, the constitution was also obliged to represent *society*. In the age of constitutionalism, the constitution's critical task was to integrate two divergent roles: to regulate the system of government and to provide the symbolic representation of a society.

The Constitution as Instrument and Symbol

Modern societies are integrated both systemically and socially. Systemic integration is achieved through mechanisms like markets and governmental institutions that regulate private actions and provide public goods. Social integration is achieved by upholding traditions and common values. But is the constitution up to the task of moving beyond its original tasks of contributing to system integration by regulating governmental institutions and advancing social integration by expressing common values? The answer depends on whether it is simply an instrument for collective decision-making or if it can also become a symbol of social unity.

As an instrument, the constitution organizes a set of mechanisms for making authoritative collective decisions, thereby contributing to the systemic integration of the regime. It formulates rules that establish and limit the powers of public bodies and render these bodies accountable. It ensures that governmental power will be made regular and predictable, offering citizens some assurance in their dealings with public bodies and providing redress should expectations be confounded. In these respects, the constitution incorporates a set of precommitment techniques that help to integrate the functionally differentiated subsystems of modern society.[2]

Once the constitution has established its authority as a system of decision-making and dispute resolution, it acquires the levels of trust needed to sustain social cohesion. Having established its normative authority, the constitution could possibly take on the symbolic role of expressing the nation's sense of collective identity. Yet this is a latent potential, not least because, as Hans Vorländer notes, "what this integration capacity rests on, what its basis, its objective and its mechanisms are, remains entirely unclear."[3] The enactment of a constitution is never sufficient to ensure its efficacy because efficacy depends on "constitutional reality."[4] Whether the constitution can acquire general symbolic importance is assumed to depend on social and cultural factors that lie beyond the realm of law.

It is possible, then, for a constitution to establish its normative authority, its legal efficacy, but still lack real influence over the maintenance of societal integration. This is because, as the Weimar jurist Rudolf Smend argued, integration through the inculcation of common values is achieved as much through the veneration of flags, anthems, and pledges of allegiance as by laws and institutions of government.[5] But herein lies the problem we have already identified: national solidarity, common religion, shared history, and uniform culture are the factors on which nation-states might have sought to build their authority but seem increasingly no longer to have. And that is why we turn to the constitution not just as an instrument but as a symbol of the values on which we might rebuild social integration in a secular, ahistorical, culturally heterogeneous society.

This has become a pressing issue in an era when many states, having broken with dictatorships, racial division, and communist rule, seek to reconstitute their regimes in circumstances when a return to traditional values as symbols of common identity is not possible. Is the modern constitution up to this formidable task? The question is addressed by considering the experience of two regimes in which the constitution has played a decisive role in promoting social integration.

The Constitution as American Myth

Since its adoption in 1787–1791, the US Constitution has been amended only seventeen times, and today it is regarded as being fixed and permanent. Its remarkable achievement is to have maintained its standing as an expression of the stability of the regime while accommodating major social, economic, and political change. It therefore seems to have succeeded in promoting not only systemic but also social integration. Its power of systemic integration is in large part attributable to the unique circumstances of its adoption. After all, the Constitution effectively established the state. That it now stands as a sacred icon of American national identity is a testament to its power of social integration.

Enlightenment thinkers recognized that establishing a system of modern republican government would necessitate bolstering the regime by promoting a civil religion, "not precisely as dogmas of Religion but as sentiments of sociability."[6] This message was fully endorsed by the American founders who, from the very beginning, positioned their founding documents—the Declaration of Independence alongside the federal Constitution—at the forefront of the nation's collective memory. The date of signing of the former—4 July 1776—has ever since been commemorated as a national holiday, while the latter has been invested with enough symbolic capital to ensure its preeminent status within America's civil religion. From the outset, the federal Constitution was touted as a work of genius, designed so that "only its great outlines should be marked, its important objects designated" because otherwise it "would never be understood by the public."[7] It was intended as a permanent framework because otherwise the system of government would be deprived of "that veneration which time bestows on everything."[8]

At the time, however, there were many who believed that no document could ever fit the needs of future generations. Each generation, they asserted, must be free to order its own affairs. Of these, Jefferson was the most prominent. "Some men look at constitutions with sanctimonious reverence, and deem them like the ark of the covenant, too sacred to be touched," he wrote in 1816, and they "ascribe to the men of the preceding age a wisdom more than human, and suppose what they did to be beyond amendment."[9] But Jefferson's criticisms went unheeded. More typical are the sycophantic words of Supreme Court Justice William Johnson, who in 1823 wrote that the Constitution is "the most wonderful instrument ever drawn by the hand of man—there is a comprehension and precision that is unparalleled; and I can truly say that after having spent my life studying it, I daily find in it some new excellence."[10] By the mid-nineteenth century, Daniel Webster, the US secretary of state, could write that the Constitution "is all that gives us a national character."[11]

Reverence for what Lincoln had called the "political religion" of the Constitution became an especially important unifying force following the rupture created by the Civil War of 1861–1865.[12] This was a period in which many believe Lincoln had acted unconstitutionally. The rupture was so severe that historians maintain that the resulting constitutional amendments (the thirteenth to fifteenth) established what was in effect a new constitution. The first had been predicated on federal union and recognition of slavery, and the second was based on the expanding power of national government and the status of individual rights.[13] Yet, this dramatic change is masked by the brilliant rhetoric of Lincoln's Gettysburg Address. "Lincoln's own placing of the birth of the nation four-score-and-seven years before 1863," notes Sanford Levinson, "itself announces that the genuine scriptural text of the new Israel is the Declaration of Independence." The Constitution is reduced to "a merely instrumental means of attaining the scriptural vision." At that moment, the Constitution was transformed from an instrument of government into an aspirational ideal. The "more perfect union" referred to in the Constitution's preamble "is provided not by compliance with what occurs beneath the Preamble, but rather by achievement of the earlier vision of 1776."[14]

Writing in the mid-1930s, Edward Corwin had argued that not only was almost every major innovation since the founding unconstitutional but that the Constitution had evolved to become "a symbol of distrust of the political process—a symbol of democracy's fear of democracy." And this "symbol of the many," he concluded, has become "the instrument of the few, and all the better instrument for being such symbol."[15] Such claims, however, have since been submerged beneath a cacophony of voices suggesting that the Constitution's sense of permanence is not founded on mere idolatry. Rather, argues Kathleen Sullivan, it is because the Constitution now expresses enduring values, including public confidence in the coherence of the basic constitutional structure, the maintenance of the boundary between law and politics to uphold the rule of law, and the safeguarding of the legitimacy of the Supreme Court in its interpretative role.[16]

Such an idealized conception of the Constitution now takes its place alongside the flag and the Declaration of Independence to form "the holy trinity" of America's civil religion. In this guise, it fulfills the vital role of promoting social integration. Writing in the year of the Constitution's bicentenary, Irving Kristol had complained that the work of so many constitutional scholars is unsatisfactory precisely because it fails to imbibe the spirit of this ideal Constitution.[17] Judging from the volume of studies over the last thirty years, this is a deficiency American constitutional lawyers have more than rectified. Today, the most prominent of them spend prodigious energy in search of the elusive spirit of the Constitution.[18] From among many, consider Jack Balkin's book *Constitutional Redemption*.

Balkin's thesis is that the legitimacy of the American Constitution depends on "our faith in the constitutional project and its future trajectory," a faith that rests, in turn, on "the story that we tell ourselves about our country, about our constitutional project, and about our place within them." Of the many stories that might be told—of progress, decline, stasis, injustices unremedied, loss, restoration, corruption, and redemption—each could yield a different constitutional interpretation. Balkin recognizes that the "great progressive narrative" could provide "a spur to improvement" but rejects it as a self-congratulatory distortion. At the same time, he also rejects the narrative of decline: William Lloyd Garrison may have rightly argued that in protecting slavery the Constitution was "a covenant with death" that would bring about its ruin, but for Balkin that "is the beginning of the story not its end." Building on the argument of Robert Cover, another Yale scholar, he instead opts for a narrative of redemption, "not simply reform, but change that fulfils a promise of the past." And central to that argument is the claim that "the Preamble to the Constitution sets a purpose that is never fully achieved but is our duty to achieve."[19]

If the Constitution is an imperfect compromise reflecting the political circumstances of the time, for Balkin, the challenge is whether it can eventually be redeemed. Can the people "live up to the promises they give themselves" and "construct a Constitution worthy of respect"? Good design is
important, but the critical factor is garnering people's beliefs and commitment to engage them in the unfolding constitutional project. This requires
faith that carries the danger of idolatry, but Balkin is more concerned about
the form of idolatry that allows debates over the Constitution "to limit our
moral imagination" such that the people "will confuse what is just with what
is constitutional." For this reason, he argues that the Supreme Court cannot
hold a monopoly on the meaning of the Constitution, advocating in its place
a sort of constitutional Protestantism: "Just as people may read the Bible for
themselves and decide what they believe it means to them, so too citizens may
decide what the Constitution means to them and argue for it in public life."[20]

Balkin nevertheless maintains that the point of constitutional government
is "the eventual redemption in history of the principles of our founding document." But the founding document is the Declaration of Independence, not
the Constitution: "American constitutionalism is and must be a commitment
to the promises that the Declaration makes about our future as a people."
Courts might not hold the Declaration to be legally enforceable, but there is
no more important constitutional text. The Declaration "is the constitution
that our Constitution exists to serve"; it "provides a legal and political framework through which those promises can be redeemed in history."[21] Viewed
as civil religion, this idealized version of the Constitution subsumes the constitutional order of the state.

Constitutional Redemption is a powerful account of the US Constitution
as a project of social integration exhorting people to identify with past ac-
complishments, connect with their forebears, and see themselves engaged in
a common project. The American people are viewed as a community bound
by a religious covenant, rather in the way that at the Passover seder Jews re-
cite the story of their enslavement in Egypt and a redemption yet to be fulfilled.[22] It is an enticing narrative—and thoroughly ideological. It is a modern
American version of the myth of the ancient English constitution whereby
the struggle for liberty called for the restoration of the ancient liberty-
preserving Anglo-Saxon constitution suppressed under the Norman yoke.[23]

Advocating Protestantism as a democratizing force, interpreters must be fervent and faithful believers in an idealized reconstruction of the Constitution.[24] "Integration through constitution" propagates a faith so deeply entrenched that all too many Americans are convinced that social progress is not realized through politics, electoral majorities, and legislative change but from such scholastic exercises in constitutional reinterpretation.

Social Integration in a Country without History

The American narrative of the Constitution as a social myth is a story of triumph. A loose nation of immigrants is forged into a singular people "conceived in liberty, and dedicated to the proposition that all men are created equal." In stark contrast, the German narrative on "integration through constitution" is born of tragedy. The German nation, possessing an ethos of state and people, existed long before the adoption of its postwar constitution. But following the catastrophe of Nazi dictatorship, the Holocaust, and the division of the state, it was impossible to restore collective identity by drawing on traditional sources.[25] In "a country without history," the task of social integration depended on the capacity of its people to adhere to the liberal principles of its new postwar constitution, the Basic Law. "Integration through constitution" required the embrace of what came to be called "constitutional patriotism."[26]

During the 1980s, German historians engaged in a heated debate over these issues. Michael Stürmer maintained that "in a country without history, the future belongs to those who give substance to memory, shape concepts, and interpret the past."[27] This caused Habermas to retort that present-day Germans "wish to reaffirm the identity of a nation committed to civil rights in a version appropriate to our history," and "those who want to see Germans return to a conventional form of their national identity are destroying the only reliable basis of our connection to the West."[28] Habermas embraced constitutional patriotism as a form of identity in which the allegiance of citizens is no longer grounded in particular historical, cultural, and geographical sources but in their adherence to the universal legal, moral, and political values of constitutionalism.[29] Claiming that the "unconditional opening of the Federal Republic to the political culture of the West is the greatest achievement of the postwar period,"[30] he raised the question of how this late modern idea of patriotism was being realized.

The conventional answer is that Germany's successful reconstruction was the result of two factors: system integration achieved by the postwar economic miracle (*Wirtschaftswunder*) and the Basic Law's promotion of social integration. Constitution-making in West Germany began "with the vacuum as complete as any that western civilization has ever known." Under the tutelage of the Allies, a constitutional democracy quickly took root, although it had an unprepossessing start. It was not the result of a democratic decision of a sovereign people; rather, it was adopted by a Parliamentary council established at the behest of foreign powers and consisting of leading representatives of the main political parties. That it was only provisional was clearly indicated by its avoiding such terms as "constituent assembly" or "constitution" and by the fact that the Basic Law was ratified by agreement of the West German states' governments and not by popular referendum. "On the birth of very few other constitutions in the history of western civilization," noted Peter Merkl, "was public opinion so silent." Constitutional scholars at the time even referred to it simply as a law for "the uniform administration of the occupation zones outside the Iron Curtain."[31]

Since the failed experiment of Weimar had been feted at birth as making the German Republic "the most democratic democracy of the world,"[32] those drafting the Basic Law were particularly concerned about aspects of the Weimar Constitution that might have facilitated Hitler's rise to power. They therefore excluded certain popular elements such as the use of referendums. There was also concern that proportional representation might lead to a fragmentation of authority that could be exploited by the emergency powers of the president. Distrusting executive power, the framers ensured that the newly established Federal Constitutional Court, rather than the president, would be entrusted with the role of guardian of the constitution.[33] The Basic Law thus established a constitutional order of "managed" or "constrained" democracy that included multiple checks on popular sentiment. It was an "attempt to reconstruct democracy without the *demos*," making the Court "a veritable demiurge of West German democracy, of which it would determine both content and form."[34]

This was very much a lawyer's constitution. So how did it become such an important symbol of social integration? A federal regime alleviated fears of big government. Placing civil rights protection under the supervision of the Court rather than legislative or executive influence may have been another

factor. But one should not underestimate the simple fact that after their cat-
astrophic experience of war, the German people retreated into a private world
that eschewed interest in political issues. In a 1955 poll, when asked whether
they approved of the Basic Law, 51 percent of respondents claimed not to
know its contents, and as many as one-third to one-half indicated a complete
lack of interest in politics.[35] The Basic Law appears to have been constructed
as a constitution for a postpolitical age. But knowledge of its contents seemed
irrelevant since it came to stand as a monument of faith, a symbol of identity
that filled the vacuum created by the loss of historical sources of political
identity.

Günter Frankenberg notes that the Basic Law contains many principles
that are not easily reconcilable. These include majority rule versus protection
of minorities, individualism versus altruism, autonomy versus paternalism,
subjective rights versus the state's protective duties, and so on. "Exactly which
and how many of these rights, principles and values," he asks, "should a constitutional consensus encompass?"[36] This misses the point. All that is required for unity is faith in the symbol together with trust in the institution
acting as its guardian. Ernst Forsthoff may have been right in claiming that
"the Constitution has ceased to be an *instrument* of unification,"[37] but this is
a secondary matter once the constitution becomes a *symbol* of unification.

This symbolic role is reinforced by Article 79(3) of the Basic Law, which
prohibits any amendment of either the provision for basic rights or the organization of the federal system. This so-called eternity clause in effect imposes
a fixed value order on the regime, an order that during the 1950s was strengthened by Constitutional Court rulings maintaining that the Basic Law was
an "objective system of values" that not only bound the state but also shaped
the entire legal order.[38]

Dieter Grimm notes that the Court's "popular esteem grew from decade
to decade, as the dedications expressed at the various jubilees testify."[39] In a
speech marking the Court's tenth anniversary, for example, Rudolf Smend
modified his Weimar thesis that social integration is a function of cultural
factors and argued instead that the Court had now assumed this integrative
role: the Court "does not interpret and apply our Constitution as the standing
orders for an economic and technical-administrative purposive association,
but as rules for a good and fair life for the German people."[40] And when four
leading constitutional lawyers produced a critical appraisal to mark sixty

years of the Court's establishment, significantly they called it a study of "the unbounded Court."[41]

Peter Häberle's influential argument that constitutional interpretation should not be fixated on the "closed community" of legal scholars further points to the Basic Law's role in promoting social integration. A constitution "that not only incorporates the state in a narrow sense, but also structures the public and constitutes society" must embrace what he calls "the open society of constitutional interpreters."[42] This has similarities to Balkin's Protestant mode of interpretation, as does Häberle's argument that preambles, though not legally enforceable, are "*the* source of insights" into understanding the constitution "as a framework for renewed harmony of citizens, of legitimacy, limitation and rationalisation of state as well as societal power and as an expression of the cultural development of a People." For Häberle, preambles "are an appeal to all citizens and a directive for lawyers" and they "bring all the interpreters of an open society together in an exemplary fashion." But while the ideology of the "open society of constitutional interpreters" performs a significant symbolic role, Häberle also acknowledges that the court must remain "the guardians of the interpretive monopoly on the main stage."[43]

The Contemporary Cult of Constitutionalism

For many decades, the American constitutional experience was regarded as unique, a product of the singular circumstances of the birth of the American nation. But, as we have just seen, the American model of constitutionalism—the Constitution as a comprehensive text authorized in the name of the people to establish a permanent framework of higher-order law whose meaning is entrusted to the judiciary—also took root in postwar Germany.

Since the 1980s, this innovation has acquired universal significance. As Grimm notes, the German experience "became a model for many states that had liberated themselves from dictatorships of every ilk." Institutional features of the American model had been devised under the influence of classical constitutionalism, but newly liberated states saw in the German constitution "a guarantor of economic prosperity and political stability" and thus "borrowed from it when they drafted their own constitutions."[44]

But what exactly do they seek to borrow? It might be something akin to the German idea of "constitutional patriotism." The phrase resonates because, being so abstract, it is one "with which people on both the left and the right could identify," standing as it does as a modern political symbol "in a society deprived of its [historic] basis for national identification."[45] But institutional infrastructure is also important. The role of the German Constitutional Court, with its sole responsibility for attending to constitutional requirements, has distinct advantages. These, as Bruce Ackerman notes, are both legal and political. Legally, "it frees judges from the reigning dogmatism of the civil law tradition and allows them to reflect self-consciously on liberal values"; politically, "it encourages the selection of judges who are untainted by close association with the old regime." A great deal of the Court's legitimacy derives from two additional features. The first is that some key values of the Basic Law cannot be amended, which enhances the Court's autonomy. The second is the breadth of its jurisdiction, which "allows the court to generate its own symbolic linkages to the ordinary citizen." This, Ackerman concludes, "symbolizes the seriousness of the new regime's commitment to limited government and individual freedom."[46]

The age of constitutionalism, then, begins with a renewed interest across the world in the nature, purpose, and potential of a constitution. But the age of constitutionalism is not simply the result of the growing number of new constitutions over the last thirty or so years. It also signifies the realization of an ambition to establish the constitution not only as the authoritative instrument of government but also as the symbol of the regime's collective political identity. The constitution is raised to the status of civil religion.

The scale of this ambition is revealed once we realize that the instrumental and symbolic dimensions of the project directly conflict. To ensure "government under law," the instrumental aspect of the constitution requires clear rules on the allocation of decision-making authority. But to achieve its symbolic purposes, the constitution must incorporate values and statements of principles pitched at a high level of abstraction and ambiguity. Reconciliation of these instrumental and symbolic dimensions becomes a key task for the court, an innovation of major legal and political significance and one that requires the judiciary to develop nothing less than a new species of law.

The legal significance of the court's task in reconciling the instrumental and symbolic dimensions of the constitution should not be underestimated.

The judiciary must advance a new conception of fundamental law that involves a return neither to natural law nor to customary law. Requiring the interpenetration of political and legal reason, it is a novel elaboration of Rousseau's concept of *droit politique,* political right. It leads to the creation of "constitutional legality," a method of reasoning in which governing according to law no longer means governing subject to enacted rules but in accordance with abstract principles of legality dependent as much on political as legal rationality.

This development forces us to reconsider the nature of constitutional jurisdiction, the appropriate method of constitutional interpretation, and the meaning of constitutional legality. It also raises new questions about how such basic values as life, liberty, and property—and equality, solidarity, and security—are to be given constitutional recognition. Finally, it highlights the possibility that the Enlightenment project of "universal reformation" is entering a phase in which the catalog of constitutional values is not simply the measure of social integration within the nation-state but also of "global society." This takes us a long way from classical constitutionalism in which the judiciary acts merely as the mouthpiece of the law and in which—to use Montesquieu's terminology—their power of judging is "null."[47] The chapters that follow take up the implications of these developments.

Chapter 9

TOWARD A JURISTOCRACY

CLASSICAL constitutionalism envisaged an interlocking arrangement of governing institutions that could check and balance one another to create "a machine that would go of itself."[1] Good rhetoric perhaps, but even its most committed proponents recognized the need for some special institution that could, in Constant's words, act as a preservative power "to defend government against division among the governing and to defend the governed against oppression by the government."[2] Within the practice of constitutionalism today, it is universally assumed that that role is fulfilled by the judiciary. This was not a preordained feature of constitutional government, and indeed the "preservative" dimension of the judiciary's constitutional role is now given a rather different twist.

In the tradition of constitutional government, this preservative role was most commonly undertaken by Parliament. As the representative body of the "communities of the realm," Parliament ensured that the Crown, the governing institution, had due regard for the liberties of the people. In the British system, Parliament—a composite institution incorporating Crown, Lords, and Commons—was supposed to represent the entire political nation and therefore possessed sovereign authority to legislate on any matter. But the Commons had a special responsibility "to express the mind of the English people on all matters which come before it" and to lay before the Crown "the grievances and complaints of particular interests."[3] Its role was to ensure that new burdens would not be imposed until the Crown provided redress of grievances. The problem today, however, is that with the transition to democracy, the Commons determines the government, which puts obvious strain on its traditional role of guardian.

A modern constitutional settlement required new contenders for the role that must be independent of both the government and the people. Discussion in nineteenth-century European circles focused on whether that status might be assigned to a constitutional monarch, but the contradictions were quickly exposed and, in any case, once modern republics were established, such considerations were overtaken by events.[4] A similar debate had taken place in the United States, where it had initially been felt that the president might assume such a role. But after the formation of political parties that vied for the office, this became implausible, and the task had quickly fallen to the Supreme Court. In Europe, the legacy of courts as agents of the Crown made that transition more treacherous.

The Weimar Debate on the Guardian of the Constitution

These issues were acutely felt in the turbulent regime of Weimar Germany. The vexed question of who guards the Constitution became the subject of a seminal debate between two of its leading constitutional lawyers, Hans Kelsen and Carl Schmitt. Borrowing from Constant, Schmitt argued that the neutral power to protect the Constitution belonged to the Reich president. Kelsen, however, maintained that the role of guardian was the preserve of a constitutional court authorized to ensure conformity with constitutional requirements. Their debate was actually at cross-purposes since Schmitt's points were directed at the maintenance of the constitution of the state while Kelsen focused on preserving the normative scheme of the Constitution establishing the office of government. But their debate remains instructive.[5]

For Schmitt, the key issue was to identify some power that "is present and indispensable" as well as "discreet and unobtrusive," and active as a neutral power "only in a state of emergency." This neutral power was purely to preserve: "it is not to compete with the other powers with a view to expanding its own influence." Schmitt argues that this is a role for the Reich president with extensive powers to declare a state of emergency. The president must hold powers independently of the legislature to act as its counterweight, be independent of party affiliation, and swear an oath to preserve the Constitution.[6]

Kelsen approached the question differently. Having helped draft the Austrian Republic's Constitution of 1920, which gave a constitutional court power to strike down legislation, and having served as a judge on that court until 1929, his main concern was with the conundrum of "the legality of law" when a constitution is enacted and a system of constitutional review instituted. His answer to the puzzle was that law-making is a matter of degree: "Constitution, statute, decree, act of administration, judicial decision, and enforcement are simply steps in the formation of the will of the community that are typical, given the way in which positive law organizes the modern state." In relation specifically to the decree, legislation is the creation of law, but since legislation is enacted according to the constitution, legislation also involves the mere application of law.[7]

On the assumption that the constitution is the highest principle of legal and political order, Kelsen argued there is no good reason why legislation should not be subject to constitutional review. Without this jurisdiction, the constitution would lack the quality of full legal bindingness, a point that becomes especially compelling in a federal state in which governmental functions could not be adequately decentralized without some institution charged with policing these boundaries.[8]

Schmitt responded by suggesting that Kelsen's argument might apply to the US system, where the Supreme Court holds a position "unique in all of world history." But that system stood in "the starkest of contrasts to the states of the European Continent." He distrusted "unthinking transfers and mythologizations," arguing that the American system was a special type of "jurisdictional state" that "subjects all public life to the control of the ordinary courts." For Schmitt, this had resonance "only if we take the term 'constitution' to refer above all to the basic rights implicit in a liberal-bourgeois understanding of the rule of law, to personal freedom and private property, which are to be protected by the ordinary courts against the state." In an explanation that prefigures what I have called Ordo-constitutionalism, Schmitt claimed that Kelsen's scheme presupposes "a neutral state, a state that does not intervene, as a matter of principle, unless it is for the purpose of restoring the disturbed conditions of free competition."[9]

The enormous changes of the twentieth century, Schmitt explained, were the product of a dialectical development of the state running in three modern phases: "from the absolute state of the seventeenth and eighteenth via the neutral state of the liberal nineteenth century to the total state characterized by an identity of state and society." In the total state that has now evolved, society is subsumed into the state to become "an economic state, a cultural state, a caring state, a welfare state, a providing state," transforming the state into a self-organized society. The state, no longer materially separate from society, "comes to encompass everything social, i.e., everything that concerns the collective life of human beings." In this total state, all social and economic problems are political problems. If they were to become issues of constitutional adjudication, what results "would not be a juridification of politics but rather a politicization of adjudication." Within such a state, "no amount of judicial procedure could veil the fact that such a . . . constitutional court would be a highly political authority" and, in so burdening it, we "endanger it."[10]

This debate took place against the backdrop of extreme political tension that came to a head in 1932 when President Hindenburg's emergency decree deposed the Social Democratic government of Prussia and appointed federal commissioners to take over their functions. Prussia challenged the legality of this decree in the *Staatsgerichthof,* the court established to adjudicate disputes between the federal government and the state. The court issued an equivocal ruling justifying the Reich's assumption of control over Prussia's governmental functions to protect public security, even though the Prussian government had not breached its duties to the Reich.[11] This equivocation marked the beginning of the end. Schmitt's account, it would appear, was more realistic: the Constitution could not be preserved by a court, although conceivably the regime might have been protected by a determined president. As it turned out, the president's actual decisions facilitated the emergence of the Nazi regime. But Kelsen's normative argument was that the problem stemmed from the failure to establish a proper constitutional court under the Weimar Constitution. The future, as we shall see, belonged to Kelsen, but Schmitt's arguments about the role of constitutional courts in the era of "the total constitution" were to prove prescient.

The Rise of Constitutional Jurisdiction

At the end of the Second World War, many European countries began the long process of reconstruction by adopting a constitution intended to take effect as fundamental law and which equipped the judiciary with the powers of constitutional review. This was a major institutional innovation. Before the war, other than the exceptional case of the United States, there was only the limited experience of Austria and Czechoslovakia on which to draw. In 1920, Austria had been the first to establish a special constitutional court, an experiment that ceased in 1934 when the Dolfuss government acquired extensive emergency powers to rule by decree, making the court redundant.[12] Only since 1945 has the role of constitutional guardian been routinely allocated to the judiciary.[13]

One notable feature of this innovation in postwar Europe is that constitutional review is commonly assigned to a specially constituted court, unlike in the United States, where it proceeds through ordinary adjudicative procedures in courts of general jurisdiction. The Austrian constitutional court was revived in 1945, followed by the establishment of similar institutions in Germany (1952), Italy (1955), France (1958), and, after their transitions from authoritarianism, in Spain (1978) and Portugal (1982). But the era of most rapid acceleration came after 1989 following the communist collapse in Central and Eastern Europe, the establishment of a post-apartheid constitution in South Africa, and the transition from dictatorship to democracy in several Latin American countries. Today, more than sixty states operate constitutional courts.

Not all are based on a single model. The French Constitutional Council is the product of a tradition that rejects judicial review.[14] But even within the more orthodox format, there are differences. The Austrian court, for example, is established on formal and limited lines with jurisdictional responsibility over governmental action but only indirectly over the constitutionality of the underlying laws. Without the power to review the constitutionality of judicial decisions in conforming to basic rights, it is not obvious that the court is the guardian of the constitution.[15] Contrast Germany, whose constitutional court has ultimate responsibility not only for interpreting the constitution but also for preserving the integrity of the constitutional order. The Austrian model conforms to the principle of checks and balances within classical constitutionalism, but it is the German model, based on the power to determine constitutional complaints, that has proved most influential. The Austrian model entrusts the court with a preservative power, whereas the German model extends the court's remit to promote the collective values of society.

The celebrated Weimar debate focused on identifying the institution that could prevent erosion of the Constitution by political forces. After the war, the debate took place on rather different premises. An era marked by what Schmitt had called "the total state" saw the emergence not only of "the total constitution" but also of constitutional courts. Their task was to maintain not only a balance of power among governmental institutions but also to protect the regime's basic values, especially against a threatened collapse of democracies into dictatorship.

This is a dramatic extension of constitutional jurisdiction. But we should not overlook its impact on regimes operating under common law or on those—as in the United States—who still entrust constitutional responsibilities to courts of general jurisdiction. Operating on the principle of parliamentary supremacy, these regimes have nonetheless recently adopted charters of basic rights that have transformed the constitutional role of their courts. Starting with Canada in 1982 and New Zealand in 1990, the United Kingdom followed suit in 1998, as did Israel which, having inherited a British-style system of parliamentary government, adopted two new Basic Laws in 1992 that had a similar impact.[16]

In these regimes, the growth in constitutional litigation has meant the creation of special legal procedures, such as a streamlined application for judicial review. With the growing constitutional caseload, apex courts have had to take control of their dockets, resulting in the rapid increase in constitutional cases determined by supreme courts over the last thirty years.[17] In regimes founded on general jurisdiction, supreme courts are being converted into de facto constitutional courts.[18] In their method of working and their style of judgment, these supreme courts now operate in ways similar to specially established constitutional courts.

Postwar developments, touted in the name of strengthening constitutionalism, have resulted in scores of countries instituting constitutional reforms that have, in Ran Hirschl's words, "transferred an unprecedented amount of power from representative institutions to judiciaries."[19] Kelsen's case for the court as guardian of the constitution has evidently prevailed, but it succeeds alongside Schmitt's claim that this must lead to a politicized judiciary exercising a politically contentious constitutional jurisdiction. The result is that the guardian of the constitution becomes in effect its master, and arguably undermines rather than safeguards the democratic foundation of constitutional democracy. Why has this happened?

The Rights Revolution

The dramatic expansion of constitutional jurisdiction presented courts with public policy questions that a generation ago seemed well beyond judicial competence and more appropriately determined by legislative and executive bodies. The reasons for this global expansion of judicial power are multifaceted.[20] But the development is undoubtedly linked to the emergence of "the total constitution," that is, the sense that the adopted constitution now expresses the constitution of society. With the increasing juridification of social relations in the second phase of modernity, a greater range of political and social issues demand judicial resolution. The driving force is an ever-expanding conception of constitutional rights.[21]

The main task of the modern constitution as originally conceived was to protect a special set of individual interests from coercive governmental interference. These were the foundational values of civil and political rights— rights to life, liberty, and property—upon which were built the freedoms of speech, religious worship, expression, and association. Protecting Locke's negative freedoms by creating a zone of individual autonomy insulated from public interference, they formed the central building blocks of a system of limited government.

This conception of basic rights has since been overhauled, and its method of protection radically reformed. It has come about in three stages. First, courts have fashioned a jurisprudence of rights that imposes positive obligations on public authorities to protect negative rights. These protective duties correlate to the idea of the constitution as an "objective order of values."[22] For freedom of expression to be made a reality, for instance, it is not enough for the government to allow the right of demonstration. It must also require public authorities to facilitate the assembly and provide the necessary protection for safety. Secondly, through what is called the "horizontal effect" of rights, courts ensure that private individuals do not violate the rights of others, in which respect charters of rights might not only bind public authorities but also indirectly apply to individuals.[23] Thirdly, recent constitutions often include a range of social and economic rights, such as access to food, water, housing, health care, social security, and education. To be effective, such rights must directly impose duties on public authorities.[24] Each of these strands contributes to the proliferation of rights claims. As institutionalized expressions of Rousseau's concept of equal liberty, they promote an aspirational constitutionalism that imposes new burdens on constitutional courts.

These radical changes to the meaning of constitutional rights raise many interpretative challenges that will be examined in Chapter 10. But they have also had a major impact on the way constitutional courts operate. One effect is that almost any interest can now be reformulated as a right. Here, courts have followed the German Federal Constitutional Court in abandoning any test to distinguish a mere interest from a constitutional right. In sketching the global model of rights that has emerged, Kai Möller resists the conclusion that all interests are now converted to rights, arguing that the lengthening list of rights can be subsumed under "one comprehensive prima facie right to personal autonomy." Yet there can be no doubt that this leads both to the blending of ethical and legal conceptions of rights and to an enormous extension of the court's jurisdiction. A comprehensive right to autonomy, Möller concludes, "would avoid the possibility of unjustifiable and unanticipated gaps, in part by deliberately releasing judges from the interpretative constraints imposed by detailed and sometimes unfortunately framed constitutional provisions."[25] The possibility that the constitution under which we live is whatever the judges say it is acquires heightened significance.

The implications of this juridical revolution are directly addressed by Mattias Kumm. Just as Schmitt claimed that the twentieth-century state had become a total state, Kumm argues that in the twenty-first century we enter the era of the total constitution. Whereas in a total state, every aspect of social life can be politicized, in the total constitution, every aspect of social life can be constitutionalized. In the total constitution, rights still accord protection against government, but they also provide a way "to constitutionalize all political and legal conflicts" by establishing the general normative standards for the resolution of all legal and political conflicts. The court now acquires the authority to pronounce on "what constitutional justice requires."[26]

The total constitution signals the transformation of the legislative state into a juristocracy. This is a regime in which judges perform the critical role of ensuring that all powers are exercised with due respect for constitutional values. Since the legitimate purposes of public action are now inscribed in the principles of the adopted constitution, legislative activity is converted into a type of executive action: "Democratic politics, executive decision-making,

and ordinary judicial decision-making becomes constitutional implementation, subject to the supervision of a constitutional court." Kumm further
argues that there is no reason why private law should not be constitutionalized: conceptually, it qualifies "as a branch of applied constitutional law."[27]
For Kumm, Schmitt's concept of the total state resulted from the decline of
classical liberalism and led, through regulation, to the politicization of private law. Such legislative interferences must now be constrained by constitutional rights: the total state must be complemented by the total constitution.

Under the total constitution, legislatures draft the laws, but courts have an
"editorial function as veto players." They provide a forum for review of legislative action by affected individuals, with the language of rights being employed to protect their interests. This, argues Kumm, simply fulfills the revolutionary promise of the Enlightenment tradition. Consequently, "those who
lament the demise of democracy and the emergence of juristocracy may be
guided by mistaken ideas both about the point of rights and the appropriate
understanding of democracy."[28] Like Rubenfeld, Kumm equates constitutionalism with democracy.

Kumm explains that, far from being neutral, the total constitution exists
to protect specific values. It can therefore prevent "radical political change
by entrenching its basic structural features—constitutional rights, democracy, and the rule of law among them—precluding their abolition by way of
constitutional amendment."[29] One illustration is Germany's "eternity clause,"
which prohibits amendments to certain clauses of its Basic Law. Far more significant, however, are prohibitions on the power to amend that have been
devised by constitutional courts. Foremost amongst these is the "basic structure doctrine" formulated by the Supreme Court of India, which holds that
no amendment can abrogate or alter the Constitution's core features, including constitutional supremacy, the rule of law, the separation of powers,
judicial review, judicial independence, federalism, and secularism.[30] This
mighty doctrine has influenced the formation of analogous concepts in Asia,
Africa, and Latin America.[31]

This global trend of judicial empowerment through the constitutionalization of rights is one of the most important governmental developments of
the contemporary era. As states have either adopted new constitutions or revised them to provide a charter of rights, they have strengthened the volume,
scope, and intensity of judicial review. This has been accompanied by re-

moving self-imposed limits on jurisdictional controls, relaxing standing rules, considering moot questions, and effectively abandoning the political question doctrine. Armed with newly acquired powers, courts are resolving a range of political and public policy questions that not long ago would have been strictly off-limits.

Wielding these tools, they have overturned contentious political decisions on such matters as speech and religion, criminal justice, immigration, health policy, national security, electoral process, fiscal policy, treatment of prisoners, and the legality of same-sex marriage. An ever-expanding constitutional jurisdiction now embraces "matters of outright and utmost political significance that often define and divide whole polities." These range from banning political parties from national elections to determining the legality of national welfare reform, from determining the constitutionality of a presidential impeachment to establishing the legitimacy of a military coup d'état, from pronouncing on the validity of amnesty laws that protect perpetrators of human rights violations to determining which parts of the state may legitimately secede.[32]

What is driving this rights movement? Hirschl offers an answer, arguing that political, economic, and legal elites either initiate or acquiesce in these reforms because they "estimate that it serves their interests to abide by the limits imposed by judicial intervention in the political sphere." Constitutionalization, he maintains, depends on the interplay between three key groups: political elites seeking to preserve their hegemony by insulating certain policies from political change, economic elites who see it as a way of protecting the market-based economic order, and judicial elites, for whom enhanced constitutionalization increases their political influence.[33]

Presenting four case studies—Canada, New Zealand, Israel, and South Africa—Hirschl argues that although the rights revolution has had a "transformative effect on political discourse," its impact on "progressive notions of distributive justice is often overrated if not outright negligible." Far from being "a reflection of a genuinely progressive revolution," it is a form of "self-interested hegemonic preservation."[34] White elites in South Africa discovered the virtues of judicial review when apartheid was collapsing. After having opposed judicial review for decades, Israel's Ashkenazi bourgeois elite embraced constitutional rights when the electoral balance was shifting. That is, even when wrapped in the rhetoric of aspirational constitutionalism, the rights revolution works primarily to bolster liberal elites against political change that threatens their status.

Hirschl's account is not definitive. His causal claims have been doubted, and his account of the impact of global developments is limited. Other comparative studies have argued that the rights revolution originates in civil society pressures from below rather than leadership initiatives from above.[35] But in shifting the focus toward social, political, and economic factors, he points in the right direction.

The Rights Revolution and Constitutional Democracy

Can the establishment of a superior constitutional jurisdiction in a democracy ever be justified? If the role of such a court is just to protect the primacy of the constitution as an expression of the constituent power of the people, the case would be unanswerable. As Hamilton recognized, constitutional review is essential because if legislation contrary to the constitution were valid, the deputy would be placed above the principal, the servant above the master, and the people's representatives made superior to the people themselves. But recent developments indicate that the matter is not so straightforward.

The constitution, Laurence Tribe asserts, now "floats in a vast and deep—and, crucially, invisible—ocean of ideas, propositions, recovered memories, and imagined experiences that the Constitution as a whole puts us in a position to glimpse."[36] But—also crucially—it is the judiciary and not "us" who "glimpse." To Bertolt Brecht's question: "All power comes from the people, but where does it go to?,"[37] we are discovering a disconcerting answer. The constitutional role of the judiciary can no longer be comfortably placed within the classic scheme of the separation of powers. We have traveled a long way from Montesquieu's assumption that, among the three powers, that of judging is null. Judges have become the arbiters of constitutional meaning. It is true that such power is subject to institutional constraints: courts have no independent power of initiative, they must restrict their decisions to the issue at hand, and they must conform to the conventions of rational argumentation. But judges now have the power to determine the conditions of "political right," and in so doing they have arrogated the critical role of overseeing the political process.

Their role in regulating democratic will-formation is particularly contentious. Issues that go to the core meaning of a constitutional democracy now
occupy the attention of constitutional courts. The US Supreme Court has
been in the vanguard of reshaping the law on such matters as campaign fi-
nancing, political corruption, gerrymandering, and the redrawing of electoral
districts.[38] Where they lead, others are following. Constitutional courts are
now ruling on a range of political disputes concerning restrictions on the activities of political parties, the tenure of presidents, corruption indictments
against heads of state, and the determination of election results.[39] The German
Federal Constitutional Court, for example, has asserted its authority to determine when and under what conditions Germany's European Union membership is compatible with its constitutional commitments as a democracy.[40]
The South African Constitutional Court refused to certify the draft Constitution adopted by the Constitutional Assembly and required revisions to bolster the protection of rights, the first case of a constitution being declared
unconstitutional.[41] The influence of constitutional courts in shaping the transition to democracy in Central Europe, Latin America, and South Africa has
been of pivotal significance.[42]

Review agencies are clearly necessary to ensure the smooth working of
democratic will-formation.[43] But whereas this was once the task of independent review commissions, it is increasingly performed by courts. The problem
is that democracy is a contested political concept, and lawyers, conditioned
to think through the prism of rights, invariably privilege a particular conception. The reprocessing of democratic will-formation through the language
of rights—the rights of speech and association, the right to vote, and the right
to political equality—leads to individualization and thus significantly undermines the ability of collective organizations like political parties and interest groups to build coalitions of interests. "Emasculating these organizations in the name of empowering individuals or isolated groups," argues
Richard Pildes, "is confused at best and political suicide at worst."[44] It leads
down a dangerous road in which the abstract idea of a rights-respecting democracy is realized only when political parties have been abolished. This is,
of course, not the whole story.[45] But the general trajectory taken by the constitutionalization of electoral politics now threatens to advance constitutionalism at the expense of constitutional democracy.

Chapter 10

INTEGRATION THROUGH INTERPRETATION

IN the age of constitutionalism, the claim that the constitution establishes a permanent framework of fundamental law that expresses the regime's collective identity is vindicated. And with this victory, the tension between the constitution's instrumental and symbolic functions becomes acute. This issue had been recognized from the outset. When in 1819 Marshall C.J. declared that one must never forget that it is a constitution we are expounding, he put his finger on the problem. If the constitution were to include every detail of governmental powers, procedures, and limits, it could hardly be grasped by the human mind let alone understood by the public. When drafting a constitution, "only its great outlines should be marked, its important objects designated."[1] How, then, is this tension between the need for specificity in regulating government and ambiguity in expressing common values to be resolved? The task, it would appear, is one for the delicate arts of interpretation.

Marshall had identified the problem but had little to offer by way of a solution. Acknowledging that the US Constitution is "intended to endure for ages to come," he recognized that it must be able to adapt "to the various crises of human affairs." He therefore accepted that although the powers of government are strictly limited, some discretion over their execution must be permitted provided their exercise is consistent with "the letter and spirit of the Constitution."[2] Yet only a few years later, emphasizing that courts are "the mere instruments of the law," he had apparently resiled from this flexible approach.[3] Such ambivalence over interpretative method is not surprising. The great adventure of building a nation through the prism of the Constitution was still in its infancy. While the symbolic role of the Constitution in shaping the character of the people remained uncertain, so too must its method of interpretation.

Marshall's ambition in crafting the work of the US Supreme Court during its first three decades is undisputed. In the landmark judicial review case of *Marbury v. Madison,* he stated that "the whole American fabric" had been erected on the idea that "the people have an original right to establish for their future government such principles as, in their opinion, shall most conduce to their own happiness." Since this original right requires "a very great exertion" that cannot be frequently repeated, its basic principles "are designed to be permanent" and must take effect as "paramount law."[4] At the time of writing it was not at all self-evident that the Constitution either incorporated that ambition or could ever achieve that status.[5] But a century later, another great American jurist expressed confidence that Marshall's ambition had been realized. "When we are dealing with words that also are a constituent act, like the Constitution of the United States," Justice Holmes declared, "we must realize that they have called into life a being the development of which could not have been foreseen completely by the most gifted of its begetters." It was quite enough for them "to hope that they had created an organism" and "it has taken a century and has cost their successors much sweat and blood to prove that they created a nation."[6] The US Constitution, Holmes was proclaiming, was not just an instrument for regulating government: it had become a symbolic expression of the constitution of American society.

This remarkably ambitious endeavor complicates the question of interpretation. It explains why the search for *the* interpretative method able to present the Constitution as a comprehensive, coherent, and compelling scheme has spawned a vast industry. At fewer than eight thousand words, the US Constitution is a short text, but over the years Supreme Court justices "have written tens of thousands of pages" explicating its terms, creating "a vast amount of meaning that is not contained in the text of the document or its original understanding."[7] To which one might add that those tens of thousands of pages have been glossed by professors of constitutional law covering hundreds of thousands of pages.

The enterprise verges on collective madness, especially if we accept Judge Posner's claim that, since most Supreme Court decisions "are written by law clerks a year or two away from graduation," professors of constitutional law are devoting their intellectual energies to assessing the work of their recent students.[8] But the stakes are great, involving nothing less than a search for the soul of the nation.[9] And because of the range, depth, and sheer intellectual energy of deliberation over interpretative fidelity to the US Constitution, the following analysis is mainly devoted to American debates.

Interpreting the Law of the Constitution

One great achievement of American jurists was to have had the Constitution accepted as a legal document so speedily. Once the Constitution takes the form of fundamental law then, as Marshall emphasizes in *Marbury*, "it is emphatically the province and duty of the judicial department to say what the law is."[10] As higher-order law, constitutional meaning must be determined as a matter of *legal* interpretation. At that time, powerful detractors like Jefferson believed that "to consider the judges as the ultimate arbiters of all constitutional questions . . . would place us under the despotism of an oligarchy," maintaining that the Constitution "has erected no such single tribunal" but "more wisely made all the departments co-equal."[11] But Marshall's skillful statecraft firmly established the Court's standing as guardian of the Constitution.

Constitutional interpretation is nevertheless an onerous responsibility. In *Federalist* 78, Hamilton recognized that "there can be few men in the society who will have sufficient skill in the laws" to qualify for that judicial task, and fewer still "who unite the requisite integrity with the requisite knowledge." Conscious that those with such special qualities might be tempted to shape the text according to their own political proclivities, he emphasized that judges must never be disposed to exercise will instead of judgment. The surest safeguard was strict adherence to the standards imposed by professional discipline. In building a consistent body of constitutional knowledge, judges "should be bound down by strict rules and precedents."

Hamilton's method became the standard criterion by which constitutional interpretation retained its authority. To meet the challenge of interpreting a document "intended to endure for ages to come" and yet be "adapted to the various crises of human affairs," the solution must be to work with tried and tested common law methods. This was strongly defended by Justice Cardozo who, in his Storrs Lectures of 1922, argued that "the vacant spaces" left by the "great generalities of the constitution" must be filled "by the same processes and methods that have built up the customary law."[12]

For others, however, common law methods conferred too much discretion. The surest way of maintaining interpretative fidelity, Justice Black declared in 1964, is to follow the text's plain meaning. The framers had wisely ensured that the Constitution would endure by designing procedures for its amendment and they gave "no such amending power to this Court." The Court's duty must be "to construe, not to rewrite or amend, the Constitution."[13] Constitutional authority is maintained by interpreting it like any other legal text.

Since the 1960s this textualist method has fallen from favor and in many quarters is entirely discredited. It has been displaced by a creative interpretation that treats the Constitution as a living entity. The value of this method was explained in the landmark ruling that declared legislation prohibiting private homosexual activity unconstitutional. Justice Kennedy stated that, although the framers' intentions provide a starting point for discerning meaning, they also knew that "times can blind us to certain truths and later generations can see that laws once thought necessary and proper in fact serve only to oppress." Every generation must therefore be free to "invoke its principles in their own search for greater freedom."[14] The appropriate interpretative method, Kennedy concluded, is to invoke principles that capture contemporary culture.

These divergent interpretative methods reflect different philosophies of law: law as a body of custom and practice, law as the will of law-making institutions of the state, and law as a set of ethical principles. They are therefore forever entangled in deeper jurisprudential disputes. The resulting difficulties are illustrated in a relatively mundane case. In *Marsh v. Chambers,* the Supreme Court was invited to rule on whether the practice of the Nebraska legislature in opening each session with a short Christian prayer violated the First Amendment provision that "Congress shall make no law respecting an establishment of religion."[15]

Following Justice Black's method of interpreting the Constitution as a legal text, the issue is straightforward: the practice is unconstitutional, being a clear case of the official establishment of religion. Following Justice Cardozo's adherence to precedents, it is also unconstitutional because it fails the test for determining whether a practice infringes on the establishment clause in the leading authority of *Lemon v. Kurtzman.*[16] And following Justice Kennedy's method of applying principles, it is reasonable to conclude that the practice directly infringes on the purpose of keeping religion out of the political arena. Nevertheless, by a majority of six to three, the Supreme Court upheld the practice.

The Court concluded that the practice did not violate the First Amendment because "it has continued without interruption ever since that early session of Congress." Accepting that "historical patterns cannot justify contemporary violations of constitutional guarantees," the Court found that in this case the historical evidence shed light on the founders' intention.[17] Avoiding plain textual interpretation, powerful precedent, and contemporary principles, the Court upheld the practice of official prayers due to historical evidence suggesting that the framers did not intend the establishment clause to apply to this situation.

Robert Post uses this case to illustrate competing theories of constitutional interpretation.[18] He suggests that the three main theories of interpretation— doctrinal rules, original intent, and contemporary purpose—are engaged in the endless competition that makes up the entire history of constitutional adjudication. But the ambiguities are even deeper: presented with three powerful normative theories, in this case the Court chose to trump norm with fact, upholding the constitutionality of the practice simply on the basis of prescription. Lacking any authoritative interpretative method, judges are transformed from guardians into masters of the Constitution. They are obliged to express their rulings in the language of right, but there is little to prevent them from being swayed by prevailing forces of power.

The Cult of Constitutional Legality

Despite the intensity of interpretative disputes, what remains uncontested is that the meaning of the Constitution is the preserve of legal artistry. In the confessional style now commonly employed by prominent constitutional lawyers, Laurence Tribe confides how he abandoned a promising academic career in literary studies for the rigors first of abstract mathematics and then of constitutional law because these were fields of disciplined argument. What makes constitutional interpretation "truly a *legal* enterprise," he explains, is that it is "genuinely disciplined by widely shared canons of the interpretive arts and by stubborn truths of text, structure, and history." Tribe's is a powerful defense of the task of understanding the Constitution both as a legal text and "a *constitutive* text."[19]

Scholars generally agree that constitutional meaning is discerned by applying legal analysis to text, structure, and history, these being the main factors that shape competing claims over original intent, doctrinal rules, and contemporary purposes. Disputes tend to revolve around their relative importance. Akhil Reed Amar rescues textualism from conservatives with a sophisticated textual interpretation of the Constitution, revealing a more progressive document than is commonly appreciated.[20] Ronald Dworkin does a similar job with doctrinal history, arguing that judges respect "the dominant lines of past constitutional interpretation" and promote "constitutional integrity" by articulating "different understandings of central moral values embedded in the Constitution's text."[21] And rescuing structural analysis from a rigid formalism, Tribe himself shows that beyond the visible Constitution, we can discern what is "invisible *within* it," thereby revealing the integrity of the Constitution's complex arrangement.[22] Transcending their differences, these jurists share an appreciation of the authoritative status of the text and a conviction that its meaning can be disclosed through skillful legal analysis.

The defining characteristic of this type of American constitutional scholarship is its fetishism. This is symptomatic of the triumph of constitutionalism. Investing the Constitution with extraordinary authority despite fundamental interpretative disagreements, such fetishism promotes a cult of uncritical devotion toward the text. It leads to what Christopher Eisgruber calls the "aesthetic fallacy," the assumption that "the Constitution has an underlying aesthetic integrity, so that we should be extremely reluctant to conclude that it is redundant, clumsy, ambiguous, or incomplete." A consequence of this fallacy is the conviction that constitutional disputes can be resolved through interpretative acumen. Yet the Constitution is not "a work of political philosophy or a sacred text or an architectural blueprint or a great work of literature"; it is a document born of compromise by practical politicians operating through committees. It is not at all surprising that in places it is "vague, turgid, or redundant" or that it contains "pedestrian provisions and unfortunate errors." It would be "silly to interpret the Constitution in the way that we interpret poetry, philosophical texts, blueprints, or the Bible," but Eisgruber's damning conclusion is that this is what most American constitutional lawyers are doing.[23]

Suppressing the fact that the Constitution was a product of political compromise has had unfortunate consequences for American constitutional jurisprudence. The evidence shows that to form "a more perfect union," the Founders had not only to compromise on basic principles but also to obscure the character of the regime they were establishing. Specifically, the Constitution was drafted to achieve a compromise over slavery, and it could only maintain its authority by preserving that compromise. The silences, ambiguities, and what Eisgruber calls "unfortunate errors" in the text were deliberate aspects of its design.

Without providing explicit protection for slavery, the Constitution ensured that governing authorities could not abolish slavery without the consent of slave-owning states. Provisions such as the fugitive slave clause (Art. IV, sec. 2, cl. 3), the moratorium on federal legislation banning the international slave trade until 1808 (Art. I. sec. 9), and the provision counting every slave as three-fifths of a person for the purpose of legislative representation (Art I, sec. 2, cl. 3) were all designed to achieve this purpose. Slavery, as Justice Daniel noted in the *Dred Scott* case, "is the only private property which the Constitution has *specifically recognized,* and has imposed it as a direct obligation both on the States and the Federal Government to protect and *enforce.*"[24]

This compromise over slavery was maintained during the early decades of the republic. It was held securely in place by the political dominance of southern states, with slave-owning Virginians controlling the presidency for all but four of the first thirty-six years. Twelve of the sixteen presidential elections between 1788 and 1848 put a southern slaveholder into the White House.[25] The compromise lasted until the mid-nineteenth century when it was strained by changing demographic patterns that gave northern states greater political power. And it was at this point that the question of the original constitutional compromise came to the fore.

Today there is overwhelming consensus among constitutional lawyers that the Court's decision in *Dred Scott* came from an incorrect theory of constitutional interpretation and is the single worst decision in Supreme Court history.[26] Yet the Court's decision was faithful to the Constitution's original settlement. *Dred Scott* has acquired such notoriety because now that the

Constitution apparently constitutes the character of the people, it must be reinterpreted as the expression of founding wisdom and the embodiment of the nation's fundamental values. In reality, what happened during a turbulent period of social, economic, political, demographic, and technological change, was that the nation was presented with a conflict between constitutional obligation and social justice. President Lincoln chose justice over obligation and, in order to vindicate that choice, chose war over peace. Whatever the rights and wrongs of that choice—and it led to the death or injury of millions in the ensuing Civil War—to say that all this turned on a matter of constitutional interpretation is to adopt winner's history and with it the cult of aspirational constitutionalism.

For Mark Graber, "Lincoln failed the Constitution by forgetting that his obligation to adopt a plausible interpretation of the Constitution that preserved the social peace was constitutionally higher than his obligation to adopt an interpretation of the Constitution that best promoted justice." Graber's conclusions also touch on five other issues of constitutional interpretation. The first is that theories of constitutional interpretation cannot address what he calls "constitutional evil," which can only be confronted with a "constitutional politics that persuades or by a nonconstitutional politics that compels crucial political actors to abandon an evil practice." That is, fancy interpretative theories provide no substitute for practical politics. Second, the US Constitution, like all constitutions, was the product of compromise. With so many different interests to be accommodated, there must be limits on any comprehensive theory of the values and principles on which a regime rests. Third, *pace* aspirational constitutionalists who discover values in abstract expressions of principles, constitutions more commonly succeed by using prosaic mechanisms of an institutional design that allows political negotiation. Fourth, "the Constitution caused the Civil War by failing to establish institutions that would facilitate the constitutional politics necessary for the national government to make policies acceptable to crucial elites in both sections of the country." And, finally, "those responsible for creating and maintaining new constitutions in heterogeneous societies cannot be Lincolnians."[27]

The logic of this argument is that we should not look to the Constitution for our collective ideals of justice. The main purpose of a constitution is to establish the authority of the system of government, requiring that it

maintains social peace among people with different visions of the good society. This purpose is found in Madison's vision of the Constitution built on
national representation, federalism, checks and balances, and judicial review, but it has given way to the equation of the Constitution with Supreme
Court jurisprudence. Given the specific historical experience of the United
States, it is conceivable that social peace can now only be maintained by a
permanent investment in this cult of constitutional legality. Even so, we
should not deceive ourselves about the consequential costs and distortions.

A rickety charter of rights containing abstract protections of life, liberty,
and property alongside a right to bear arms and insisting that enumerated
rights "shall not be construed to deny or disparage others retained by the
people" is hardly the acme of modern rationality. It fails to include "the right
to travel, the right to vote, the right to marry, the rights of parents to conduct the upbringing of their children, the right to choose a vocation and earn
a living, and, most glaringly, any sort of equality right" leaving these and
other basic rights to be devised by the Supreme Court on an ad hoc basis and
subject to political trade-offs according to the composition of the Court.[28] It
culminates in the peculiar belief that one of the most important powers of
the president, the most powerful political office on earth, is the right to nominate judges to sit on the Court.

Interpreting the Constitution

A critical aspect of the Weimar debates over method was the distinction between the constitution and constitutional law. Constitutional lawyers go
wrong, argues Schmitt, by focusing on the *relative* concept of the constitution, the constitution understood as "a multitude of individual, formally
equivalent laws." Coherent constitutional interpretation, he maintains, depends on an *absolute* concept that expresses the constitution of the state as a
real or reflective whole.[29] From this perspective, American jurists go wrong
in conflating the text (the relative concept) with the manner in which their
state is constituted (the absolute concept). This is symptomatic of the fetishism
of constitutionalism.

This quality of constitutionalism is masked by the unique standing of the
Constitution in American public life. American jurisprudence divides into
two broad schools: strict constructivists and aspirationalists.[30] Once it is ac-

cepted that objective interpretation of a text—its plain meaning—is impossible,[31] these schools can be seen to present competing accounts of an absolute concept, the constitution of the state. They seek to present a cogent interpretation of the character of the *regime* and then show, implicitly, how it finds expression in the Constitution. Schmitt argues that there are two accounts of the absolute concept, the existential and the normative, reflecting the two-sided character of the state. Yet American theorists invariably present normativist interpretations. Despite their evident differences, Amar, Balkin, Dworkin, and Tribe all espouse normativist interpretations of the character of the regime and this then determines their reading of the US Constitution. Some, such as Amar and Tribe, do so while remaining focused on the text, while others—including Balkin and Dworkin—explicitly adopt a broader method in which marginalia—declarations, preambles, and footnotes[32]—have greater significance.

The most critical challenge to normativist interpretation comes from those who do not overlook the existential aspects of constitutional analysis. Glimmerings are seen in those textualists called "originalists" for whom the Constitution expresses what the text meant when it was first adopted.[33] This method might have resonance in a recently adopted constitutional text but seems little short of bizarre with respect to the US Constitution, which was drafted almost a quarter of a millennium ago.

The most influential existential analysis, however, is Bruce Ackerman's monumental study *We the People,* which is an account of the Constitution as a dynamic process in which the political unity of a people is continuously reconstituted.[34] In a three-volume study of 1,300 pages written over a period of twenty-five years, Ackerman's method has undoubtedly evolved, but its central theme remains fixed. He argues that a cult of constitutional legality has come to dominate constitutional discourse to such an extent that Americans cannot now grasp the significance of the changes made since the founding era. They know that the Constitution has changed in fundamental ways, but their fixation on Supreme Court opinions has meant they are taught "to conceptualize these changes in ways that trivialize them." Only when we are clear about "*what* we should be interpreting" can we appreciate "*how* to interpret." In place of the text, he argues, the focus should be on the regime, "the matrix of institutional relationships and fundamental values that are usually taken as the constitutional baseline in normal political life."[35]

Ackerman argues that a regime-centered analysis offers insights "into the interpretive dilemmas of the past" and clarifies "many modern problems of constitutional interpretation." What must be interpreted is neither the text nor some ideal normative scheme but "an evolving historical practice, constituted by generations of Americans as they mobilized, argued, resolved their ongoing disputes over the nation's identity and destiny." This point has been obscured by the formal amendment power in Article V which, combined with a cult of constitutional legality, skews appreciation of the real nature and extent of constitutional change. There is dissonance between a legal formalism that projects continuity and a "nation-centered substance" that establishes "the dynamic force behind the living constitution."[36]

The message is that in its legal form the Constitution expresses the values of classical constitutionalism, but in political reality it has become a total constitution, the constitution of the regime rather than simply the constitution of its office of government. The critical shift happened during post–Civil War Reconstruction. This was the moment when the 1787 Constitution, founded on a division of powers between the states and the federal government within which change took the form of an amendment, was effectively supplanted by substantive constitutional change forged in a consensus of president, Congress, and court. Reconstruction Republicans brought in reforms that stretched the 1787 Constitution "beyond the breaking point." Instead of holding a second Constitutional Convention, they "adapted the separation of powers between Congress, President, and Court as a great new engine for refining the constitutional will of the American people."[37]

Reconstruction, Ackerman argues, was as profound a constitutive act as that of the founding. At its core lay the principle of presidential leadership in which the president's initial claim to have a mandate from the people for change was most importantly taken up by Congress and later endorsed by the court. This principle was strengthened during the New Deal, when elements of the nineteenth-century constitutional settlement were superseded, and a system of government that could meet contemporary economic and social challenges was established. This system then laid a platform for the mid-twentieth-century civil rights revolution.

By focusing on the constitution of the regime, Ackerman explains, we see how the original "decentralized federal system enabling white men to pursue their self-interest within a market economy" has been replaced by "a powerful national government with unquestioned authority to secure the legal equality and economic welfare of all its citizens." The change results from interaction among all the major political actors, of which the court is only one element, and it brings about real change, not just the promise of abstract rights. Whereas aspirational normativists laud landmark rulings like *Brown v. Board of Education of Topeka,*[38] in reality it was when the president and Congress bolstered the ruling with a series of momentous statutes "that *Brown*'s promise became a fundamental premise of the modern republic." Tending not to treat legislation as a source of constitutional principle, lawyers fail to see how statutory reforms provided "the primary vehicle for the legal expression of popular sovereignty in the twentieth century."[39]

Ackerman argues for a reorientation that interprets the regime rather than the text. He shows that critical moments like Reconstruction or the New Deal, while giving a formal nod to the lightly amended Constitution of 1789–1791, are also "acts of constituent authority."[40] His thesis shows how a relational conception of constituent power does its work, illustrating what Schmitt meant with his concept of the constitution as a dynamically-evolving reconstitution of political unity. It also throws into relief the gulf that has arisen in US scholarship between constitutional theory and practice. Ackerman's is not the only account to do so—Post's analysis of *Marsh v. Chambers* also shows how theories of constitutional interpretation reflect different conceptions of constitutional authority.[41] But no one has surpassed Ackerman's account of why, contrary to the cult of constitutional legality, any sound theory of constitutional interpretation in a world of the total constitution must begin by interpreting the regime.

The Limits of Integration through Interpretation

One defining feature of the present age of constitutionalism is the abiding faith placed in the judiciary to determine the legitimacy of laws enacted by democratically elected legislatures. This they do with reference to principles that, whether or not explicitly stated, are assumed to be inscribed in the state's constitution. Across the world—from Costa Rica to Indonesia, Hungary to South Africa—newly-established constitutional courts are charged with propagating the faith.[42] Local variations exist, but they have a common theme: to explicate, through interpretation, the liberal values implicit in the regime's "invisible constitution."

Responding to these post-1989 developments, Ackerman strikes a different chord. Asserting the primary importance of "the creative role of constitutionalism," he argues that adopting an entrenched constitution must take priority because "constructing a liberal market economy, let alone a civil society, requires decades . . . and the project can easily be undermined without the timely adoption of an appropriate constitutional framework." He accepts that a "piece of paper calling itself a constitution" can be "an empty ideological gesture" without the means of ensuring that it becomes "a profound act of political self-definition." But the failure to entrench liberal gains, he maintains, will lead only to the erosion of any revolutionary achievement.[43] Ackerman here reveals a renewed faith in an entrenched constitution, a faith later affirmed by his suggestion that Roosevelt's failure to entrench the liberal gains of the New Deal had "a profound [sc. negative] impact on the next sixty years of constitutional development."[44]

There appear to be two Ackermans: the analyst and the advocate. The advocate promotes the entrenchment of liberal values in a new constitution while the analyst warns that this leads to a cult that distorts understanding of political change. The advocate endorses liberal normativism, while the analyst highlights its dangers.[45] But does not his advocacy overvalue the benefits of entrenchment? If liberal reforms are not working for the benefit of the many, then they are likely to unravel, with or without entrenchment.[46] The post-1989 experience in Central and Eastern Europe suggests that the adoption of a liberal constitutionalism that exchanges "pluralism for hegemony" and signifies "modernization by imitation and integration by assimilation" is leading to the rejection of what can only be "an inferior copy of a superior model."[47]

The evident absence of authoritative methods of constitutional interpretation is now contributing to a growing entanglement of courts in political controversy that can, it seems, only lead to an erosion of their legitimacy. This leads to two divergent types of response.

The first openly acknowledges these conflicts between theories of constitutional interpretation and recognizes that they rest on differing substantive visions about the meaning of the constitution, but argues that, rather than threatening the constitution's legitimacy, they actually help to sustain the constitution's authority. This argument, labeled "democratic constitutionalism," explicitly advances constitutional litigation as a surrogate political process. Accepting that no general normative methodology for deciding constitutional issues exists, Robert Post and Reva Siegel instead simply place their faith in the constitutional order's responsiveness to these competing political visions.[48] Tocqueville had argued that in a democracy, people obey the law because it is their own work and it can be changed if it does not command acceptance.[49] In a bold and rather implausible maneuver, Post and Siegel now implicitly appropriate Tocqueville's defense of democracy to justify the rather different regime of constitutionalism.

A second, widely touted response has been to shift the focus from theory to practice. Since no authoritative interpretative method exists, might a consensus nevertheless be formed over how judges actually undertake constitutional review? A proposed solution adopts a technique that, it is claimed, "entails very little interpretation," renders the underlying conception of rights "almost irrelevant," and enables judges "to evaluate the work of the political branches of government from a common perspective and without regard to their own political and moral philosophies."[50] This technique comes into its own once all interests are capable of being expressed in the language of rights. With the proliferation of rights discourse, rights are effectively converted into mere claims and, since most disputes involve competing claims, the court's role is transformed. Rather than inventing rights through interpretation, they simply need a method of weighing competing claims.

The solution is proportionality analysis. This technique requires the court to assess: (1) whether a measure that infringes a constitutionally protected interest serves a legitimate purpose, (2) whether the measure actually furthers that purpose, (3) whether the measure is necessary to realize that purpose (or whether there a less intrusive but equally effective measure exists), and (4) having met the previous tests, whether the benefits of infringing the interest are greater than the loss incurred. This test, first devised in German jurisprudence, has since been widely adopted as a standard technique for constitutional litigation addressing rights claims.[51]

Proportionality analysis illustrates a change in the role of the judiciary under the total constitution. Some claim that it institutionalizes "a practice of Socratic contestation" in which, rather than applying rules or interpreting

principles, courts assess justifications.[52] Constitutional courts therefore resolve the dilemma of interpretation by becoming a forum for reviewing the
public reasons that justify public action.[53] On this basis, argues David Beatty,
the practice of judicial review "has nothing to do with solving interpretive
puzzles"; instead, it instigates "a distinctive kind of discourse that operates,
in Habermas's terms, in an intermediate zone between facts and norms."[54]
Constitutional review, no longer an exercise in interpretation, becomes a
forum of policy review analogous to auditing.

With the emergence of proportionality analysis, Schmitt's quaintly named
"motorized legislator" is compounded with that of the algorithmic adjudi-
cator.[55] Losing their unique character as constitutional guardians, judges now
engage in policy review and enter into dialogue with legislatures and executives.[56] Any residual elements of classical constitutionalism, such as the separation of powers or strict rule of law enforcement, disappear to be replaced
with an auditing technique that ostensibly resolves all the legitimacy problems of constitutional interpretation. Integration through interpretation is
displaced by integration through system rationality. And in place of democratic constitutionalism's open embrace of aspirational constitutionalism, the
culture of justification promoted by proportionality analysis now aligns constitutional review more closely with the precepts of Ordo-constitutionalism.
This, as will be shown in Chapter 13, is considerably strengthened by global
developments.

Chapter 11

A NEW SPECIES OF LAW

WE must now examine further the cult of constitutional legality, which, as Chapter 10 indicated, is a key feature of contemporary constitutionalism. To do so, I first return to the early phases of adoption of a modern constitution. But rather than focusing on the United States and Europe as cradles of these ideals, I begin by highlighting developments in Latin America. This is because it is here that we see accentuated the scale of the challenge involved in trying to uphold the authority of the constitution against the background of intense political upheaval.

Throughout the nineteenth century, and in various parts of the world, many liberal political movements sprung up that sought to institute progressive reforms through the vehicle of a constitution designed to consolidate a new regime of limited government. Across Europe, the constitutions of France's satellite states, including Spain, had been dictated by Napoleon's policies. But the US Constitution, though generally overlooked in Europe, was paid "the sincere flattery of general imitation" by Latin American countries which, after declaring independence from Spain from 1811, sought to devise new forms of government. Despite their noble aims, however, and except for rare intervals, their experiences were "conspicuously lacking in justice, domestic tranquility and the blessings of liberty."[1]

The problem was that Latin American republics had acquired their independence in inauspicious circumstances. Years of war had ravaged their economies, and the Spanish imperial legacy left them not only without effective administrative and fiscal systems but also without any traditions of liberalism, republicanism, or representative government on which they might build a national political identity. They declared themselves republics and adopted constitutions that imitated the American model, with presidential

government and protection of basic rights, but they singularly failed to realize their goals. Imbibing the rationalist schemes of Enlightenment philosophers was not enough because the material conditions for success were altogether lacking. Following the demise of the Spanish Empire's religiously
inscribed rule, even the task of bolstering the authority of a bourgeois,
property-owning elite proved insurmountable.

The obstacles they faced should not be underestimated. These included "racial and class antagonisms, great inequalities of wealth and income, concen-
tration of land and power in the hands of a small ruling elite, the vestiges of
the monarchical tradition . . . appropriated by Latin American presidents and
the quasi-autonomy and privileges of the Catholic Church and military." In
all, over one hundred constitutions were adopted in sixteen Latin American
countries during the nineteenth century, with some—such as Bolivia and the
Dominican Republic—having enacted more than a dozen each.[2]

In such a turbulent social and political environment, Latin American constitutions all provided for emergency powers to be invoked in times of internal strife or external threat, most of which were modeled on powers acquired by the French during the revolutionary upheavals of the 1790s. These
powers provided the template for the modern concept of the state of siege
(état de siège).[3] Since the regimes were regularly threatened with civil strife,
these powers were frequently invoked. And since the powers provided for the
suspension of basic rights, these constitutional republics in reality functioned
as "regimes of exception." This led to the formation of constitutionally authorized systems of authoritarian government.

Most Latin American constitutions formally prohibited military participation in politics, but the reality turned out quite differently. The regular need
to invoke emergency powers made attempts to maintain civil control over the
military impossible. By the mid-nineteenth century, as Brian Loveman's research shows, every Latin American constitution had made some provision
for regimes of exception, and in over 80 percent of these the constitution
explicitly defined the military's role. Giving it responsibility for protecting
the constitution against internal subversion and for maintaining law and
order, the military was established as "a fourth branch of government with a
constitutionally defined status and a political mission." Since almost any coup
might be justified as intending to preserve the constitution from governmental abuses, Latin American constitutional republics soon became military dictatorships.[4]

These military dictatorships were not explicitly created by usurpation. They claimed to have been established in accordance with constitutional rules for the purpose of defending the constitution. The military became a key element of the regime's political system not just by force of circumstance but by deliberate constitutional design. The foundations of this system, laid down in the nineteenth century, later provided the pillars of twentieth-century Latin American constitutions.

Between 1900 and 2008, Latin American countries were under authoritarian rule for an average of over sixty-five years. Moreover, most of their twentieth-century constitutions were made or influenced by authoritarian rulers.[5] These were drafted for many reasons, including the need to legitimate their authority both internally and internationally, to regulate relations between governing institutions within the authoritarian regime, and to preserve their legacy at the end of military rule. Consequently, although the era of military rule in Latin America has now ended, with most countries since 1990 established as constitutional democracies, the influence of these practices remains. The legacy persists most clearly in a presidential system that, through a "winner-takes-all" process, exacerbates rather than alleviates political tensions,[6] in a weak judiciary that cannot protect basic rights,[7] and in a military power that has come to conceive itself as the guardian of the constitution.[8]

The Latin American experience throws up a more general question about the modern constitution. The template of emergency powers in these constitutions was borrowed from European models, has been widely adopted across the world, and has been acknowledged as a critical element not only of classical constitutionalism but also of Ordo-constitutionalism.[9] It therefore raises questions about the meaning of "the rule of law" under the modern constitution and the way that idea evolves under the total constitution. The distinction between normal and exceptional conditions has been accommodated in modern constitutional thought, as has the idea that, in exceptional situations, aspects of the rule of law might have to be qualified. But can this distinction persist in a world of the total constitution?

Norm and Exception

The classical doctrine of constitutionalism was devised on assumptions drawn from late-eighteenth-century conditions. One was that within the tripartite division of power, the legislature was likely to be the most dangerous branch.[10] Another was that the burdens of government would not be especially onerous. A third was that with the emergence of the age of commerce, warfare would decline, conflict would be replaced by trade, and constitutional democracies would exist in a hospitable world.[11] Each of these assumptions proved ill founded. The rapid pace of modern social and economic change led to a dramatic extension of governmental functions. With the challenges of maintaining the security of the total state against the threats of war, economic crises, natural disasters, and epidemics, the government had to shift to an administrative mode. Administrative rationality became the logic of modern government. As Weber said, "everything else has become window dressing."[12]

Designed for a world of peace and limited government, the "normal" workings of constitutional democracies have often been strained when confronted with crises and emergencies. Emergencies can arise from many sources. Natural disasters, foreign threats, serious policy failures, or economic collapse may not always lead to crisis in the sense of a governmental inability to act or the perceived illegitimacy of governmental action. But responses to emergencies commonly require extraordinary executive action in situations that cannot be controlled by legislatures and courts. The dilemma is that facing an emergency, a constitutional democracy cannot avoid adopting exceptional measures, yet it cannot survive if those measures permit unbridled executive action. This is the dilemma of norm and exception: How can exceptional executive powers be granted without normalizing them and thereby converting constitutional democracy into an authoritarian regime?

Writing on the cusp of modernity, Locke was one of the earliest scholars to address this issue. As an advocate of keeping legislative and executive powers in separate hands, he is regarded as a pioneer of classical constitutionalism. But recognizing that the government is entrusted with a distinct set of powers, he also argues that these must include discretionary powers to act "for the publick good, without the prescription of the Law, and sometimes even against it." This enables the government to respond to an indeterminate range of risks that cannot be regulated by general rules. Locke's argument accords with the logic of norm and exception. The "normal" sovereign authority is the legislature, which holds the supreme power of rule-making. But because life cannot be governed entirely by general rules, the executive must have "an Arbitrary Power in some things left in the Prince's hand to do good."

Acknowledging the two-sided character of the state, Locke sought to reconcile reason with necessity, adherence to law with pursuit of the common good, maintenance of the norm with accommodation of the exception.[13]

These tensions become ever more acute in the modern era. If, as Paine indicated, the constitution must contain the complete set of governmental principles, what provision is made for exceptional action during an emergency? Among the American Founders, we find Jefferson thinking along similar lines to Locke. "A strict observance of the written laws is doubtless one of the highest duties of a good citizen," he notes, but "it is not the highest" because the "laws of necessity, of self-preservation, of saving our country when in danger, are of higher obligation."[14] Jefferson's speculations became issues of intense practical significance during the 1860s when the American republic faced the prospect of secession and civil war.

Confronted with armed rebellion in the southern states, President Lincoln had to decide whether Jefferson was right and, if so, what was required. Following the fall of Fort Sumter on 13 April 1861, he called a special session of Congress but scheduled it to convene only on 4 July. In the intervening eleven weeks, acting alone and without clear constitutional authority or precedents, he took dramatic action. For Lincoln, maintenance of the Union was more important than adherence to the Constitution, and this licensed him to take action beyond the executive powers conferred by Article II. In a series of proclamations he summoned the militia of several states to help suppress the rebellion, blockaded the ports of seceded states, called on volunteers to serve in the regular army for a period of three years, and ordered the suspension of the writ of habeas corpus in the vicinity of any military action.[15] Most of these measures, based on powers within the authority of Congress, were unconstitutional, as was Lincoln's disobedience of Chief Justice Taney's ruling that suspension of habeas corpus was beyond presidential power.[16] But by the time Congress convened, Lincoln had set in place "a complete program—executive, military, legislative, and judicial—for the suppression of the insurrection."[17]

When Congress did meet, the president explained his actions, arguing that they were either legal or required by public necessity, and invited Congress to ratify them. "Are all the laws, *but one,* to go unexecuted, and the government itself, go to pieces," he declaimed, "lest that one be violated?"[18] Presented with this fait accompli, Congress could only register approval of the president's measures. A year or so later, the Supreme Court upheld the legality of the blockade, stating that the question of whether the president was justified in regarding the insurrection as the action of belligerents was a matter for the "political department of the Government."[19]

Clinton Rossiter suggests that Lincoln's actions exemplify one of history's most important manifestations of what he calls "constitutional dictatorship."[20] Daniel Farber cautions that Lincoln "was not arguing for the *legal* power to take emergency actions contrary to statutory or constitutional mandates" but only that, while unlawful, these actions "could be ratified by Congress if it chose to" and that they remained "morally consistent with his oath of office." Lincoln chose the lesser of two evils, Farber explains, and it is only by reading them out of context that we can claim they stand for some more general proposition.[21]

Rossiter's use of the term "dictatorship" in describing the exercise of presidential power in a constitutional democracy is controversial. Dictatorship suggests that government is above rather than subject to the law, making "constitutional dictatorship" an oxymoron. His usage is drawn from the ill-fated German Republic. When the Weimar Constitution was adopted, the notion of law as the command of the sovereign power had apparently been replaced by a higher-order arrangement of modern constitutional law. But because of volatile circumstances surrounding its adoption, Article 48 of the Constitution gave the president broad powers of action, including suspension of basic rights, if "public security and order are seriously disturbed or endangered." Owing to the economic and political upheavals of the period, the power to rule by decree was extensively invoked.[22]

Carl Schmitt was maturing as a constitutional scholar during these turbulent times. In 1921 he published a historical study of dictatorship from its Roman origins to its role in the Weimar Constitution. His thesis was that modern dictatorship was changing from a commissary function, in which a mandate is given to suspend the constitution in order to preserve it, into a sovereign dictatorship with powers beyond an interposing constitution.[23] Following this, he wrote a more polemical account of sovereign power, opening with the dramatic claim that: "Sovereign is whoever decides on the exception."[24] Schmitt argued that despite the tendency of all modern constitutional development to seek elimination of the sovereign, this could not be realized.

Constitutional norms might regulate public action in normal times, but they could not govern during exceptional circumstances when constitutional norms must be displaced to protect the constitution of the state.

Schmitt's point is that whether a state of exception exists is a political decision, a decision of the sovereign power. Constitutionalism might contemplate the death of the sovereign, but that is impossible. Arguing that "the exception is different from anarchy and chaos" and that "order in the juristic sense still prevails even if it is not of the ordinary kind," Schmitt is describing a type of commissary dictatorship. If the written law is displaced, it is because the state "suspends the law in the exception on the basis of its right of self-preservation."[25] That normativists are blind to this point, Schmitt argues, is a serious weakness. They too readily assume the authority of the enacted normative order and cannot explain how that order can suspend itself. How is it logically possible, he asks, "that the norm is valid except for one concrete case that it cannot factually determine in any definitive manner?"[26]

Unable to account for the distinction between norm and exception, Schmitt argues that liberal constitutionalists try "to regulate the exception as precisely as possible" and "to spell out in detail the case in which law suspends itself."[27] This is precisely how Rossiter approaches the task. Rossiter offers many criteria for controlling the institution, operation, and termination of the state of exception. It should not be initiated unless indispensable to the preservation of the state and its constitutional order. The decision to initiate should not be made by those who will hold these exceptional powers. At the moment of initiation, a specific provision must be made for its termination. All uses of emergency powers should comply with legal requirements. No rights or procedures should be altered any more than is necessary, and no adopted measures should be made permanent. Powers should be exercised by representative officers who retain ultimate responsibility for emergency actions. The decision to terminate the emergency should not be made by those exercising emergency powers. And none of these powers should extend beyond the end of the crisis when the antedating constitutional arrangements immediately apply.[28]

Some of Rossiter's criteria are sound prudential precepts. They reveal, for example, why Latin American practice, especially in giving the military a role as constitutional guardian, fails to prevent a commissary function from becoming a sovereign dictatorship. Other criteria, such as compliance with legal requirements or that infringements should be no greater than necessary, are either too vague for any practical guidance or exercises in wishful thinking. None directly addresses the jurisprudential question Schmitt raises.

Successive waves of Islamist terrorist attacks from 11 September 2001 onward made these questions once again prominent. Many have followed Rossiter's method, seeking precise criteria for invoking and constraining emergency powers. Highlighting the threat to civil liberties imposed by emergency regimes, for example, Ackerman argues for short-term emergency measures only. These should impose strict limits on unilateral executive action and powers of detention and provide for extensions of the measures only after legislative approval by an escalating supermajority.[29] More radically, Oren Gross argues that the adoption of what he calls an "extra-legal measures model," in which violation of constitutional norms is sanctioned, might serve the protection of those norms better than the accommodations that are commonly made to deal with emergencies and that end up eroding the standing of constitutional norms.[30]

These reprise earlier debates, but one important limitation of recent proposals is a tendency to be formulated with terrorist threats in mind. Seeking to minimize the impact of special powers of detention on civil liberties, they treat the question of emergency powers too narrowly. The challenge raised by emergencies extends way beyond terrorism to include economic matters such as the 2008 financial crisis as well as natural crises caused by hurricanes, tsunamis, and pandemics. In this wider context, any attempt to define an emergency powers regime that ensures the crisis period is limited and normal conditions are quickly restored becomes a much more complex undertaking.

In the face of these growing challenges, constitutional lawyers apparently continue to be guided by the model of classical constitutionalism. Yet the issue of how to design governmental powers to address emergencies is only tenuously related to tensions between executive and legislature in the conferral of powers or between executive and judiciary over how those powers are exercised. In the world of the total state in which risks—economic, political, natural, ecological, technological—are rapidly increasing, the challenges are unlikely to be resolved by falling back on classical constitutionalism. The implications of incorporating emergencies within the framework of the total constitution have not yet been adequately addressed.

Normalizing the Exception

The jurisprudential issues presented by addressing emergencies in the context of the total constitution are only now coming to the fore. In a world in which every aspect of social life can be constitutionalized and no disputes fall outside the framework of constitutional norms, there can be no room for a regime of exception. This presents a new challenge that normativists embracing the total constitution must address.

The challenge is taken up by David Dyzenhaus. Acknowledging that the norm-exception distinction skews the debate about emergencies, he accepts that no true legal order can make room for a regime of exception; a legal order that compromises is not only morally but also legally compromised. Dyzenhaus argues that the essential criterion of governmental legitimacy is adherence to a universal rule of law project. The critical issue in emergencies is not to maintain a separation of powers or establish appropriate checks; it is to ensure that all public institutions—not just the judiciary—protect the "fundamental constitutional principles" that are "inherent in the constitution of law itself." In rejecting the norm-exception distinction, Dyzenhaus also rejects all versions of the two-sided theory of the state: "the state is totally constituted by law." Consequently, we face a stark choice between "government under the rule of law and government by arbitrary power." For constitutionalists, the distinction between norm and exception is analogous to that between legitimacy and illegitimacy.[31]

When Dyzenhaus switches from theory to practice, however, his analysis becomes much more ambiguous. He recognizes the need for special regimes provided that "there is both an absolutely explicit legislative mandate for such experiments and that the experiments be conducted in accordance with the rule of law." Criticizing Rossiter's account for relying on a "hope" that those exercising emergency powers will return to the ordinary way of doing things as soon as possible, he nevertheless argues similarly that judges should simply use "the legal protections provided as a basis for trying to reduce official arbitrariness to the greatest extent possible." In endorsing experiments that balance security and rights, so modifying normal legal procedures, Dyzenhaus moves away from a strict conception of legality to a sense of legality appropriate to the circumstances. In place of strict legality as the norm and arbitrary power as the exception, his abstract appeal to a "spirit of legality" incorporates a proportionality calculation that normal-izes the exception.[32]

Criticizing Dyzenhaus's argument as being "grounded in a Kantian ethics made up of synthetic a priori moral propositions," Nomi Claire Lazar presents an alternative theoretical framework founded on an "ethics of experience." Recognizing that virtually all rights claims are now subject to proportionality assessment, she extends that principle to emergencies. Arguing that emergency regimes show "salient continuities" with normal situations, she maintains that the exercise of emergency powers "are justified, when they are justified, because they embody principles that already function under normal circumstances." The state, Lazar concludes, cannot be ruled by law alone, not least because "the rule of law" is only ever a matter of degree.[33]

These differences reflect different jurisprudential traditions of law and the meaning of the rule of law, but they now erect barriers to understanding. No jurist maintains that there can be a regime of exception that is entirely norm-free. In the early modern period, it was accepted that when urgent action was required, it was not unjust for the ruler to take actions contrary to law, a claim formalized as "reason of state."[34] But by this jurists meant free from formal written rules, not a sphere of entirely arbitrary action. In this respect, Schmitt, like Locke, argues that to protect the state—that is, the *constituted* order—the *written law* may have to be displaced. But he does recognize that in responding to emergencies, "order in the juristic sense still prevails." Lazar's position is close to the orthodox view that once a state has adopted a constitution, there can be no regime free from institutional review, but circumstances exist in which the rules may need to be qualified. This is analogous to what Carl Friedrich in 1957 calls "constitutional reason of state."[35] And Dyzenhaus, implicitly accepting the idea of the total constitution, argues that all governmental action must be governed by some ineffable "spirit of legality."

These arguments circle around the critical issue. Dyzenhaus rejects the norm-exception dichotomy but in doing so presents a crude account of Schmitt's argument, claiming that Schmitt believes that "emergencies are a black hole." He then simply replaces these with "grey holes," combined with a plea that judges must maintain oversight.[36] Lazar adopts a similarly unrefined approach, arguing that "Schmitt's conception of sovereign dictatorship is impossible" and that it is "as abstract and unworkable as [Dyzenhaus's] liberal ideal theory."[37] The critical task surely must be to move beyond invocations to "the rule of law" and "constitutional reason of state" and directly examine the reason of the constitutional state. If norm-exception does not work, "experiential ethics" is a fudge, and "spirit of legality" is a retreat into abstraction, can a more appropriate formulation be found?

The Concept of Constitutional Legality

In the era of the total constitution, reason of state is absorbed into constitutional reason. The constitution now regulates the procedures both for declaring a state of emergency and for judicial control of its processes.[38] Since the process is now institutionalized, it is no longer simply a matter of the ruler's conscience. Governments cannot now claim the authority to act unlawfully, even for what Friedrich calls "constitutional reasons of state." They either invoke formal constitutional procedures, such as a state of emergency, or they exercise broad discretionary powers conferred on them by legislation. In either case, governments make no claim to act by virtue of necessity, emergency, or higher good; they invoke an already existing lawfully conferred power. In the total constitution, the exception, being constitutionalized, is normalized.

In this totalizing era, a new species of law is emerging that advances the "invisible constitution" as the overarching edifice of legality. This is constitutional legality, a type of super-legality that is depersonalized, abstract, and ahistorical. It begins to emerge as the constitution, having acquired the status of "higher law" with the judiciary its authoritative interpreter, becomes the expression of a society's fundamental principles. In the total constitution, all public authority emanates from and is conditioned by the written constitution; there can be no sovereign beyond it. But it is no longer just a system of rules; it is a set of abstract principles, an "invisible constitution" that articulates the values of social order. And, crucially, the constitution no longer derives its authority from the constituent power of the people who adopted the text; once that historical link is broken, the constitution is treated as an order of values that evolves as social conditions change.

The modern idea of law as a system of rules enacted by the legislature still performs an extensive regulatory function. But it is overlaid by a new species of law—constitutional legality—that shapes the entire regime. Ordinary law—legislation—is a product of will, while super-legality evolves through an elaboration of reason. Legality is determined by explicating "the invisible constitution." Political disputes are managed by applying the principles of super-legality. And all governmental action, including legislation, is subject to a principle of objective justification: Can the measure in question be justified as necessary and proportionate?

Normativist jurists see the emergence of constitutional legality as an entirely progressive development. But it is far more equivocal. Although its implications are only now coming to the fore, constitutional legality was built into the foundations of constitutionalism. Consider, for example, Hamilton's contention in *Federalist* 23 that because the government is entrusted with the safety and well-being of the state and the factors that endanger this are infinite, the president's powers must be given a generous interpretation. "No constitutional shackle can wisely be imposed on the power" because failure to confer enough power would be "to violate the most obvious rules of prudence and propriety" and "no precise bounds could be set to the national exigencies." Maintaining that "a power equal to every possible exigency must exist somewhere in the government," Hamilton concludes that, if not otherwise specified, that power is the president's.

Hamilton never countenanced the possibility that governmental power could be exercised contrary to law or that special regimes should be created to deal with emergencies. For him, the Constitution conferred broad executive discretionary powers to act proportionately to perceived threats. The question of whether extraordinary executive powers are constitutional has since provoked intense debate, but under a total constitution there can be no doubt. Reason of state has been institutionalized and the exception normalized.

Contemporary constitutionalism envisages a regime of governing according to law. But the concept of constitutional legality makes this an indeterminate prospect. Government cannot act in direct contravention to law simply because the institutional safeguards of the constitution do not permit it. But legislatures now delegate broad powers to executives not only to deal with emergencies but also to act in a general regulatory capacity, and the principle of "proportionate empowering" confers wide latitude to take whatever action is deemed necessary. Through a wide range of mechanisms, governments now play a major role in enacting, shaping, interpreting, implementing, and reviewing legal rules and determining the government's own legal responsibilities.[39] In this process, legal principle and political necessity become fused.[40]

In the era of the total constitution, government according to law no longer means governing subject to independently promulgated formal rules. It means governing in accordance with abstract principles of legality whose explication is as much a political as legal exercise, as much a governmental as a judicial undertaking. Abstract principles acquire meaning only when infused with values, with no rational method existing for choosing between contestable values claiming to be the best iteration of the principle. The rule of law no longer means conformity to rules; it requires a judgment on whether liberal principles of liberty and equality can be reconciled with claims of necessity and security. Constitutional legality emerges as a powerful and intensely contestable political phenomenon.

Chapter 12

THE STRUGGLE
FOR RECOGNITION

CLASSICAL constitutionalism is a liberal but not necessarily democratic governing philosophy. The modern idea of the constitution puts "the people" in a pivotal position, with the type of formulation adopted in the preamble to the US Constitution—"We the people of the United States . . . do ordain and establish this Constitution"—now being almost universally adopted.[1] The claim of "government by the people" was the banner under which American colonists sought freedom from British rule, the French third estate demanded the abolition of hereditary privileges, and that has since inspired all movements for constitutional modernization. But it was never so simple. The claim that power had been traded for right and force replaced by a narrative of a people who have agreed about the terms by which they are to be governed remains highly ambiguous.

Erected on a distinction between public and private, classical constitutionalism assumed that only active citizens, those men whose wealth gave them the freedom to deliberate on public matters, were fit to participate in the public business of governing. The rest—the great majority of "dependent" persons (women, domestic servants, laborers)—might be given basic civil rights, but they could not form part of the political nation. Indeed, those countries in the vanguard of promoting modern freedoms invariably perpetuated regimes of slavery or other forms of indentured servitude.[2] Only active citizens could be entrusted with the task of attending to "the rule of law"; the rest could expect, at best, only to be "ruled by law."

The great political struggle ever since has been against the institutionalized conviction that gender, race, and economic dependence render people unfit for active citizenship. Governing in accordance with the precepts of classical constitutionalism not only enforced a regime of hierarchy and inequality; through its stories of "peoplehood," it also legitimated it.[3] The critical question today is whether this political struggle to overthrow these classical assumptions by democratization brings about major changes in the values of constitutionalism or whether the ideological power of constitutionalism has been able to tame democracy and bring it into alignment with constitutionalism's founding ideals.

Enfranchisement and Emancipation

In most liberal regimes, political struggles for enfranchisement led to legislative reforms that incrementally brought the vote to the laboring classes and women. These were invariably long drawn-out processes, with Britain achieving universal suffrage in 1928, France in 1945, and Switzerland finally realizing it only in 1991. But emancipation from slavery raised more acute issues.

Since slavery had been institutionalized through the US Constitution, the struggle to overcome it inevitably had a constitutional aspect. By 1860, emancipation seemed a remote prospect: the institution was deeply entrenched, with eleven of the republic's fifteen presidents and seventeen of the twenty-eight Supreme Court justices slave owners.[4] Only a few years earlier the Supreme Court had struck down an Act of Congress authorizing the outlawing of slavery in certain states on the ground that it infringed the Fifth Amendment's prohibition on the deprivation of property without due process of law.[5] Tensions over this issue reached a head during the 1860s but were completely resistant to political resolution. A bloody civil war followed.

The Unionist victory resulted in a sustained attempt to reunite the nation on the foundations of liberty and equality. Reconstruction included a rewriting of the Constitution through the Thirteenth, Fourteenth, and Fifteenth Amendments, which provided for the abolition of slavery, the equal protection of the laws, and protected the right to vote against discrimination by race. Congressional legislation advanced these constitutional principles, notably in the Civil Rights Act of 1875, which provided for equal treatment in access to public facilities.

However, enforcement of this new settlement, not being actively taken up by the political branches, was left to the Supreme Court. In a series of rulings over the following three decades, the Court delivered consistently restrictive interpretations of the Fourteenth and Fifteenth Amendments and the Civil Rights Act.[6] In 1896 the Court then delivered the coup de grâce. *Plessy v. Ferguson* upheld the constitutionality of a Louisiana statute that required railway companies to "provide equal but separate accommodations for the white, and colored, races," stating that the Fourteenth Amendment "could not have been intended to abolish distinction based on color, or to enforce social, as distinguished from political equality." Adding insult to injury, Justice Brown stated that if, as the plaintiff argued, enforced separation stamped people of color with "a badge of inferiority," it could only be "because the colored race chooses to put that construction upon it."[7]

By the end of the nineteenth century, these rulings had effectively marginalized the significance of Reconstruction Amendments and legislation. Giving wide latitude to the states had deprived African Americans of any real protection from federal provisions. Throughout the south, states passed legislation prohibiting freedom of association and mandating strict segregation on the grounds of race. Covering the entire range of public facilities—transportation, parks, libraries, municipal housing, courtrooms and, above all, schools—these Jim Crow laws gave official sanction to the inferior status of African Americans and also legitimated their discriminatory treatment in private facilities. Slavery had been officially abolished in the 1860s, but as the twentieth century opened it had been converted into a caste system.[8]

From the outset, the notion of "separate-but-equal" facilities was a sham.[9] Yet the constitutional struggle to overcome this failed to achieve much success until the latter half of the twentieth century. Only in the landmark cases known as *Brown v. Board of Education of Topeka* in 1954 did the Supreme Court begin to reconsider the constitutional principle, finding that in public education, "the very foundation of good citizenship," the doctrine of "separate but equal" had no place and concluding that separate education facilities "are inherently unequal."[10] There is no doubt that the Court had grasped the significance of this ruling. It had held its first hearings in 1952 but, unable to reach a decision, it rescheduled hearings for the following year. In 1954 it then made a unanimous ruling but issued no decree. Only a year later did the Court determine how to implement desegregation; holding that it required local solutions, they remanded the process to local courts with no date for the end of segregation fixed.[11]

The *Brown* ruling related only to public schools, but it was the catalyst for a civil rights movement that eventually brought about the desegregation of all public facilities.[12] To give them real force, however, the school rulings needed to be backed by determined governmental action, and neither the president nor Congress took the initiative.[13] It was not until the Kennedy-Johnson era of the 1960s that the pace of desegregation gained momentum, reinforced by the Civil Rights Act of 1964. Later still, in the 1970s, it extended to the North where, because races largely lived apart and neighborhood schools were racially unmixed, comprehensive desegregation involved the pairing of schools and the contentious issue of mandatory bussing policies.

Given the lack of legislative action to address discriminatory practices, these issues had to be addressed by constitutional litigation. This gave courts significant new responsibilities that could neither be classified as dispute adjudication nor as legislation. And yet the task could hardly be called constitutional interpretation: the Fourteenth Amendment was so abstract as to defy precise interpretation and, in any event, its drafters were unlikely to have had such a matter in mind since during the 1860s there was no such thing as a public school system in the South. What the Court in fact did in *Brown* was to presume to exercise constituent power. In its role as guardian of the Constitution, it spoke "in the name of the people" to determine the contemporary meaning of the values of the regime. The Court held that it "must consider public education in the light of its full development and its present place in American life throughout the Nation."[14] This was not an interpretation of the law of the Constitution so much as a political judgment about the significance of social, economic, and cultural change on the constitution of the state.[15]

Can the allocation to the judiciary of the task of determining society's fundamental political values of liberty, equality, and solidarity be justified? The Constitution, as we have seen, has both instrumental and symbolic functions. And although lawyers are well equipped to attend to the former task of interpreting the rules concerning the allocation of decision-making responsibilities, there is little in their education, training, and professional experience to suggest that they are suited to the latter. Why, for example, should Justice Brown, who delivered the majority judgment in *Plessy* and whose professional expertise lay primarily in maritime law, be trusted with such questions? One answer is that judges are bound to act according to principles. But are not these principles of such formality and abstraction that they only acquire determinate meaning once imbued with (contestable) values? Placing this onerous responsibility on the judiciary can be justified, Alexander Bickel famously suggested, only when judges are prepared to "immerse themselves in the tradition of our society" and "in the thought and the vision of the philosophers and the poets" so that they might "extract 'fundamental presuppositions' from their best selves."[16]

Bickel's answer suggests that the judiciary now assumes the key role of acting as a legitimating force. But at what cost? This process reinforces the false narrative that since the United States was established on a universal principle of equal dignity, the constitutional task of the courts is essentially one of redeeming that promise. Treating slavery as a moral flaw rather than a vital component of a socioeconomic regime leads to an identitarian politics of formal equality that masks substantive inequality.[17] But it also absolves the political branches from having to face up to intractable political questions. It is certainly not accurate to suggest that judges are simply usurping the powers of the legislature and executive. The point, rather, is that constitutionalism establishes a scheme that offers incentives to democratic representatives to evade their most basic civic responsibilities. Diverting these issues to a forum that is relatively remote, unaccountable, costly, and operates on the principle of individual complaint, constitutionalism pushes ever more political issues into an institution that is insulated from the cut and thrust of ordinary life. Elsewhere, as the issue of enfranchisement illustrates, the political struggle is often long, intense, incremental, and the product of accommodation and compromise, but its consequences have at least been thrashed out in accountable institutions. By signaling that the people should turn to the forum of principle to deliver social change, aspirational constitutionalism carries the danger of draining the lifeblood from democracy, not just as a system of collective decision-making but, perhaps more importantly, as a way of life.

Constitutionalism as Imperialism

Constitutionalism is presented as a regime that marks the emergence of humanity from what Kant called "self-incurred immaturity."[18] It propagates a story of progress, one that eventually leads in 1917 to the US entry into the First World War, not from self-regarding interests but to free the world of imperialism and make it safe for democracy.[19] But this narrative has its detractors. Erected on the principle of equal liberty, constitutionalism, they contend, is advanced to justify inegalitarian institutions and practices. It is a historically specific European experience masquerading as a universal that has been purposely employed by European powers to legitimate imperial conquests.

When European powers established settled colonies across the world, they did not base their claims purely on conquest. Force might be sufficient to acquire colonies, but a discourse of legitimation was necessary to retain them; power had to be tempered by right. The doctrine of discovery provided one such justification. This was the claim, contrary to the plain facts, that colonized lands were unoccupied. Its real purpose evidently was to assert a claim against other European powers.[20] Sir Edward Coke, the "great" English common lawyer, was more blunt. In 1608, he simply ruled that "all infidels are in law . . . perpetual enemies" and could therefore be subjugated to the prerogative authority of a Christian king.[21] Conquest was justified as the spread of Christianity to people who "as yet live in Darkness and miserable Ignorance" and that "may in time bring the Infidels and Savages . . . to human Civility."[22]

The canonical text for North American colonists was Locke's *Second Treatise,* which proclaimed, "In the beginning, all the world was *America.*" Without nationhood or territorial jurisdiction, Native Americans were in a "state of nature," whereas European societies had advanced to the "civilized" stage and established modern governing institutions. Since the indigenous population had neither the concept of sovereignty nor that of property, Locke concluded that Europeans were free to establish settled colonies and to appropriate uncultivated land without their consent provided enough was left in common for others.[23] The basic elements of his thesis were incorporated into US constitutional law in *Johnson v. M'Intosh,* in which the Supreme Court held that discovery by European powers conferred sovereignty by conquest, including the right to nullify any occupancy rights of the indigenous population.[24]

James Tully argues that Locke's account masks the real history: "The invasion of America, usurpation of Aboriginal nations, theft of the continent, imposition of European economic and political systems, and the steadfast resistance of the Aboriginal peoples are replaced with the captivating picture of the inevitable and benign progress of modern constitutionalism."[25]

Dispossessed through wars and treaties, indigenous populations had no rights in the new constitutional order. Such practices, argues Robert Williams, "provided a vital legacy for those English-Americans to whom, by virtue of their rebellion against the English Crown, devolved the mandate to civilize the Indian's wild country." The history of the American Indian in Western legal thought, he concludes, reveals that "a will to empire proceeds most effectively under a rule of law," since it permitted "the West to accomplish by law and in good conscience what it accomplished by the sword in earlier eras."[26]

The adoption of a uniform language of constitutionalism throughout settled colonies first excluded and then assimilated indigenous peoples. Later, constitutional democracies promoted accommodation, which required indigenous people seeking recognition of their status to present their case in that language. They were obliged to "seek recognition as 'peoples' and 'nations,' with 'sovereignty' or a 'right of self-determination,' even though these terms distort or misdescribe the claim they would wish to make if it were expressed in their own languages." The struggle for recognition of their own way of collective being, Tully argues, presents "as fundamental a challenge to modern constitutionalism as Paine's theory was to the vision of the ancient constitution."[27]

The treatment of indigenous peoples during colonization is an extreme illustration of the way that modern nation-building suppresses linguistic, cultural, ethnic, or religious differences to construct a homogeneous national identity. The multitude is represented as the "sovereign people" who are presumed to have consented to the constitution that rules their lives. This is the "civilizing mission" by which peoples are to be led out of savagery and barbarism into a civilized state. As they evolve out of hunting and pastoralism into agriculture and commerce, their forms of government must similarly evolve from tribal leadership, despotism, and monarchy toward constitutional government.

Tully argues that constitutionalism goes further than just legitimating the historic practices of European imperialism. Instituting a uniform system of constitutional thought over a diverse range of cultures within contemporary states, it is a generalized cultural imperialism that now prevents us from thinking creatively about contemporary political challenges. As a plea to restore the traditional idea of a constitution as a general framework within which conventional practices gradually acquire authority through mutual recognition and accommodation, his argument extends far beyond the treatment of indigenous populations and the need for dialogue between peoples who do not share universal principles,[28] to embrace differing conceptions of justice arising from race and gender differences.[29] It can even be read as an argument in support of the variable practices of constitutional democracy and against the universal philosophy of constitutionalism.

Constitutionalism and the Inclusionary Dynamic

Constitutionalism, Tully argues, imposes an inappropriate set of universal principles on culturally differentiated populations. But far from leading to the restoration of the traditional idea of a constitution, the solution most often advocated is aspirational constitutionalism. Sometimes labeled "transformative constitutionalism," aspirational constitutionalism acknowledges these differences but uses the constitution to bring about social change by promoting inclusivity.

Consider two recent illustrations: South Africa and Ecuador. Charged with drafting a post-apartheid constitution of South Africa, the Constitutional Assembly undertook an elaborate participatory exercise of involving people in the constitution-making process with the purpose of ensuring that the constitution could express the views of a nation "united in diversity."[30] In addition to adopting a wide-ranging charter of civil, political, and social rights, its 1996 Constitution recognizes eleven official languages, protects customary and tribal law, promotes regional diversity, and institutionalizes multiculturalism.[31] But Ecuador went even further. Their 2008 Constitution promulgated a vast array of social rights (food, water, health, social security, education, housing, work, and cultural identity) as well as recognizing extensive antidiscrimination rights (covering ethnicity, age, sex, culture, civil status, language, religion, politics, sexual orientation, and disability). Declaring all these rights equally important, the Constitution imposed a duty on the government to "adopt affirmative action measures that promote real equality for the benefit of the rights-bearers who are in a situation of inequality."[32]

Subsequent experience has revealed that drafting ambitious principles is much easier than making them a practical reality.[33] By making the constitution the pivot for delivering social revolution, however, such experiments reinforce the belief that the practical task of bringing about these momentous changes must fall to lawyers and courts.

Using the constitution as a vehicle for social change exposes a dilemma commonly faced in postcolonial contexts between promoting a modernizing universalism and embracing local particularism. Should the constitution project an idealized homogeneity of a newly liberated people or acknowledge the actual heterogeneity—racial, religious, linguistic, and cultural—of its peoples? This question was first played out on the great stage of India, a land of communities and caste, of racial, religious, and linguistic minorities.

After partition in 1945, when Muslim leaders declared their intention of forming the separate state of Pakistan, the Indian Constituent Assembly had a great many issues to resolve. Gandhi advocated a decentralized, village community–based system of government, but this traditionally rooted conception of constitution was rejected in favor of a modern centralized parliamentary system based on universal adult suffrage.[34] Many of the remaining dilemmas were embodied in the person of Bhimrao Ambedkar, chair of the drafting committee of the Constituent Assembly. An "unalloyed modernist" who believed in "the modern state as the site for the actualization of human reason," he was also, as a Dalit, aware that independence could easily lead to rule by the upper castes.[35] Since provision had been made for separate representation of Muslims, Ambedkar argued that reserved seats must also be given to the so-called depressed castes. Facing opposition from Gandhi, who objected to the notion that upper castes could not represent all Hindus, Ambedkar prevailed. Constitutional provision was made not only for the legislative representation of "scheduled castes" but also for a program of positive action to ensure a proportionate representation in public employment.[36] Social equality, the drafters recognized, required more than the establishment of formal legal and political equality.

Ever since 1947 there has been debate on whether India's independence Constitution simply marked a transfer of power or signaled real social transformation. A strong case can be made that the Constitution did establish a framework for social transformation and that considerable progress has been made.[37] But this is counteracted by studies indicating that public interest litigation, which was developed to overcome structural barriers to constitutional change, has singularly failed to deliver on its transformative ambitions.[38] And once the inquiry shifts from constitutional litigation strategy to governmental practices, continuity with colonial rule becomes more apparent. Here, the citizens of constitutional theory become the subjects of administrative practice. From a governmental perspective, in which the population is counted, classified, and made the objects of policies, practices adopted under colonial rule have seamlessly continued in the postcolonial regime.

This continuity claim, a variant of the dual state thesis, is given a radical twist by scholars of the subaltern school. Partha Chatterjee presents the argument not just with respect to India but also to "most of the world," by which he means the three-quarters of humanity who "were not direct participants in the history of the evolution of the institutions of modern capitalist democracy." He argues that "civil society" is in practice confined to a small section of "culturally equipped" Indian citizens, and it is this select group who are "the people" of the constitutional imagination. The great majority of the population, by contrast, are "only tenuously, and even then ambiguously and contextually, rights-bearing citizens in the sense imagined by the constitution."[39] This majority must be attended to by governmental agencies, but this is as a matter of administrative policy rather than any expression of constitutional right. Many operate on the borders of legality, living in illegal squatter settlements, working in the informal sector, and interacting with public authorities only as a matter of necessity. To the extent that their claims are addressed at all, it is not through the medium of constitutional rights but on the different terrain of prudential political negotiation.

The great play made of the role of the Constitution as a vehicle of inclusion and transformation, we conclude, too readily absorbs the rhetoric of constitutionalism. In underestimating the depth of the class cleavage Chatterjee highlights, the Constitution's capacity to achieve its integrative ambitions is grossly overestimated. The distinction between active and passive citizens remains, with the former governed by constitutional processes and the latter governed through administrative processes that are negotiated politically. But that is not all. By taking on political tasks well beyond its competence, the Court is in danger of losing legitimacy among certain sectors of the population. Once it is seen as a partisan institution that promotes liberal or aspirational values, its efficacy in performing more mundane constitutional tasks is diminished.[40]

Constitutionalism and the Exclusionary Dynamic

Although in early phases of development, the state must often bolster its authority by drawing on traditional sources of commonality, constitutionalism rejects such primitive sources of nationalism. If all are to be included

in an imagined political community, it is not possible to found unity on ethnicity, religion, language, or even common history. Constitutional recognition requires that the "community of fate" be transcended, and the people
adhere to the principles of equal liberty inscribed in the constitution.[41] This
raises troubling questions for states in which it is difficult to build collective
unity even on ostensibly universal principles. But can constitutional authority
be maintained if regimes adopt exclusionary practices? In such "divided
societies," the practical challenges of institutional design are intense. Solutions commonly touted include power-sharing arrangements, special protection for minorities, or practices that avoid having to confront the lack of
unity.[42] Can this type of state persist in the age of constitutionalism?

Nepal is an instructive case. Its 1990 Constitution signaled major regime
change, from authoritarianism to constitutional monarchy, but it sought to
build the new order on a homogenizing idea of the nation. Despite Nepal
comprising around one hundred ethnic groups or castes with a similar
number of languages and at least ten religions, the Constitution privileged
the country's Hindu religion, Aryan culture, and Nepali language, thereby
discriminating against millions on the basis of religion, caste, gender, language, and ethnicity. This attempt to institute exclusionary rule failed to
garner popular acceptance. The new Constitution simply fueled mounting
unrest that then erupted into civil war. The conflict was only finally resolved
with the promulgation in 2007 of an interim Constitution establishing Nepal
as a federal, democratic republic on inclusionary principles—a constitutional
settlement made permanent in 2015.[43] As this experience suggests, across
many regions of the world, the symbolic power of inclusion is now so great
that regimes seeking to build constitutional authority on exclusionary
grounds simply cannot establish their legitimacy.

The most contentious case of exclusionary constitutionalism is that of Israel. Established in 1948 after the end of British colonial rule over mandatory Palestine, Israel had committed to adopting a constitution. But this was
postponed, initially because of the 1948 war and subsequently because of lack
of agreement.[44] In its place, the Knesset passed a series of nine Basic Laws,
three of which referred to Israel as a "Jewish and democratic state." Formally
adopted only in 1985, in reality this formula had been used from the beginning when Arab inhabitants were invited "to participate in the upbuilding
of the State on the basis of full and equal citizenship."[45] Ambivalence was

therefore built into the foundation. Although pledging to respect the citizenship rights of the indigenous population, it would appear that "the people" are constituted exclusively by its Jewish members.

This inclusionary-exclusionary tension has driven constitutional development. Israel's symbols of national identity are exclusively Jewish, and so too are its processes of nation-building, especially the 1950 Law of Return, which gives every Jew in the world the right to settle in Israel. What, then, is the status of Palestinians who comprise around 20 percent of the population? Possessing civil and political rights, formally they have equal status, but the manner of Israel's founding and development suggests that sovereignty and constituent power vest in its Jewish citizens, implying that "the people" does not include all the people of the territory.[46] In a variant of Chatterjee's claim that the majority of Indians are part of the population but without full citizenship rights, Mazen Masri argues that Israeli-Palestinians may be citizens but are not part of the constituent "people." Israel's regime, he argues, is founded on "exclusionary constitutionalism."[47]

Masri's argument has been contested by Israeli jurists who draw a distinction between Israel's national identity (Jewish) and its civic and political identity (democratic). They argue that Israel is no different than many constitutional democracies that contain national or ethnic minorities but whose public character is determined by the majority.[48] That may have been the liberal aspiration, but it seems beyond question that this is not the present reality, not least because the "Jewish and democratic" formula is no longer purely symbolic or cultural; it has become a structural—and exclusionary—characteristic of the state.

This structural characteristic was built into its foundation when it was assumed that two states—Israel and Palestine—would be established. It is the continuing failure to realize this objective that now makes this exclusion so contentious. Confronted with an existential threat it has faced since its founding, and seeking to establish a constitutional democracy mainly comprising immigrants without any experience of democracy and in a territory without strong democratic traditions, Israel has faced grave challenges. Recent political developments, including a 2018 nationality Basic Law that reduces the position of Arabic to "a language with a special status" and declares Israel the nation-state of the Jewish people,[49] strengthen the argument that Israel is being transformed "from one based on constructive legal ambiguity into one rooted in exclusive ethno-theological values."[50] In the case of India, exclusion is attributable to social facts rather than to the constitution. In Israel, by contrast, exclusion exists at the normative core of its constitution.

The Peoples of the Constitution

In an age in which the constitution is no longer just an instrument for regulating government but has become a key symbol of social and political unity, "the people" in whose name that constitution is adopted is an intensely contested subject. Invented as a device to wrest power from the aristocracy and protect the liberties of the emerging bourgeoisie, the adoption of a written constitution signifies progress. Yet the original people of the constitution were invariably "men of property" who, in justifying this new regime, differentiated the people into active and passive citizens. Thereafter, the constitutional struggle has been to extend its benefits of protection and participation to the multitude. This, too, has been a progressive development.

Nevertheless, many radicals were suspicious of the entire constitutional project. Seeing the constitution as a device to protect the interests of the wealthy, and therefore as a barrier to be overcome, they sought social change either by elected majorities and legislative reforms or, in extremis, revolutionary overthrow of the entire regime. These are the political strategies that advocates of constitutionalism have tried to displace. Having established the authority of the constitution as a permanent but flexible framework, they aimed to constrain the powers of legislative majorities, to entrust the protection of its values to the judiciary, and to define "the people" through the prism of that constitution. All changes must be negotiated through the process of constitutional review. This in outline is the American story, most graphically illustrated in the treatment of indigenous populations, in the struggle of African Americans to realize citizenship rights, and latterly in such struggles as the rights of women to reproductive freedom or of homosexuals to equal treatment.

It is an innovation that has been widely embraced and greatly extended. Contemporary constitutions do not simply institute the negative rights regime of limited government; they incorporate aspirational values and ambitious schedules of civil, political, and social rights. Across the world, the constitution is now seen as the only medium through which to realize the promise of an inclusive regime of equal rights. The multitude is now vested with citizenship rights. Constitutionalism has come of age.

And yet, for all its progressive rhetoric, there is scant evidence that aspirational constitutionalism has been able to deliver the fundamental social change it promises. This is not so surprising: social reform still depends on political movements imposing their will on political parties that must then win control of the government to redistribute resources. But constitutionalization shifts the action away from legislatures and governments into courts and away from collective will-formation toward individualized rights-based claims. That constitutionalization has extended furthest in regimes where economic inequality is rising most rapidly offers corroboration.[51] But what must surely occur when the total constitution finally reigns is a blurring of the distinction between government and society. State sovereignty is discredited in the name of advancing status rights.

As political movements are replaced by legal strategies and collective will-formation made subservient to rights arguments, regimes become depoliticized by the individuation of claims. The concept of "the people" is disaggregated into a multiplicity. It is unclear how, under such conditions, a state maintains the loyalty of its citizens. The question, most acute in divided societies where loyalties are already strained, is whether constitutionalization now makes exit a legitimate option. Can the concept of "the people" be disaggregated so that different peoples comprising a nation can claim a right to independence? In other words, is there a constitutional right to secede from the state?

The orthodox position was that concisely stated by Lincoln in 1861 when he stated that perpetuity "is implied, if not expressed, in the fundamental law of all national governments" and "no government proper ever had a provision in its organic law for its own termination."[52] But can this view persist in an age of constitutionalism? Permanence, it is argued, is a precondition of order and stability, and it provides the basis on which democratic deliberation can evolve, whereas a constitutional right to secede would promote factionalism and reduce the chances of achieving political compromise in the face of religious, ethnic, or linguistic differences. On the other hand, the right to secede offers a guarantee to minority groups that the majority will not adopt discriminatory practices. Nevertheless, there is an important difference between claiming that a group has good reason to secede from the state and claiming that it has the constitutional right to do so. But once the constitution is felt to express the collective values of society, this distinction between prudential political concession and constitutional right is blurred.[53] Political negotiation of group differences is replaced with constitutional adjudication of an asserted right.

This has been a quandary mainly in multinational states with territorially concentrated national minorities that already have a degree of self-government, such as Catalans, Québécois, Corsicans, and Scots. In these circumstances, David Haljan argues that the state should be conceived as founded on the principles of "associative constitutionalism," in which the constitutional right of secession is implied in the original consensus that founded the state.[54] Haljan draws support from the Canadian Supreme Court's ruling in its Quebec secession reference of 1998. This determined, first, that the principles of Canada's invisible constitution are those of federalism, democracy, constitutionalism, the rule of law, and respect for minorities and, second, that these principles indicate that "the clear expression of the desire to pursue secession by the population of a province would give rise to a reciprocal obligation on all parties to Confederation to negotiate constitutional changes."[55]

Some constitutional scholars have suggested that in this case the Court performed the valuable service of channeling into legal form a dispute that might otherwise lead to the breakup of the state by more violent means.[56] But it also strengthens the claim that the constitution's values are not just in the text but implicit in the structure of society, and that there are no limits to the judiciary's competence to identify basic values and determine the rights that derive from them. This trajectory has led to some recently adopted constitutions expressly including rights of secession.[57] The struggle for the constitutional right of minority groups to secede from the state is a stark illustration of the ways in which political bonds of allegiance are stretched and how principles forged in the crucible of the nation-state are, under the extending influence of constitutionalism, evolving as self-standing principles of legitimate collective ordering. This evolving constitutional discourse is reinforced by developments in the arena of international law, an issue to which we now turn.

Chapter 13

THE COSMOPOLITAN PROJECT

WHEN in 1795 Kant wrote his essay on "perpetual peace," international law was languishing in neglect. Grotius, Pufendorf, and Vattel, the great pioneers of the *ius publicum Europaeum,* were in his estimation merely "sorry comforters," providing a cloak of justification for the aggressive behavior of leading European powers. Their elaborate codes of rules lacked all legal force because states were not subject to any common external constraint.[1] In its place, Kant advanced an idealistic project through which, "after many revolutions . . . a universal cosmopolitan existence will at last be realised as the matrix within which all the original capacities of the human race may develop."[2] Since then the codes of international law have expanded, but by the end of the twentieth century his ambition seemed no closer to being realized. Concluding his study of the modern history of international law in 2002, Martti Koskenniemi acknowledged that "power and law have been entangled in much more complex relationships than the conventional imagery would allow."[3]

After the end of the Cold War, however, the project of establishing a cosmopolitan right acquired a new impetus. In the mid-1970s, "seemingly from nowhere," the idea of human rights emerged and came to "define people's hopes for the future as the foundation of an international movement and a utopia of international law."[4] In the area of commerce, the workload of transnational commercial arbitration and international investment arbitration expanded dramatically and in 1995 the World Trade Organization was established to provide a set of global trade rules and a process for dispute resolution. In the field of humanitarian law, developments were marked by the establishment in 2002 of the International Criminal Court to prosecute those accused of genocide and war crimes. These, together with related initiatives,

kindled extensive discussion about the prospects for "the constitutionalization of international law."[5] Once infused with constitutional principles, these
developments in international law seemed to mark a major step toward realizing a regime of global constitutionalism.

This thesis has been systematically advanced by Jürgen Habermas. His
earlier work had sketched the modern development of state forms, with each
stage resulting in increasing formalization of social relations by means of law.
Since the most recent form, the democratic welfare state, had been experiencing crisis tendencies since the 1970s, this caused him to reexamine the
foundations of contemporary constitutional democracy. By the 1980s he was
presenting constitutionalism not as an institutional arrangement but as a set
of principles, and this provided the basis of his argument about "constitutional patriotism." If constitutionalism is founded on the general principle
of equal liberty, it must be of universal significance, an insight that led him
to reconsider the constitutional dimensions of European integration and subsequently to the question of global constitutionalism.

The drafting of a European constitution dominated debate in the early
2000s. Adherence to the principles of constitutionalism, Habermas argued,
would enable diverse national traditions to be shaped into a cohesive European identity.[6] The challenge, he explained, "is not to *invent* anything but to
conserve the great democratic achievements of the European nation-state, beyond its own limits." This was not just about bolstering global markets but
of protecting the achievements of social democracy and the "European way
of life." And he recognized the risks: a constitution might have the "catalytic
effect" of enhancing the European Union's (EU) capacity to act, but it could
not provide a remedy for the legitimation deficit unless there could be a
European-wide public sphere that can give citizens of member states "an
equal opportunity to take part in an encompassing process of focused political communication."[7]

The project did not develop in that way. After failing to approve a constitution, the EU experienced the Euro crisis of 2008, to which it responded by
reinforcing a regime of "executive federalism" and strengthening "a post-
democratic exercise of political authority." Criticizing politicians who have
"long since become a functional elite," Habermas recognized that the crisis
exposed the need for transformative politics. But he also emphasized that not
only the financial markets but also "the functional systems of world society

whose influence permeates national borders" were challenges that neither states nor coalitions of states could solve. The postnational constitutional challenge could no longer be addressed at the level of the EU alone. "The *international* community of states," he concluded, "must develop into a *cosmopolitan* community of states and world citizens."[8]

Cosmopolitan Constitutionalism

To meet the challenge of moving toward a global society, Habermas returned to Kant. Recognizing that Kant's concept of a cosmopolitan order must be reformulated in the light of a global system that has dramatically changed, he asserted that we are at "a transitional stage between international and cosmopolitan law."[9] But how is cosmopolitan law different from international law or, rather, what precisely *is* cosmopolitan law?

Cosmopolitan law "bypasses the collective subjects of international law and directly establishes the legal status of the individual subjects by granting them unmediated membership in the association of free and equal world citizens." It rests on an idea of human rights that has its origins not in morality but in legal and political liberties. Cosmopolitan law is novel in that it establishes "a symmetry between the juridification of social and political relations both within and beyond the state's borders" and is, he maintains, "a logical consequence of the idea of the constitutive rule of law."[10]

Having identified its character, Habermas assesses its constitutional significance. Recent trends—the demise of embedded capitalism, the associated rise of globalized markets, the expanded reach of international law, and the growth of international organizations—are leading to the displacement of the nation-state's pivotal role in constitutional thought.[11] A gap has opened up between the need to legitimate governing power beyond the nation-state and the revealed limitations of the modern arrangements of democratic legitimation within the nation-state. International law must therefore be constitutionalized. But unless democracy is to be abandoned as a legitimating principle, new models must be devised. His solution is to present a new type of "political constitution for world society."[12]

This blueprint rejects establishing a world state in favor of a politically constituted world society comprising states and citizens. Legitimation is generated not only by the involvement of citizens in will-formation within states but also through the influence of cosmopolitan citizens on the international community. Through these diverse processes, a "transnational negotiation system" is established with responsibility *within the framework* of the international community, for issues of global domestic politics" and ultimately a "General Assembly of the world organization" would assume responsibility for constitutional development of this world society.[13] Habermas's response to the objection that a regime without centralized world government would lead to fragmentation and underenforcement of norms is a differentiated arrangement in which governance varies according to policy field. In areas like the maintenance of international peace and human rights protection, a hierarchical world organization would be established with the power to impose sanctions, although governance arrangements in transnational arrangements are more likely to emerge gradually as functional necessities.

Critical to the success of this scheme is the need for learning by both states and citizens, leading to new meanings of modern concepts like sovereignty and constituent power.[14] The distinction between sovereignty and government would need to be further attenuated,[15] and constituent power would have to be reformulated as a dual concept, including not just the power of citizens to establish a national constitution but also the capacity of world citizens to contribute to will-formation internationally.[16]

The juristic aspects of cosmopolitan constitutionalism are taken up by Mattias Kumm. Present puzzles exist, he suggests, because of the way constitutional lawyers continue to imagine constitutional law. Agreeing with Habermas that a "paradigm shift" in constitutional thinking is required, Kumm argues that the entire state-based way of thinking about constitutionalism must be replaced by "the cosmopolitan paradigm." This is not simply a thought experiment: cosmopolitan constitutionalism is a jurisprudential account that explains "the deep structure of public law" as practiced today. Core issues, such as human rights practice and the complexity of governance at the interface between national and international law, can only be addressed by taking this move toward cosmopolitanism.[17]

Today, the concept of the state, Kumm suggests, is meaningful only to the extent that it operates according to principles of constitutionalism that now establish an autonomous and authoritative conceptual framework that legitimates governmental action both nationally and internationally. The constitution's authority no longer rests on collective will or authorization by "we the people" but on its adherence to principles of cosmopolitan constitutionalism determined by a standard of public reason tested by legality, rationality, due process, proportionality, and subsidiarity. These principles frame a system of "constitutional pluralism," an overarching regime that "allows for the possibility of conflict not ultimately resolved by the law," but which nonetheless provides common constitutional principles that create "a framework that allows for the constructive engagement of different sites of authority with one another."[18]

Since cosmopolitan constitutionalism is founded on the rights of free and equal citizens, the national constitution is legitimate only to the extent it protects those rights. Any claim to authority that rests on the will of the legislator, including a will expressed as constituent power, must be reinterpreted within a rights-based framework.[19] Kumm accepts that many rights claims are contested, and their resolution vests a great deal of power in the judiciary. But he justifies this on the grounds that rights discourse is a "highly cooperative endeavour in which courts and other politically accountable institutions are partners in a joint enterprise" in which governing institutions assume different roles.[20]

This analysis indicates just how much the cosmopolitan project is indebted to Kant's worldview, not least in requiring political power to bend the knee before right. But what, if anything, gives this thought experiment authority? If cosmopolitan constitutionalism is not dependent on a conventionally understood exercise of constituent power, whence comes its authority? Kumm's answer is that its power derives simply from the cogency of its account of legitimate authority. And this comes from a "*holistic* construction of legitimate public authority" that achieves a "foundational significance" by retaining as its normative point of reference "the idea of *free and equal persons . . .* governing themselves through and by law."[21] If this argument seems circular, that's because it is. Cosmopolitan constitutionalism takes its authority from its faith in the power of reason.

Ordo-constitutionalism as a Global Project

In the last chapter of *The Road to Serfdom*, Hayek claims that there is little hope of achieving a stable international order or bringing about a lasting peace where every state is free to pursue whatever is in its own immediate interest. But the solution is not world government because no international planning project can avoid being "a naked rule of force." International authority is necessary to keep order and enable people to flourish, but the powers it requires—to check powerful economic interests and act as an impartial umpire—are "essentially the powers of the ultra-liberal 'laissez-faire' state," which must be "strictly circumscribed by the Rule of Law." A federal principle of organization on a global scale must bind the supernational authority strictly to its own constitution.[22]

There was, however, very little international dimension to Hayek's thought during the postwar period. It is largely absent from his studies *The Constitution of Liberty* (1960) and *Law, Legislation and Liberty* (1973–1979), presumably because his emphasis on evolutionary orders could not be reconciled with such a constructivist project as the creation of international authority. Yet many of his disciples, especially those associated with the Mont Pèlerin Society, founded in 1947, took up his argument.[23] Since the war they have adopted and expanded the Ordo-liberal argument about the need for an economic constitution at the national level. Extending the principle of "thinking in orders" to world society, they developed "a set of proposals designed to defend the world economy from a democracy that became global only in the twentieth century."[24]

Their project is called neoliberal because unlike classical liberals, the objective is not just to minimize all governmental interference with market activity. Neoliberals recognize that markets rarely work spontaneously and need the support of state-enforced rules. Governmental action must ensure that markets operate efficiently and insulate them from the popular pressures of democratic politics. In an era of globalized economic activity, similar action is needed internationally. These developments at the interface between national and international governance are of pivotal importance to the neoliberal project and require the establishment of a regime of Ordo-constitutionalism at the global level.

This project needs some historical perspective. The first phase, classical constitutionalism, ended with the First World War. The war was the watershed leading to the second phase of democracy and big government, the era Sartori calls the "intensification of politics" and Schmitt that of "the total state." In neoliberal terms, the first phase ended the era of classical liberalism, and the second phase was framed by the collapse of the gold standard and the fracturing of the economic unity of the world. It is during this second phase that Ordo-liberals, concerned about governmental interference in the economy, propose the need for a "strong state" to protect "free markets." The third phase emerges from the revolt of the Global South and the end of empires during the 1970s and is consolidated by developments resulting from the end of the Cold War. If the world of empires marks the first wave of globalization, the era since the 1970s is indicative of the second wave. Marked domestically by the idea of the total constitution, this second wave of globalization provides the platform for promoting Ordo-constitutionalism worldwide.

Economic developments in this era of globalization contribute to the decline in the authority of national governments and enhance the authority of supranational institutions. Hayek's proposal to establish an international authority within a federated regime of government now comes into its own. No single authority is created, but an interlocking network of institutions rapidly evolves over the postwar period. The International Monetary Fund and the World Bank were both established in 1944 to secure global financial stability, promote international trade, and aid economic development. Regional institutions such as the EU, the Association of Southeast Asian Nations, and the North American Free Trade Agreement came into being. The World Trade Organization was established in 1995 to promote free trade. Independent central banks are formed, and systems of international commercial arbitration and international investment treaty arbitration expand greatly.

Hayek believed that the method of creating a range of institutions designed to regulate specific activities approached the task "from the wrong end," complicating the objective of creating "a true international law which would limit the powers of national governments to harm each other." The challenge for neoliberals was to meld this incrementally evolving network into a coherent regime to protect the world economy from political interference by democratizing movements. The objective, in Hayek's words, was "the dethronement of politics."[25]

Cosmopolitan scholars recognized that the incremental development of transnational systems had created a legitimation gap: collective power was being exercised without democratic authorization or accountability. Habermas's solution was to democratize those institutions. But this overlooks the salient fact that such institutions had been created specifically to advance the neoliberal project of a world economic order freed from political interference. The neoliberal project contemplates the formation of a global economic constitution to restrict the legitimate range of actions of constitutional democracies. The paradigm shift envisaged by cosmopolitan scholars, comprising liberal principles of legality, rationality, proportionality, and subsidiarity, locks nation-states into a world federation founded on neoliberal premises. Habermas and Kumm advance their claims of right without fully appreciating just how far the power dynamics that drive their movement fulfill the objectives of the neoliberal project.[26]

From a global perspective, Ordo-constitutionalism is designed to ensure that constitutional democracy safeguards economic freedoms. This is achieved at the national level with a regime of constrained democracy, a model that constitutional courts have the critical role of safeguarding. At the international level, the aim is to establish a regime that protects the rights of international capital and also, through the scheme of multilevel governance advocated in cosmopolitan constitutionalism, provides additional protection to rights within national systems. Constitutionalization defends economic freedoms against attempts by democratic legislatures to enact protectionist or redistributive policies.

Ordo-constitutionalists are therefore more than willing to embrace the rights revolution. Recognizing that the constitutionalization of social and economic rights is a response to the diminished capacity of legislatures to implement programs of redistribution, they fully support the idea of individualized litigation monitored by constitutional courts. It is a small price to pay for a revolution with the potential to break the authority of the sovereign nation-state and establish a cosmopolitan regime with enhanced protection not just for individual freedom in general and economic freedom in particular. Cosmopolitan constitutionalism, Ernst-Ulrich Petersmann argues, marks an advance by strengthening protection for all types of rights, including those of property.[27]

Ordo-constitutionalism operates at the intersection between international law and domestic law. It works most effectively when international tribunals make rulings that can be directly enforced in domestic courts. One powerful illustration is the system of international investment treaty arbitration that protects the economic rights of foreign investors through an international arbitration system and enforces the award of damages in domestic courts.[28] But its most powerful articulation comes in the shape of the EU.

As a regime in which member states pool many of their sovereign rights, the EU moves beyond traditional international relations conducted by sovereign states. It establishes a common market that protects four economic freedoms—freedom of movement of goods, services, labor, and capital—and promotes undistorted competition. But the project also envisages moving beyond the internal market to establish a federation, a governmental order in which the federal tier is insulated from democratic accountability.[29] As we have noted, there has been a failed initiative to legitimate the EU through the adoption of a constitution, but the fact that from the outset the EU has pursued a policy of constitutionalization by juridification should not be overlooked.[30] The EU has always conceived of itself as a new type of order that pursues its ends by integrating the legal orders of member states. This movement is promoted and policed by the European Court of Justice which, by means of an "invisible constitution," enforces EU law not just by the European Court itself but by domestic courts of member states which, if faced with conflicting national law, must give effect to EU law. The judiciaries of member states are thereby co-opted to become the enforcement agencies of Ordo-constitutional principles.

The age of empires drew to a close in the decades following the Second World War and with it a system that had provided relative stability in world trade. How, neoliberals asked, could the free flow of capital and goods be maintained in a world of independent, sovereign, and democratizing nation-states? Their solution was an international order that would oversee the removal of national barriers to trade and investment and establish an integrated global economic regime policed by law. To achieve this, a paradigm shift in legal and constitutional thought was necessary. A system of sovereign states interacting as formal equals through public international law had to be displaced by a federated cosmopolitan order.[31] This would erode distinctions between public and private and national and international in favor of a tiered order of individual civil, social, and—crucially—economic rights. Through these processes of constitutionalization, a global regime of Ordo-constitutionalism was instituted. Cosmopolitans conceptualize it normatively as a regime of right. Neoliberals explain how right-ordering is necessarily tied to changing economic relations of power.

Constitutionalism with a Cosmopolitan Purpose

Constitutionalism was devised as a philosophy of government to reconcile order and freedom. Forged in the crucible of the modern state, it has gone through various iterations. But cosmopolitan jurists now contend that, because of globalization, the state's authority has been displaced by a constitutionalism that has evolved into an autonomous discourse of legitimation. The international implications of this have been introduced, but we have yet to consider their impact on the constitution of the nation-state.

Globalization, it is argued, is leading to a new type of national constitution. In calling it "the cosmopolitan constitution," Alexander Somek is careful to explain that this label does not designate some constitutional formation beyond the nation-state; rather, it captures the constitution of a nation-state "under conditions of international engagement."[32] The most basic change it advocates is to institute the principle of open statehood. There are many implications of this, but the most important concern is the status of basic rights. That the constitution was devised to protect basic rights is hardly novel; what is new is the enhanced status they are accorded. This enhancement is the consequence of two developments: first, the adoption of an abstract idea of human rights as the universal standard of legitimacy and, second, international agencies' beginning to actively police that standard.

Germany led the way with its Basic Law, stating that the German people "acknowledges inviolable and inalienable human rights as the basis of every human community, of peace and of justice in the world."[33] The significance of this formulation has recently been transformed by the sheer range of human rights in question and by the way they are increasingly determined by international judiciaries. The result has been the rapid globalization of standards enforced by comparative evaluation and extensive borrowing. By making the Basic Law relative, the authority of national constitutional law is diminished.

This development is now a feature of many regimes. Consider the example of India. Indian courts now "roam freely over American, English, South African, Israeli, or even Pakistani jurisprudence" and regularly "read international law principles into the Constitution." To engage with Indian constitutional law "is not to enter into a world of parochial concerns, derived from the peculiarities of a political tradition; it is to enter a global conversation on law, norms, values, and institutional choices."[34] This trade is strengthened and ratified through international judicial networks that regularly exchange "best practice," making international human rights the benchmark against which all states are measured.[35] The inclusion of such rights within the constitution is no longer a matter of local political choice. Increasingly, it is no longer even possible to subject them to purely domestic judicial interpretation.

Open statehood and enhanced rights protection are also eroding the distinction between citizens and resident aliens. National constitutional authority is again relativized. In the context of high levels of international migration, enhanced protection against discrimination on the grounds of nationality gives rise to the expectation that the civil rights and social benefits of citizenship will be equally accorded to nonnationals. This weakens the political bond on which the authority of the social contract is founded and with it the assumptions that have underpinned the modern discourse of state sovereignty.

In the cosmopolitan-orientated constitution, the idea of the state as an authoritative political association loses its purchase. At home in the world rather than just in one's own state, the cosmopolitan is a depoliticized being. Like citizens of the state, they have basic rights, and they depend on the provision of collective goods. But apart from that, all that is required is the effective protection of their rights and efficient mechanisms to deliver services. Cosmopolitans may have need for administrators, regulators, service providers, and auditors, but the practices of democratic deliberation become redundant.

In this age of constitutionalism, the meaning of constitution is transformed almost beyond recognition. It is no longer the written text, and constitutional adjudication is no longer concerned with the text's intended meaning. The constitution has become a set of the constitutional court's changing standards of reasonableness and rationality. In his classic nineteenth-century study *The English Constitution*, Walter Bagehot claimed that the duty of parliamentarians was "to know the highest truth which the people will bear, and to inculcate and preach that."[36] This pedagogic task is now assumed by the judiciary as they strive to uphold the highest standards of rationality they think the polity can bear. Constitutions, Somek notes, "were made in order to prevent change," but with the emergence of the cosmopolitan constitution, they are now "to be tacitly amended on the basis of cross-cultural exchanges about the optimal protection of rights."[37]

The cosmopolitan constitution, then, is a national constitution that has become receptive to cosmopolitan influences. The trajectory is clear: it requires the judiciary, as guardian of the constitution, to live up to universal standards in the protection of rights and to yield, "for the purpose of self-correction, to the judgment of one's peers."[38] The radical character of the innovation is highlighted by comparison with the founding assumptions of modern constitutional thought.

First, the collective entity of "the people" is disaggregated if not entirely dissolved. As Somek explains, the notion "is now experienced as even slightly embarrassing, as if there were something intrinsically xenophobic or otherwise obnoxious about an entity called a 'people.'" Second, when the distinction between citizens and foreigners is permeated by the influence of antidiscrimination rights, even the idea of nationality becomes suspect. And a cosmopolitan interpretation of liberty and equality makes the third element—the modern clarion call of solidarity—merely superfluous. In the eyes of cosmopolitans, migrants have become "successors of the proletariat." They are "agents of change," and their movement renders societies "more diverse and multicultural." As a consequence, the task of redistribution is replaced with that of "inclusion." Postnational citizenship discourse, Somek concludes, "is neoliberalism with a leftist face" in that it envisages migrants "exercising a transformative force similar to the proletariat." It is a transformation far removed from that of moving toward greater equality.[39]

Cosmopolitan constitutionalism ushers in a world of markets, voluntary associations, and service agencies in networks that transcend national boundaries. It is a constitutional discourse for a world of interacting orders and permeable boundaries. To the extent that it conjures a world without boundaries, constitutionalism with a cosmopolitan purpose envisages a world if not quite yet without states, then perhaps without politics, and certainly without the pivotal significance of democratic practices.

CONCLUSION

Overcoming Constitutionalism

CONSTITUTIONALISM has recently gone through a remarkable rejuvenation. Languishing in the mid-twentieth century as an anachronistic doctrine reflecting an eighteenth-century vision of limited government, it has been transformed into the world's most powerful philosophy of governing. The constitution has accordingly been elevated from its original task of regulating relations between governmental institutions to the symbolic representation of social unity. Driven by a rights revolution that dramatically strengthens the power of the judiciary, these developments have generated a novel concept of constitutional legality which, marking the fusion of legal and political reason, upholds an "invisible constitution" of abstract principles that is rapidly acquiring universal influence. But how did constitutionalism become such a powerful ruling philosophy?

One explanation can immediately be discounted. Constitutionalism was cemented as the ideology underpinning the world's first experiment in organizing government through a constitution. Whatever the reasons for its extending influence, they are not attributable to the model characteristics of the US Constitution itself. A century ago, Harold Laski complained that the Constitution "is the worst instrument of government that the mind of man has so far conceived,"[1] a judgment that subsequent developments have done nothing to rebut. In his 2006 book *Our Undemocratic Constitution*, Sanford Levinson examines its many egregious features. These include the equal representation of states in the Senate, despite the fact that the largest has a population seventy times greater than the smallest; an Electoral College to formally elect the president, resulting in candidates entering the White House without winning the popular vote; Supreme Court justices' appointments for life, leading to infirm octogenarians unable to discharge their onerous responsibilities; and an amendment procedure that makes the Constitution the most difficult to alter of any in the world. Levinson concludes that the Constitution erects "almost insurmountable barriers in the way of *any* acceptable notion of democracy."[2]

American experience has undoubtedly influenced contemporary developments but not because of the constitutional text. Much more powerful has been the great number of sophisticated theories of constitutionalism propagated by American jurists. Written primarily as idealized visions of their own "invisible constitution," they have been dusted down and offered to states with more recently adopted constitutions. Bruce Ackerman was only half joking when he opened his third volume of *We the People* with a "familiar conversation" between himself and a government official, explaining that "since 1989, the State Department had been badgering me to serve on delegations to advise one or another country on its constitutional transition to democracy."[3] We might harbor doubts about the value of these culturally specific insights to regimes only recently seeking the transition to liberal democracy, but there can be no doubt about the global influence of American constitutional jurisprudence.

That influence has been most keenly felt in countries that have reached a critical point in their development and need a clean break with the past.[4] When circumstances decree that almost nothing from historic practices can be retained, constitutionalism presents itself as a legitimate scheme for modern government. States facing "year zero," the complete rupture caused by a break with fascism, colonialism, communism, or other forms of authoritarian rule, have discovered that constitutionalism offers an alluring basis for reconstruction. In these circumstances, nations cannot draw on an existing culture as the source of constitutional renewal. The modern state is a two-sided entity comprising both normative and material aspects but, when a clean break is necessary, the normative power of the factual is precisely what must be rejected. Presented as a comprehensive normative scheme for a fundamentally reconstructed state, the image of the constitution proposed by the theory of constitutionalism offers a blueprint for the good society to come, promising to bridge the gap between present reality and future ideals.

This is one reason why classical constitutionalism, once an institutional arrangement to protect the liberties of the propertied class, is now an anachronism. Far from instituting a scheme of limited government, recent constitutions impose manifold duties on government that seek the conversion of its inscribed values into political reality. These aspirational constitutions convert the legislative role into executive action directed toward the realization of those values. This is constitutionalism as emancipatory project. But it encounters a powerful rival in Ordo-constitutionalism which, reworking classical constitutionalism for contemporary conditions, skews the constitution toward the quite specific end of preserving individual freedom by protecting a market-based order. Of much greater significance than these diverse political ends, however, is the fact that each project seeks to advance its claims through the template of constitutionalism. In the real world of global politics, where ideal expressions of right must bend to the dynamic forces of power, such a template imposes stringent constraints on any aspirational ambitions.[5]

But it is not just the growing numbers of states making radical breaks with their pasts that has so dramatically expanded the reach of constitutionalism. Deep-seated socioeconomic changes have altered the conditions of constitutional government as profoundly as those marking the movement from traditional to modern constitutions. These changes are a consequence of what has been called the second phase of modernity. It begins once mass production capitalism reaches the critical point of creative destruction, a stage that many advanced economies have reached over the last few decades. In this second phase of modernity, the effectiveness and legitimacy of many collective institutions of modern life—factory systems, big bureaucracies, major corporations, and even nation-states—are undermined by a series of structural changes falling under the general heading of "individualization."[6]

Extending its influence across the range of social, economic, political, and cultural fields, individualization has had a major impact on all systems of government. Its momentum has led to the erosion of hierarchies, the outsourcing of many collectively organized tasks, and the displacement of collective decision by individual judgment. This in turn has meant the fragmentation of institutional arrangements as bureaucracies are broken down through policy-operational differentiation and the outsourcing of activity, the perforation of boundaries between public and private, and the increased influence of rights discourse. A further feature of second-phase modernity is the growing dominance of systems organized on a global scale. Because of this, national governments have seen their authority challenged, both from above by global systems and from below by the blurring of public and private and the demands of individual rights. Such rapid structural changes have unsettled conventional expectations and generated yet more formal and transparent arrangements, transforming the role of the constitution in the social life of the nation.

This transformation leads to constitutionalism taking a reflexive turn. Individualization encourages this in numerous ways. The constitution is reinterpreted through the prism of individual rights rather than institutional powers. The center of action shifts away from legislatures into the courts, where a determinate decision by legislative will is replaced by deliberative judgment through judicial reasoning. The growing social influence of constitutional discourse leads to the emergence of the total constitution, which is reimagined according to universal principles such as rationality, proportionality, and subsidiarity. Finally, reflexive constitutional reasoning permeates all social and political discourse, leading to the reconceptualization of state and society on the foundation of individual rights. The name I have given to this entire process is constitutionalization.

The contemporary period is not "the age of constitutionalism" just because of a growing number of states that are reconstituted in ways that mark a clean break with the past. It is so designated because, as a result of these socioeconomic changes, the role of the constitution in all regimes of constitutional government is revitalized. The dramatic impact that constitutionalization has had on constitutional jurisprudence was examined in Part III. If we focus only on domestic developments, it is tempting to see the move toward a principled, rights-based, universalizing jurisprudence of aspiration as an entirely progressive change. But this overlooks the way that constitutionalization dissolves the sharp lines dividing the national from the international.[7]

A particularly insidious aspect of the second phase of modernity is the increasing amount of governing power now exercised by international institutions. Established as intergovernmental arrangements to coordinate action in a world of growing interdependencies, constitutionalization reinforces their authority. Yet these institutions are not established by democratic authorization, that is, by an expression of the people's constituent power. If they are legitimated at all, it is according to certain universal precepts of public reason. And as these global networks of governance extend their power and influence, Ordo-constitutionalism comes of age. Working through the constitutionalization of international institutions and the interpenetration of national and international, its neoliberal cosmopolitan and market principles not only permeate national constitutional discourse but even impose structural constraints on its range of operation. Despite the apparently competing rhetorics of aspirational and Ordo variants, it is the disciplinary template of constitutionalism itself that determines their relative influence.

The impact of this reflexive turn can be summarized by revisiting the six main criteria of constitutionalism specified in the Introduction. The first principle, that the constitution establishes a *comprehensive scheme of government*, must be extended: the constitution now provides a blueprint for a *comprehensive scheme of society*. The second, the principle of *representative government*, is converted to the constitution as the *symbolic representation of collective political identity* and, with respect to international institutions, signifies a reinstatement of the principle of virtual representation once vehemently opposed by the American colonists. The third, the *division, channeling, and constraining of governmental powers*, devised to establish limited government through the horizontal allocation of powers between legislative, executive, and judiciary, now also expresses the *vertical differentiation of powers* between global, regional, national, and local authorities in a scheme of total government. The fourth, that the constitution creates a *permanent governing framework*, now bolsters the legitimacy of international institutions through the *constitutionalization of intergovernmental arrangements*. The fifth, that the constitution establishes a system of *fundamental law*, is globalized and so loses its link to collective political will, becoming the embodiment of *universal public reason*. Finally, the principle that the constitution assumes its status as the regime's *collective political identity* becomes the common template of an *invisible constitution of neoliberal values with a global reach*.

~

Do these rapid developments signal the waning of constitutional democracy? The most compelling argument to the contrary seems to be the dramatic growth in the numbers of states classified as constitutional democracies in the last few decades. At the end of the Second World War, only twelve established constitutional democracies were left standing in the world.[8] By 1987, the number had grown to 66 of the world's 193 United Nations member states and, by 2003, that figure had almost doubled again, to 121.[9] Almost every state seeking to legitimate its rule in the eyes of its citizens and the world now feels it must present itself as a constitutional democracy.

But these statistics are deceptive and must be qualified. Constitutional democracy's key feature is to maintain the tension between two basic concepts of freedom: freedom as collective self-rule and freedom as individual autonomy. These must be kept in a state of productive irresolution because it is this that confers on constitutional democracy its open and dynamic character. Like all modern regimes, constitutional democracy involves governing by an elite. But it is distinctive in conferring the equal right on citizens to elect and be elected, and in requiring all major decisions to be subject to the ultimate verdict of the people.

Vital though it is, the practice of constitutional democracy is not reducible to regular elections based on universal suffrage. For elections to be meaningful, there must be a culture of active political engagement facilitated by a free press, vibrant civil society associations, and transparency in public decision-making. Constitutional democracy also promises advancement toward what Tocqueville called a growing equality of conditions. For this to be realized, we look for an increase not just in the number of those with a right to participate in decision-making but also in the number of arenas in which this right can be invoked.

Constitutional democracy cannot be defined simply as a form of government. The regime might be presidential or parliamentary, unitary or federal, and its electoral procedures can vary, as can the ways in which it identifies and protects rights. Constitutional democracy is both local and pluralistic, and justly so since it owes its authority to a particular people of a defined territory. In these respects, the adopted constitution must be seen to have been erected on the foundation of an already existing constitution of the state. It is this constituted order that invests with precise meanings principles of popular authorization, transparency in public decision-making, political equality, and accountability. Crucial to the flourishing of the regime are active civil society associations that educate and formulate, strong political parties that convert diverse views into a common will, a relative equality of income and wealth, and a civic culture that tolerates difference. As John Stuart Mill appreciated, these strenuous conditions are most likely to be met by a people "united among themselves by common sympathies."[10]

Few of the constitutional democracies appearing in recent global trends qualify according to these more rigorous criteria. This is not just because they are populous, culturally diverse states with complicated histories and a wide variety of governmental arrangements. The crucial point is that all too often they have been invested with the institutional trappings of constitutional democracy without the underpinning political culture to sustain it. Quantitative studies classify as constitutional democracies those regimes that have been modernized by the imposition of constitutionalism as a technical fix. Yet the ambition behind this exercise is daunting. It often requires newly independent nation-states with little prior experience on which to draw to quickly establish functionally effective market systems, vibrant civil society networks, strong and competitive political party systems, and workable mechanisms for ensuring transparent and accountable government.

Given the scale of this task, it is hardly surprising that so many newly established constitutional democracies are not functioning as many had hoped.[11] And yet, the apparent failure of the experiment has not led to the overthrow of these regimes. Rather than being ousted by coups d'état or other revolutionary action, they have kept the institutional trappings of constitutional democracy but without adhering to the norms and values by which they are supposed to work. Such constitutional democracies are degraded by being hollowed out from within.

This phenomenon is not just a feature of newly established regimes. It also afflicts relatively mature constitutional democracies. The strains are felt on multiple fronts. Constitutional democracy builds its authority on the pivotal role of the legislature as the primary institution of representative democracy. Yet legislatures are now losing authority to governments, regulatory officials, and courts. This erodes the principle of popular authorization, simultaneously weakening legislatures and political parties. Organized as vehicles for the formation of popular will, political parties now seem remote from their members and beholden to powerful backers. The result is that most established political parties have experienced a serious decline in support.[12] These domestic political trends are reinforced by the sense that governing power is increasingly exercised by officials in international organizations whose remit is opaque and who are insulated from established methods of control and accountability. Together, these trends indicate a marked decline of trust not just in political elites but also in governing institutions.[13]

The decline in political authority is accentuated by the impact of recent social and economic changes. Of particular importance has been the accelerating growth of economic inequality in all constitutional democracies.[14] In direct contrast with Tocqueville's principle of a growing equality of conditions, this erodes the sense of common feeling that sustains constitutional democracy. The cause is not just the corrosive effects of the threat of economic power being converted into political power, but also, in a new take on Sieyes's views of the nobility, the wealthy no longer seeing themselves as part of a territorially bounded political nation. Compounded by historically unprecedented levels of migration into advanced democracies, it is a trend that fragments the sense of "the people" and loosens the "common sympathies" that sustain constitutional democracies.[15]

The cumulative effect of these changes on the status of constitutional democracy has been profound. The challenges of accommodating the interests of large heterogeneous societies through representative politics, of securing both economic growth and acceptable wealth distribution, of maintaining territorial controls in a world of porous borders, and of curbing the power of transnational institutions all put enormous strain on the capacity and legitimacy of constitutional democracy.

∼

Such somber developments considerably complicate any defense of constitutional democracy against constitutionalism. But at least they present a more realistic basis for analysis. Recent developments have triggered numerous studies examining how and why constitutional democracies are in decline and what might be done to protect them.[16] The startling fact, however, is that these studies assume that the regime under attack is a constitutional democracy. Invariably conflating constitutional democracy with constitutionalism, they fail to consider whether the problem is not with constitutional democracy but with the way that rampant constitutionalism transforms constitutional democracies.

There have been many discussions about the emergence of so-called illiberal democracies in states like Hungary and Poland, about the growing electoral success of nationalist parties such as the Front National in France (since 2018 renamed Rassemblement National), Alternative für Deutschland (AfD) in Germany, the Freedom Party of Austria (FPÖ), Lega Nord (in 2018 rebranded as Lega) in Italy, or the Bharatiya Janata Party (BJP) in India, and about the erosion of constitutional norms following the emergence of authoritarian leaders. But these studies have focused determinedly on sources of dissatisfaction with constitutional democracy. They have not engaged with the possibility that these developments might be reasonable responses to how constitutional democracies have been undermined by the extending influence of constitutionalism.

The contemporary crisis is widely considered to have its source in the looming specter of "populism."[17] This label has been applied to a range of political movements whose manifestations vary according to circumstances. Unlike liberalism, socialism, or indeed constitutionalism, populism is not a specific ideology giving rise to a distinctive political movement. Populism is a syndrome, a set of symptoms indicating an ailment afflicting contemporary democracies.[18] Born of dissatisfaction with the ways in which constitutional structures and party politics are working, populist politics seek more direct means by which popular opinion can influence governmental decision-making. In this respect, the aim is to restore the voice of the majority as the authentic expression of constituent power. It is not difficult to denigrate the movements falling under this label as nationalist, xenophobic, simplistic, antipluralist, a revolt of the "left-behinds," and downright dangerous if transformed from syndrome to project for power. Populism is undoubtedly a reaction to the impact of deep-seated social and economic changes falling under the umbrella of globalization. But it can also be seen as the inevitable political response to the reflexive turn taken by contemporary constitutionalism.

This is not how the rise of populism is seen in contemporary constitutional scholarship, which invariably assumes it is simply an expression of antagonism to constitutional democracy.[19] These studies offer an inventory of solutions: imposing bans on radical political parties and curbs on free speech, adopting "eternity clauses" that prohibit the amendment of basic principles of the constitution, instituting threshold voting arrangements, and strengthening the powers of arms-length reviewing institutions.[20] The solution commonly touted to threats associated with the rise of populism is to strengthen the institutional mechanisms of constitutionalism. Having wrongly diagnosed the ailment, what is proposed as a remedy is an intensification of the treatment that is one of the main sources of the original disorder.

Many if not most of these populist movements have arisen in opposition not to constitutional democracy but to the way it has been reshaped by constitutionalism. Consider for example the rise of populism in central and eastern European states that have undergone a rapid transition from Soviet-style socialism to market capitalism. Here, the growth of populism seems directly linked to the imposition of constitutionalism. In these regimes, argue Ivan Krastev and Stephen Holmes, "discontent with 'the transition to democracy' was . . . inflamed by visiting foreign 'evaluators' with an anaemic grasp of local realities." The rise of populism, they suggest, is born of "humiliations associated with the uphill struggle to become at best an inferior copy of a superior model."[21]

Indeed, some radical theorists have argued that populism is less a symptom of decline than a sign of the possible renewal of democracy.[22] Populism provokes us to inquire more deeply into the sources of these recent constitutional developments, but it is best seen as a warning symptom of how the political foundations of constitutional democracy are being eroded.[23] If rampant constitutionalism is part of the problem, a more productive way forward must be to restore the basic values of constitutional democracy.

≈

Is constitutional democracy a twentieth-century phenomenon whose time has passed? That certainly is the view of cosmopolitans who believe that the second phase of modernity has demolished the foundations of modern state-based constitutional democracy. They argue that the project of building constitutional authority on the foundation of the modern idea of the state—the union of territory, people, and sovereign authority—is over, claiming that authority now depends on the degree to which governmental practices conform to an ideal "invisible constitution."

The invisible constitution does not prescribe a particular arrangement of governing institutions but comprises a set of universal principles explicated by a network of judicial bodies. The modern idea of the constitution as a text in which the people, through an exercise of constituent power, outline the terms by which they govern themselves is relegated to secondary matter. The hierarchical relationship between ordinary law made by legislatures and the fundamental law of the constitution has been superseded. In the new cosmopolitan paradigm, the constitution no longer has ultimate authority since it is now subject to the creative powers of judicial interpretation that render it compliant with the principles of the invisible constitution. Super-legality reigns.

This looks like progress: who could object to the subjection of govern-mental decision-making to rationality review? In fact, it is political naivete. Cosmopolitan constitutionalism promotes the authority of a set of self-sustaining principles, but these principles only acquire meaning when in-fused with values. And these values become clear when it is seen that the invisible constitution is closely linked to a powerful global network of in-visible power.

In the 1980s, Norberto Bobbio drew attention to the ways in which the values of democracy as a system of open government by a visible power were being eroded by the growth of a corporate state wielding influence through invisible methods beyond the reach of democratic control and account-ability.[24] The world has much changed since then. Second-phase modernity has resulted not in a diminished state but in a much more fragmented one. With the proliferation of semiautonomous agencies, the blurring of public-private boundaries, and the growing power of global networks, invisible power has now become a more pervasive phenomenon even less susceptible to political accountability. Constitutionalization might therefore be seen as an attempt to regulate invisible power. But whatever benefits constitu-tionalization might confer—and it does at least operate on the principle of openness—it ends up legitimating a system that is no longer the project of a people and no longer subject to popular control. The new species of law it brings in its wake is itself a new type of invisible power. In the nineteenth century, Tocqueville recognized that, by neutralizing the vices inherent in popular government, lawyers inevitably become the conduits of constitu-tional democracy. Continuing to value liberty and being attached to order above all other considerations, they have now become effective agents in bolstering the new global system.[25]

At the beginning of the twentieth century, Weber outlined the thesis that modern capitalism had its origins not in the Enlightenment and the processes of secularization, but in the emergence of new forms of religious conviction that preached individual responsibility, required more methodical control over conduct, and embraced acquisition as the ultimate purpose of life. He concluded his argument by suggesting that no one knows "who will live in this cage in the future." It is surely not fanciful now to see in the triumph of constitutionalism the culmination of Weber's claims.[26] Marking the apotheosis of individual rights, it contributes to the hollowing out of democracy and the retreat of the individual into a privatized society in which few participate in public affairs. And as Tocqueville foresaw, this will lead to a void that can only be filled by an extensive regulatory network operating in a governing mode that is "absolute, minute, regular, provident, and mild."[27]

There are many powerful forces directing contemporary change and subverting the authority of a political worldview founded on equal liberty in solidarity.[28] Yet the fact remains that civilized life still requires an extensive governmental apparatus to provide the physical and social infrastructure essential for peace, security, and welfare, and no more effective method of ensuring the realization of these goals has been devised than the political conception of constitutional democracy I have outlined. Ultimately, the argument against constitutionalism rests on the claim that it institutes a system of rule that is unlikely to carry popular support, without which only increasing authoritarianism and countervailing reaction will result.

NOTES
ACKNOWLEDGMENTS
INDEX

NOTES

Preface

1. Thomas C. Grey, "Constitutionalism: An Analytical Framework," in *Constitutionalism,* ed. J. Roland Pennock and John W. Chapman (New York: New York University Press, 1979), 189–209, 189.

2. For a recent study equating constitutionalism with constitutional government, see Bruce Ackerman, *Revolutionary Constitutions: Charismatic Leadership and the Rule of Law* (Cambridge, MA: Belknap Press of Harvard University Press, 2019), 2: "Constitutionalism, as I understand it, involves the imposition of significant legal constraints on top decision-makers." For a recent study equating constitutionalism with having adopted a modern type of written constitution, see Linda Colley, *The Gun, the Ship and the Pen: Warfare, Constitutions, and the Making of the Modern World* (London: Profile Books, 2021), 218: "It was Magna Carta . . . that lay at the root of all subsequent written efforts at constitutionalism." In "Constitutionalism: A Skeptical View," Waldron comes closer to the key issue but then equivocates over its meaning and focuses his criticisms on the equation of constitutionalism with limited government: Jeremy Waldron, *Political Political Theory: Essays on Institutions* (Cambridge, MA: Harvard University Press, 2016), chap. 2.

Introduction

1. Charles Howard McIlwain, *Constitutionalism: Ancient and Modern* (Ithaca, NY: Cornell University Press, 1940), 13. Wheeler states that "McIlwain performed an astounding *tour de force.* Laying down what was to become acclaimed as the bible for all succeeding theorists of constitutionalism, he purported to display the essence of the topic and did so . . . without carrying his essential story beyond England of 1630." Harvey Wheeler, "The Foundations of Constitutionalism," *Loyola of Los Angeles Law Review* 8 (1975): 507–586, 564.

2. McIlwain, *Constitutionalism,* 21.

3. Edward S. Corwin, "The 'Higher Law' Background of American Constitutional Law," *Harvard Law Review* 42 (1928): 149–185, 153.

4. Francis D. Wormuth, *The Origins of Modern Constitutionalism* (New York: Harper, 1949), 3. The allusion to "auxiliary precautions" is a reference to James Madison, Alexander Hamilton, and John Jay, *The Federalist Papers* [1787–1788], ed. I. Kramnick (London: Penguin, 1987), no. 51 (Madison).

5. Montesquieu, *The Spirit of the Laws* [1748], trans. A. Cohler, B. Miller, and H. Stone (Cambridge: Cambridge University Press, 1989).

6. M. J. C. Vile, *Constitutionalism and the Separation of Powers*, 2nd ed. (Indianapolis: Liberty Fund, 1998), 2.

7. Thomas Paine, "Rights of Man" [1791], in his *Rights of Man, Common Sense and Other Political Writings*, ed. M. Philp (Oxford: Oxford University Press, 1995), 83–331, 122.

8. Paine, "Rights of Man," 92.

9. See Gary Jeffrey Jacobsohn, *Constitutional Identity* (Cambridge, MA: Harvard University Press, 2010), 8–9: "This approach to identity [is] *deeply constitutive*, as it reflects an understanding of the constitution as the foundation for both legal and social relations within a polity. . . . [W]hat is constitutive of the identity of a polity seems to us to be rooted in extra-constitutional factors such as religion and culture than in the language of a legal document" (emphasis in original).

10. Jed Rubenfeld, *Freedom and Time: A Theory of Constitutional Self-Government* (New Haven, CT: Yale University Press, 2001), 163, 177, 163.

11. Karl Marx, *Critique of Hegel's "Philosophy of Right"* [c. 1843], ed. J. O'Malley (Cambridge: Cambridge University Press, 1970), 29–30.

12. See, e.g., Larry D. Kramer, *The People Themselves: Popular Constitutionalism and Judicial Review* (New York: Oxford University Press, 2004); Richard Bellamy, *Political Constitutionalism: A Republican Defence of the Constitutionality of Democracy* (Cambridge: Cambridge University Press, 2007); Mark Tushnet, "Authoritarian Constitutionalism: Some Conceptual Issues," in *Constitutions in Authoritarian Regimes*, ed. Tom Ginsburg and Alberto Simpser (New York: Cambridge University Press, 2014), 36–50.

13. Thomas Jefferson, "Letter to James Madison, 6 September 1789," and "Letter to Samuel Kercheval, 12 July 1816," in *Thomas Jefferson: Political Writings*, ed. J. Appleby and T. Ball (Cambridge: Cambridge University Press, 1999), 593–598, 210–217.

14. *Federalist* 57 (Hamilton). See also *Federalist* 43 (Madison): "The express authority of the people alone could give due validity to the Constitution."

15. François Furet, *Interpreting the French Revolution*, trans. E. Forster (Cambridge: Cambridge University Press, 1981), 4.

16. See Hans Kohn, *The Idea of Nationalism* (New York: Macmillan, 1961), chap. 1.

17. See Gary Gerstle, *Liberty and Coercion: The Paradox of American Government from the Founding to the Present* (Princeton, NJ: Princeton University Press, 2015), 55: "European theory has driven studies of the state . . . and this has meant

an emphasis on the nature and activities of the central state. . . . It is obvious that this singular term does not work well for a polity such as the United States, in which multiple institutions carry out 'state' activities." See also Max M. Edling, *Perfecting the Union: National and State Authority in the US Constitution* (New York: Oxford University Press, 2021), 12, 14: "The American union reserved to the states the power to regulate the social, economic, and civic life of their citizens and inhabitants with only limited supervision and control from the national government. . . . The federal government did not replace the states as the central locus of power before the middle of the twentieth century."

18. Somerset v. Stewart, 98 ER 499 (1772); Aziz Rana, *The Two Faces of American Freedom* (Cambridge, MA: Harvard University Press, 2010), 80.

19. Johnson v. M'Intosh, 21 US 543 (1823); United States v. Rogers, 45 US 567, 572 (1845), Taney C.J.: "The native tribes who were found on this continent at the time of its discovery have never been acknowledged or treated as independent nationals by the European governments, nor regarded as the owners of the territories they respectively occupied. On the contrary, the whole continent was divided and parcelled out, and granted by the governments of Europe as if it had been vacant and unoccupied land, and the Indians continually held to be, and treated as, subject to their Dominion and control."

20. Dred Scott v. Sandford, 60 US 393, 406, 407 (1857), Taney C.J.: "The question then arises, whether the provisions of the Constitution . . . embraced the negro African race. . . . They had for more than a century before been regarded as beings of an inferior order, and altogether unfit to associate with the white race, either in social, or political relations; and so far inferior, that they had no rights which the white man was bound to respect."

21. US Const., art. I, § 8: "The Congress shall have the Power. . . . To regulate Commerce with foreign Nations, and among the several States, and with the Indian Tribes."

22. US Const., art. I, § 2, cl. 3; art. I, § 9; art. IV, § 2, cl. 3.

23. "Letter from Jefferson to George Rogers Clark, 25 December 1780," National Archives, Founders Online, https://founders.archives.gov/documents/Jefferson/01-04-02-0295. See also Adam Burns, *American Imperialism: The Territorial Expansion of the United States, 1783–2013* (Edinburgh: Edinburgh University Press, 2017), chap. 1.

24. Paul W. Kahn, *Origins of Order: Project and System in the American Legal Imagination* (New Haven, CT: Yale University Press, 2019), 40.

25. Kahn, *Origins of Order,* 10.

26. Edward S. Corwin, *John Marshall and the Constitution: A Chronicle of the Supreme Court* (New Haven, CT: Yale University Press, 1919), chaps. 1, 5; James F. Simon, *What Kind of Nation? Thomas Jefferson, John Marshall, and the Epic Struggle to Create a United States* (New York: Simon & Schuster, 2002).

27. David Jayne Hill, *Americanism, What It Is* (New York: Appleton & Co., 1916), 49: "The Civil War . . . did not involve a denial of the fundamental principles upon which American constitutionalism is based. It consisted, on the contrary, merely in a difference of documentary interpretation."

28. Hill, *Americanism*, 40.

29. David Runciman, *The Confidence Trap: A History of Democracy in Crisis from World War I to the Present* (Princeton, NJ: Princeton University Press, 2013), 77; McIlwain, *Constitutionalism*, 134: "In parts of Europe, it will be noted, the incompetence of constitutional governments led to their replacement by despotisms."

30. Hill, *Americanism*, 56.

31. Quotations from Franklin D. Roosevelt, Address on Constitution Day, September 17, 1937, the American Presidency Project, https://www.presidency.ucsb.edu/documents/address-constitution-day-washington-dc. There is, of course, a more complex story to be told: Bruce Ackerman, *We the People*, vol. 3, *The Civil Rights Revolution* (Cambridge, MA: Belknap Press of Harvard University Press, 2014), 26: "A funny thing happened to Americans on the way to the twenty-first century. We have lost our ability to write down our new constitutional commitments in the old-fashioned way. This is no small problem for a country that imagines itself living under a written Constitution." The issue is taken up in Chapter 10.

32. Basic Law, art. 79(3).

33. Basic Law, art. 21(2). On constrained democracy, see Karl Loewenstein, "Militant Democracy and Fundamental Rights," *American Political Science Review* 31 (1937): 417–432 (pt. I); 638–658 (pt. II).

34. *Lüth*, BVerfGE 7, 198 (1958).

35. Basic Law, art. 146.

36. See Christoph Möllers, "'We Are (Afraid) of the People': Constituent Power in German Constitutionalism," in *The Paradox of Constitutionalism: Constituent Power and Constitutional Form,* ed. Martin Loughlin and Neil Walker (Oxford: Oxford University Press, 2007), 87–106.

37. For the complexities, see Adom Getachew, *Worldmaking after Empire: The Rise and Fall of Self-Determination* (Princeton, NJ: Princeton University Press, 2019).

38. McCulloch v. Maryland, 17 US (4 Wheat.) 316, 407 (1819), Marshall C.J.

39. Speech by B. R. Ambedkar, "Constituent Assembly of India, 4 November 1948," cited in Madhav Khosla, *India's Founding Moment: The Constitution of a Most Surprising Democracy* (Cambridge, MA: Harvard University Press, 2020), 42–43. The quotation on "paramount reverence" is taken from same speech and is cited in Sujit Choudhry, Madhav Khosla, and Pratap Bhanu Mehta, eds., *The Oxford Handbook of the Indian Constitution* (Oxford: Oxford University Press, 2016), 3.

40. Khosla, *India's Founding Moment*, 22.

41. Kesavananda Bharati v. State of Kerala, AIR 1461 (1973); Minerva Mills Ltd v. Union of India, AIR 1789 (1980). See also Upendra Baxi, "Law, Politics, and Constitutional Hegemony: The Supreme Court, Jurisprudence, and Demo-sprudence," in Choudhry et al., *The Oxford Handbook of the Indian Constitution*, 94–109.

42. Choudhry et al., *The Oxford Handbook of the Indian Constitution*, 6.

43. See "Timeline of Constitutions" of the Comparative Constitutions Project, https://comparativeconstitutionsproject.org/chronology/, accessed August 25, 2021.

44. For empirical analysis, see David S. Law and Mila Versteeg, "The Evolution and Ideology of Global Constitutionalism," *California Law Review* 99 (2011): 1153–1257.

45. Samuel Issacharoff, "Populism versus Democratic Governance," in *Constitutional Democracy in Crisis?*, ed. Mark A. Graber, Sanford Levinson, and Mark Tushnet (New York: Oxford University Press, 2018), 445–458, 445. Many of these regimes are now under stress, an issue considered in the Conclusion.

46. Tom Ginsburg and Mila Versteeg, "Why Do Countries Adopt Constitutional Review?," *Journal of Law, Economics & Organization* 30 (2014): 587–622, 587: "By our account, some 38% of all constitutional systems had constitutional review in 1951; by 2011, 83% of the world's constitutions had given courts the power to supervise implementation of the constitution and to set aside legislation for constitutional incompatibility."

47. See Martin Loughlin, "What Is Constitutionalization?," in *The Twilight of Constitutionalism?*, ed. Petra Dobner and Martin Loughlin (Oxford: Oxford University Press, 2010), chap. 3.

48. Ran Hirschl, *Towards Juristocracy: The Origins and Consequences of the New Constitutionalism* (Cambridge, MA: Harvard University Press, 2004), 8–9.

49. Gordon J. Schochet, "Introduction: Constitutionalism, Liberalism, and the Study of Politics," in *Constitutionalism*, ed. J. Roland Pennock and John W. Chapman (New York: New York University Press, 1979), 1–15, 6.

50. Eric Hobsbawm, *The Age of Revolution, 1789–1848* (New York: Vintage Books, 1962); Hobsbawm, *The Age of Capital, 1848–1875* (New York: Scribner, 1975); Hobsbawm, *The Age of Empire, 1875–1914* (London: Weidenfeld & Nicolson, 1987); Hobsbawm, *The Age of Extremes: The Short Twentieth Century, 1914–1991* (London: Abacus, 1995).

51. For critical assessment of Hobsbawm's account of twentieth century developments, see Tony Judt, "Downhill all the Way," in his *When the Facts Change: Essays 1995–2010* (New York: Penguin, 2015), chap. 1.

52. Max Weber, "Science as a Vocation," in *From Max Weber: Essays in Sociology*, ed. H. H. Gerth and C. Wright Mills (London: Routledge & Kegan Paul, 1948), 129–156.

53. *Federalist* 1 (Hamilton): "It seems to have been reserved to the people of this country . . . to decide the important question, whether societies of men are really capable or not of establishing good government from reflection and choice, or whether they are forever destined to depend for their political constitutions on accident and force."

54. Ulrich Beck, Wolfgang Bonss, and Christophe Lau, "The Theory of Reflexive Modernization: Problematic, Hypotheses and Research Programme," *Theory, Culture & Society* 20 (2003): 1–33, 1.

55. Ulrich Beck and Edgar Grande, "Varieties of Second Modernity: The Cosmopolitan Turn in Social and Political Theory and Research," *British Journal of Sociology* 61 (2010): 409–443.

56. See the discussions in Dobner and Loughlin, *The Twilight of Constitutionalism?*

57. This promise led to the advocacy of "transformative constitutionalism" in a number of postwar regimes: see, e.g., Gautam Bhatia, *The Transformative Constitution: A Radical Biography in Nine Acts* (Uttar Pradesh: HarperCollins, 2019); Armin von Bogdandy et al., eds., *Transformative Constitutionalism in Latin America: The Emergence of a New Ius Commune* (Oxford: Oxford University Press, 2017); Karl Klare, "Legal Culture and Transformative Constitutionalism," *South African Journal on Human Rights* 14 (1998): 146–188; Michaela Hailbronner, "Transformative Constitutionalism: Not Only in the Global South," *American Journal of Comparative Law* 65 (2017): 527–565.

58. Stephen Gill and A. Claire Cutler, eds., *New Constitutionalism and World Order* (Cambridge: Cambridge University Press, 2014); Quinn Slobodian, *Globalists: The End of Empire and the Birth of Neoliberalism* (Cambridge, MA: Harvard University Press, 2018), 11: "Neoliberalism has been less a discipline of economics than a discipline statecraft and law."

59. See, e.g., Kwame Nkrumah, *Neo-Colonialism: The Last Stage of Capitalism* (London: Thomas Nelson, 1965); Getachew, *Worldmaking after Empire,* chap. 1.

60. F. A. Hayek, "New Nations and the Problem of Power," *The Listener,* November 10, 1960, 819: "I believe that limiting the powers of democracy in these new parts of the world is the only chance of preserving democracy in those parts of the world. If democracies do not limit their own powers they will be destroyed." Cited in Slobodian, *Globalists,* 4. See further F.A. Hayek, "A Model Constitution," in *Law, Legislation and Liberty,* vol. 3, *The Political Order of a Free People* (London: Routledge & Kegan Paul, 1979), 105–127.

61. Compare Gary Jeffrey Jacobsohn and Yaniv Roznai, *Constitutional Revolution* (New Haven, CT: Yale University Press, 2020). Presenting valuable studies of developments in Germany, India, and Israel, this work comes unstuck on the concept of "constitutional revolution." The authors are unable to distinguish between "revolution" and "evolution" because they fail to recognize that the "paradig-

matic shift" they identify, being the product of constitutionalization, reshapes these constitutions in accordance with the precepts of constitutionalism.

1. Constitutions

1. See, e.g., Giovanni Sartori, "Constitutionalism: A Preliminary Discussion," *American Political Science Review* 56 (1962): 853–864; Dieter Grimm, "The Origins and Transformation of the Concept of the Constitution," in his *Constitutionalism: Past, Present, and Future* (Oxford: Oxford University Press, 2016), 3–37, 3.

2. Charles Howard McIlwain, *Constitutionalism: Ancient and Modern* (Ithaca, NY: Cornell University Press, 1940), 26.

3. M. J. C. Vile, *Constitutionalism and the Separation of Powers*, 2nd ed. (Indianapolis, IN: Liberty Fund, 1998), 37.

4. Ptolemy of Lucca, *On the Government of Rulers: De regimine principum*, trans. J. M. Blythe (Philadelphia: University of Pennsylvania Press, 1997); James M. Blythe, *Ideal Government and the Mixed Constitution in the Middle Ages* (Princeton, NJ: Princeton University Press, 1992).

5. The term first appeared in Theodore Beza, *Du droit des magistrats* (1574), where it was invoked to bolster his argument that magistrates had the right to have the king deposed if he failed to keep within the lawfully conferred powers under "les loix fondamentales d'un Royaume": *Constitutionalism and Resistance in the Sixteenth Century: Three Treatises by Hotman, Beza and Mornay*, ed. J. H. Franklin (New York: Pegasus, 1969). On ideological dispute, see Martyn P. Thompson, "The History of Fundamental Law in Political Thought from the French Wars of Religion to the American Revolution," *American Historical Review* 91 (1986): 1103–1128.

6. See J. W. Gough, *Fundamental Law in English Constitutional History* (Oxford: Clarendon Press, 1955).

7. See respectively, "The Act Erecting a High Court of Justice for the King's Trial, 6 January 1649," in *The Constitutional Documents of the Puritan Revolution, 1625–1660*, ed. S. R. Gardiner, 3rd ed. (Oxford: Clarendon Press, 1906), 357; *Commons Journal*, 28 January 1688, cited in Steve Pincus, *1688: The First Modern Revolution* (New Haven, CT: Yale University Press, 2009), 284.

8. "Sentence of the High Court of Justice upon the King, 27 January 1649," in Gardiner, *The Constitutional Documents of the Puritan Revolution*, 372.

9. Gerald Stourzh, "Constitution: Changing Meanings of the Term from the Early Seventeenth to the Late Eighteenth Century," in *Conceptual Change and the Constitution*, ed. Terence Ball and J. G. A. Pocock (Lawrence: University Press of Kansas, 1988), 35–54, 43.

10. Anonymous, *Touching the Fundamentall Laws, or Politique Constitution of this Kingdom* (London: Thomas Underhill, 1643), in *The Struggle for Sovereignty:*

Seventeenth-Century English Political Tracts, ed. Joyce Lee Malcolm, vol. 1 (Indianapolis, IN: Liberty Fund, 1999), 261–279, 264.

11. McIlwain, *Constitutionalism,* 23: "Glanvill frequently uses the word 'constitution' for a royal edict. . . . At this time [the thirteenth century], and for centuries after, 'constitution' always means a particular administrative enactment much as it had meant to the Roman lawyers."

12. "The Instrument of Government," 16 December 1653, in Gardiner, *The Constitutional Documents of the Puritan Revolution,* 405.

13. "The Fundamental Constitutions of Carolina, 1 March 1669," The Avalon Project, Yale Law School, Lillian Goldman Law Library, https://avalon.law.yale .edu/17th_century/nc05.asp.

14. Stourzh, "Constitution," 45: "The use of the word 'unconstitutional' suddenly spread in North America, once it had been first used in 1764/65 in Rhode Island."

15. Dieter Grimm, "The Concept of Constitution in Historical Perspective," in his *Constitutionalism,* 89–124, 90.

16. Emer de Vattel, *The Law of Nations, or Principles of the Law of Nature Applied to the Conduct of Affairs of Nations and Sovereigns* [1758] (Indianapolis, IN: Liberty Fund, 2008), § 27.

17. Viscount Bolingbroke, "A Dissertation upon Parties," in his *Political Writings,* ed. D. Armitage (Cambridge: Cambridge University Press, 1997), 1–191, 88.

18. Montesquieu, *The Spirit of the Laws* [1748], trans. A. Cohler, B. Miller, and H. Stone (Cambridge: Cambridge University Press, 1989), book 3.

19. Montesquieu, *The Spirit of the Laws,* book 9, chap. 1. But note that Montesquieu here may have influenced the American founders with his claim that a confederation, composed of small republics, "enjoys the goodness of the internal government of each one; and, with regard to the exterior, it has, by the force of the association, all the advantages of large monarchies."

20. Montesquieu, *The Spirit of the Laws,* book 11, chap. 4.

21. Montesquieu, *The Spirit of the Laws,* book 11, chap. 5.

22. Montesquieu, *The Spirit of the Laws,* book 11, chap. 6.

23. Judith N. Shklar, *Montesquieu* (Oxford: Oxford University Press, 1987), 112.

24. Grimm, "The Origins and Transformation of the Concept of the Constitution," 20.

25. John A. Hawgood, *Modern Constitutions since 1787* (London: Macmillan, 1939), 3. See further Ernst-Wolfgang Böckenförde, "The Historical Evolution and Changes in the Meaning of the Constitution," in his *Constitutional and Political Theory,* ed. M. Künkler and T. Stein (Oxford: Oxford University Press, 2017), chap. 6.

26. See Kelly L. Grotke and Markus J. Prutsch, eds., *Constitutionalism, Legitimacy, and Power: Nineteenth-Century Experiences* (Oxford: Oxford University Press, 2014).

27. Hawgood, *Modern Constitutions since 1787,* 81: "The story of Bonapartist constitutionalism was very much the same everywhere. Republics one and indivisible on the model of 1795 were succeeded by republics dependent and variable on the model of 1799, and these in their turn gave place to monarchies consanguineous and subservient on the model of 1802–4. . . . Everywhere the shadow of representative government and popular sovereignty was conceded and their substance denied."

28. Hawgood, *Modern Constitutions since 1787,* chaps. 8–10; Markus J. Prutsch, "'Monarchical Constitutionalism' in Post-Napoleonic Europe: Concept and Practice," in Grotke and Prutsch, *Constitutionalism, Legitimacy, and Power,* chap. 4; Volker Sellin, "Restorations and Constitutions," in Grotke and Prutsch, *Constitutionalism, Legitimacy, and Power,* chap. 5.

29. See Johannes Althusius, *Politica: Politics Methodically Set Forth and Illustrated with Sacred and Profane Examples* [1603], trans. F. S. Carney (Indianapolis, IN: Liberty Fund, 1995).

30. See J. G. A. Pocock, *The Ancient Constitution and the Feudal Law: A Study of English Historical Thought in the Seventeenth Century,* rev. ed. (Cambridge: Cambridge University Press, 1987). This trope is replicated in European political thought of the period: see, e.g., François Hotman, *Francogallia* [1573], ed. R. E. Giesey and J. H. M. Salmon (Cambridge: Cambridge University Press, 1972).

31. Montesquieu, *The Spirit of the Laws,* book 11, chap. 6.

32. Joseph de Maistre, "Study on Sovereignty" [1794–1795], in *Works,* ed. J. Lively (New York: Macmillan, 1965), 93–129, 107, 103.

33. Edmund Burke, *An Appeal from the New to the Old Whigs* [1791], ed. J. M. Robson (Indianapolis, IN: Bobbs-Merrill, 1962), 134.

34. Edmund Burke, *Reflections on the Revolution in France* [1790] (London: Penguin, 1968), 106: "A state without the means of some change is without the means of its conservation."

35. G. W. F. Hegel, *The Philosophy of Mind* [1830], trans. W. Wallace (Oxford: Clarendon Press, 1971), § 540.

36. Ernst-Wolfgang Böckenförde, *Staat, Gesellschaft, Freiheit: Studien zur Staatstheorie und zum Verfassungsrecht* (Frankfurt am Main: Suhrkamp, 1976), 60.

37. Claude-Henri de Saint-Simon, "L'industrie ou discussions politiques, morales et philosophiques" [1817], in his *Oeuvres,* vol. 2 (Paris: Edition Anthropos, 1966), 82–93; Lorenz von Stein, *The History of the Social Movement in France, 1789–1850* [1850], trans. K. Mengelberg (Totowa, NJ: Bedminster Press, 1964), 75–79; Ferdinand Lassalle, "Über Verfassungswesen" [1862], in his *Gesamtwerke,* ed. E. Blum (Leipzig: Pfau, 1901), 72–93.

38. Charles A. Beard, *An Economic Interpretation of the Constitution of the United States* (New York: Macmillan, 1913); Bertrand de Jouvenel, *On Power: The Natural History and Its Growth* [1945], trans. J. F. Huntington (Indianapolis, IN: Liberty Fund, 1993), 240–242.

2. The Ideology of Constitutionalism

1. Clifford Geertz, "Ideology as a Cultural System," in his *The Interpretation of Cultures* (London: Fontana, 1973), 193–233.

2. Giovanni Sartori, "Constitutionalism: A Preliminary Discussion," *American Political Science Review* 56 (1962): 853–864, 855.

3. Sartori, "Constitutionalism," 856, 855.

4. Sartori, "Constitutionalism," 859.

5. Sartori, "Constitutionalism," 859, 860.

6. For empirical analysis of the degree to which contemporary regimes fail to protect the rights enacted in their constitutions (and therefore meet Sartori's category of "façade constitution"), see David S. Law and Mila Versteeg, "Sham Constitutions," *California Law Review* 101 (2013): 863–952.

7. John Adams, "Novanglus no. 7," in *Works,* ed. C. F. Adams, vol. 4 (Boston: Little, Brown, 1856), 106.

8. A. V. Dicey, *Introduction to the Study of the Law of the Constitution,* 8th ed. (London: Macmillan, 1915), 191–195.

9. Dicey, *Law of the Constitution,* 197.

10. F. A. Hayek, *The Constitution of Liberty* (London: Routledge & Kegan Paul, 1960), 193.

11. Immanuel Kant, *Metaphysical Elements of Justice* [1797] (Part I of the *Metaphysics of Morals;* known as the *Rechtslehre*), trans. J. Ladd (Indianapolis, IN: Hackett, 1999), § 45.

12. Exemplary of the conservative account is Friedrich Julius Stahl, *Die Philosophie des Rechts nach geschichtlicher Ansicht* [1833–1837], 2 vols. (Tübingen: Mohr, 1878). With respect to the liberal version, see Robert von Mohl, *Die Polizeiwissenschaft nach den Grundsätzen des Rechtsstaates* [1832], 3rd ed. (Tübingen: Laupp, 1866). For discussion, see Ernst-Wolfgang Böckenförde, "The Origin and Development of the Concept of the *Rechtsstaat,*" in his *State, Society and Liberty: Studies in Political Theory and Constitutional Law,* trans. J. A. Underwood (New York: Berg, 1991), 47–70.

13. See, e.g., Rudolf von Jhering, *The Struggle for Law* [1872], trans. J. J. Lalor (Chicago: Callaghan & Co., 1915). Jhering argued that the state's power must be restrained by the concept of self-limitation (*Selbstbeschränkung*): that is, the state maintained its authority by binding itself to certain liberal norms.

14. Dicey, *Law of the Constitution,* 189.

15. Hayek, *The Constitution of Liberty,* 200.

16. Dicey, *Law of the Constitution,* 324–325.

17. Hayek, *The Constitution of Liberty,* 201: "To the men who devised the system, especially to its main architect, Rudolf von Gneist . . . this creation of a system of separate administrative courts . . . appeared as the crowning piece of

the *Rechtsstaat,* the definite achievement of the rule of law." See Rudolf von Gneist, *Der Rechtsstaat* (Berlin: Springer, 1872). And on France, see H. S. Jones, *The French State in Question: Public Law and Political Argument in the Third Republic* (Cambridge: Cambridge University Press, 1993), chap. 2.

18. A. V. Dicey, *Lectures on the Relation between Law and Public Opinion in England during the Nineteenth Century* (London: Macmillan, 1905), 309.

19. Dicey, *Law of the Constitution,* xxxv–cxxi.

20. Cited in M. J. C. Vile, *Constitutionalism and the Separation of Powers,* 2nd ed. (Indianapolis, IN: Liberty Fund, 1998), 131. Similarly, in the Maryland Declaration of Rights, 1776, art. VI: "That the legislative, executive and judicial powers of government, ought to be forever separate and distinct from each other."

21. *Federalist* 47. Madison also notes that those state constitutions, such as Virginia and Maryland, that supposedly are designed to institute a separation of powers, do, in fact, provide for balancing. In Maryland's constitution, for example, the executive magistrate is appointable by the legislature and the judiciary by the executive.

22. This is the basic thesis of Gordon S. Wood, *The Creation of the American Republic, 1776–1787,* rev. ed. (Chapel Hill: University of North Carolina Press, 1998).

23. See Lance Banning, *The Jeffersonian Persuasion: Evolution of a Party Ideology* (Ithaca, NY: Cornell University Press, 1978).

24. Jean-Jacques Rousseau, *The Social Contract and Other Later Political Writings,* ed. V. Gourevitch (Cambridge: Cambridge University Press, 1997), 39–152.

25. Emmanuel-Joseph Sieyès, "What Is the Third Estate?" [1789], in his *Political Writings,* trans. M. Sonenscher (Indianapolis, IN: Hackett, 2003), 92–162, 137, 139.

26. See Alec Stone, *The Birth of Judicial Politics in France: The Constitutional Council in Comparative Perspective* (Oxford: Oxford University Press, 1992), pt. I.

27. See Stephen Holmes, *Benjamin Constant and the Making of Modern Liberalism* (New Haven, CT: Yale University Press, 1984); Harold J. Laski, "The Political Theory of Royer-Collard," in his *Authority in the Modern State* (New Haven, CT: Yale University Press, 1919), chap. 4; François Guizot, *The History of the Origins of Representative Government in Europe,* trans. A.R. Scoble (Indianapolis, IN: Liberty Fund, 2002).

28. On the French debates, see Jones, *The French State in Question,* chaps. 5–7.

29. Sartori, "Constitutionalism," 862.

30. See, e.g., in the United States, Woodrow Wilson, *Constitutional Government in the United States* (New York: Columbia University Press, 1908); in Germany, Ernst Forsthoff, *Rechtstaat im Wandel: Verfassungsrechtliche Abhandlungen 1950–1964* (Stuttgart: Kohlhammer, 1964); in France, Georges Burdeau, "Zur Auflösung des Verfassungsbegriffs," *Der Staat* (1962): 389–404.

3. The Constitution of What?

1. Thomas Hobbes, *Leviathan* [1651], ed. R. Tuck (Cambridge: Cambridge University Press, 1996), 75.

2. Georg Jellinek, *Allgemeine Staatslehre,* 3rd ed. (Berlin: Springer, 1922), 337–344 ("die normative Kraft des Faktischen").

3. Carl Schmitt, *The Nomos of the Earth in the International Law of the Jus Publicum Europaeum* [1950], trans. G. L. Ulmen (New York: Telos Press, 2003), 48.

4. French Constitution of 1791, Art. 1, title 2. This form was retained in the 1793 and 1848 republican constitutions. Art. 1 of the 1958 Constitution states: "France shall be an indivisible, secular, democratic and social Republic." The National Convention declaration is cited in Westel W. Willoughby, *The Fundamental Concepts of Public Law* (New York: Macmillan, 1924), 66.

5. For a recent illustration, see Yaniv Roznai and Silvia Şuteu, "The Eternal Territory? The Crimean Crisis and Ukraine's Territorial Integrity as an Unamendable Constitutional Principle," *German Law Journal* 16 (2015): 542–580.

6. Ernest Renan, *Qu'est-ce qu'une nation?* (Paris: Calmann Lévy, 1882); Benedict Anderson, *Imagined Communities: Reflections on the Origins and Spread of Nationalism,* 2nd ed. (London: Verso, 1991); Ernest Gellner, *Nations and Nationalism* (Oxford: Blackwell, 1983), 55.

7. Poindexter v. Greenhow, 114 U.S. 270 (1885), 290.

8. Texas v. White, 74 U.S. 700 (1868), 700.

9. C. F. von Gerber, *Grundzüge eines Systems des deutschen Staatsrechts* (Leipzig: Tauchnitz, 1865); Paul Laband, *Das Staatsrecht des deutschen Reiches,* 4 vols. (Tübingen: Laupp, 1876–1882).

10. See Ernst-Wolfgang Böckenförde, "The Concept and Problems of the Constitutional State," in his *Constitutional and Political Theory: Selected Writings,* ed. M. Künkler and T. Stein (Oxford: Oxford University Press, 2017), chap. 5.

11. Jean Bodin, *The Six Bookes of a Commonweale* [1576], ed. K. D. McRae, trans. R. Knolles [1606] (Cambridge, MA: Harvard University Press, 1962), 199, 249–250.

12. Carl Schmitt, *Political Theology: Four Chapters on the Concept of Sovereignty,* trans. G. Schwab (Chicago: University of Chicago Press, 2005), 17.

13. Dieter Grimm, "The Origins and Transformation of the Concept of the Constitution," in his *Constitutionalism: Past, Present, and Future* (Oxford: Oxford University Press, 2016), 3–37, 3: "Every political unit is constituted, but not every one of them has a constitution."

14. Rudolf Smend, *Verfassung und Verfassungsrecht* (Munich: Duncker & Humblot, 1928), 78: "Die Verfassung ist die Rechtsordnung des Staats, genauer des Lebens, in dem der Staat seine Lebenswirklichkeit hat, nämlich seines Integrationsprozesses." Excerpts are found in Arthur J. Jacobson and Bernhard

Schlink, eds., *Weimar: A Jurisprudence of Crisis* (Berkeley: University of California Press, 2000), 213–248.

15. Carl Schmitt, *Constitutional Theory* [1928], trans. J. Seitzer (Durham, NC: Duke University Press, 2008), §§ 1, 2, 67.

16. Schmitt, *Constitutional Theory*, 62–63 (emphases in original). Schmitt evidently has in mind Hans Kelsen's influential normative positivist state theory, but his account also applies to nonpositivist variants. See Hans Kelsen, *General Theory of Law and State*, trans. A. Wedberg (Cambridge, MA: Harvard University Press, 1945).

17. Schmitt, *Constitutional Theory*, 65, 75, 60, 61 (emphases in original).

18. Hermann Heller, *Staatslehre* [1934], in his *Gesammelte Schriften*, vol. 3 (Leiden: A. W. Sijthoff, 1971), 79–395; part III has been translated by D. Dyzenhaus as Hermann Heller, "The Nature and Function of the State," *Cardozo Law Review* 18 (1996): 1139–1216, 1179, 1180.

19. Heller, "The Nature and Function of the State," 1187, 1190–1191.

20. Heller, "The Nature and Function of the State," 1214.

21. Heller, "The Nature and Function of the State," 1214–1215, 1216.

4. The Path to Ordo-constitutionalism

1. Ron Chernow, *Alexander Hamilton* (London: Penguin Books, 2005), 291, 87.

2. See, e.g., Edward L. Rubin, *Beyond Camelot: Rethinking Politics and Law for the Modern State* (Princeton, NJ: Princeton University Press, 2005); Paul Tucker, *Unelected Power: The Quest for Legitimacy in Central Banking and the Regulatory State* (Princeton, NJ: Princeton University Press, 2018).

3. See, e.g., Carl Schmitt, "The Motorized Legislator" [1950], in *High-Speed Society: Social Acceleration, Power, and Modernity*, ed. Hartmut Rosa and William E. Scheuerman (University Park: Pennsylvania State University Press, 2009), 65–73, 65: "Since 1914 all major historical events and developments in every European country have contributed to making the process of legislation ever faster and more summary, the path to realizing legal regulation ever shorter, and the role of legal science ever smaller." On "statutorification," see Grant Gilmore, *The Ages of American Law* (New Haven, CT: Yale University Press, 1977); Guido Calabresi, *A Common Law for the Age of Statutes* (Cambridge, MA: Harvard University Press, 1982).

4. Carl Schmitt, "The Plight of European Jurisprudence" [1943–1944], *Telos* 83 (1990): 35–71, 63.

5. Franz Neumann, *Behemoth: The Structure and Practice of National Socialism* (London: Gollancz, 1942).

6. Ernst Fraenkel, *The Dual State: A Contribution to the Theory of Dictatorship*, trans. E. A. Shils (New York: Oxford University Press, 1941), 5, 58, 107, 71.

7. Jens Meierhenrich, *The Remnants of the Rechtsstaat: An Ethnography of Nazi Law* (Oxford: Oxford University Press, 2018), 40. See also Douglas G. Morris, *Legal Sabotage: Ernst Fraenkel in Hitler's Germany* (Cambridge: Cambridge University Press, 2020), chap. 4.

8. Michael Oakeshott, "On the Character of a Modern European State," in his *On Human Conduct* (Oxford: Clarendon Press, 1975), 185–326, 200–201.

9. Oakeshott, "Modern European State," 251–252, 268.

10. Oakeshott, "Modern European State," 320, 323.

11. Paul W. Kahn, *The Origins of Order: Project and System in the American Legal Imagination* (New Haven, CT: Yale University Press, 2019), x–xi, 47.

12. Kahn, *The Origins of Order,* xi, 249.

13. Kahn, *The Origins of Order,* 157.

14. Kahn, *The Origins of Order,* 187–188.

15. Kahn, *The Origins of Order,* xiv.

16. Friedrich A. Hayek, *The Road to Serfdom* [1944] (Chicago: University of Chicago Press, 1975), 12, 83, 72, 167, 6.

17. F. A. Hayek, *The Constitution of Liberty* (London: Routledge & Kegan Paul, 1960), 85, 103, 156.

18. Hayek, *The Constitution of Liberty,* 181, 182, 205.

19. F. A. Hayek, *Law, Legislation and Liberty,* vol. 1, *Rules and Order* (London: Routledge & Kegan Paul, 1973), 2 (hereafter *Rules and Order*).

20. Hayek, *Rules and Order,* 14.

21. Hayek, *Rules and Order,* 100, 133, 134.

22. F. A. Hayek, *Law, Legislation and Liberty,* vol. 2, *The Mirage of Social Justice* (London: Routledge & Kegan Paul, 1976), 64, xii.

23. F. A. Hayek, *Law, Legislation and Liberty,* vol. 3, *The Political Order of a Free People* (London: Routledge & Kegan Paul, 1979), chap. 17 (hereafter *The Political Order of a Free People*).

24. Hayek, *The Political Order of a Free People,* 109, 110.

25. Hayek, *The Political Order of a Free People,* 113, 114, 119, 121.

26. Chandran Kukathas, "Hayek and the State," in *Law, Liberty and State: Oakeshott, Hayek and Schmitt on the Rule of Law,* ed. David Dyzenhaus and Thomas Poole (Cambridge: Cambridge University Press, 2015), 281–294, 294.

27. See John Finnis, *Aquinas* (Oxford: Oxford University Press, 1998), 20–29.

28. Ordo-liberalism, strictly a general movement rather than a school, comprises three main strands. First, the Freiburg School of lawyers and economists, who issued the "Ordo Manifesto" of 1936. Second, the "sociological neoliberals," represented mainly by Wilhelm Röpke and Alexander Rüstow. See Alexander Rüstow, *Freedom and Domination: A Historical Critique of Civilization* [orig. 3 vols., 1950, 1952, 1957], trans. S. Attanasio (Princeton, NJ: Princeton University Press, 1980). And third, the postwar advocates of the social market economy (*soziale Marktwirtschaft*), represented by Ludwig Erhard, minister of economic af-

fairs from 1949 to 1963 and then chancellor of the Federal Republic from 1963 to 1966. For an overview of Ordo-liberalism, see Carl J. Friedrich, "The Political Thought of Neoliberalism," *American Political Science Review* 49 (1955): 509–525.

29. Franz Böhm, Walter Eucken, and Hans Grossman-Doerth, "The Ordo Manifesto of 1936," in *Germany's Social Market Economy: Origins and Evolution,* ed. Alan Peacock and Hans Willgerodt (London: Macmillan, 1989), 15–26, 23.

30. Walter Eucken, *The Foundations of Economics: History and Theory in the Analysis of Economic Reality,* trans. T. Hutchinson (London: William Hodge & Co., 1950), 118, 57.

31. Franz Böhm, "Rule of Law in a Market Economy," in Peacock and Willgerodt, *Germany's Social Market Economy,* 46–67, 50, 62–63, 63–64.

32. Basic Law of the Federal Republic of Germany, Art. 79(3); *Lüth* BVerfGE 7, 198 (1958).

33. See, e.g., the constitutional structure of the European Union, which is established as "a highly competitive social market economy" (Art. 3.3 TEU) and promotes a monetary union policed by an independent European Central Bank (Art. 130 TFEU).

34. Note, e.g., the Basic Law of the Federal Republic of Germany, art. 21(2): "Parties that, by reason of their aims or the behaviour of their adherents, seek to undermine or abolish the free democratic basic order or to endanger the existence of the Federal Republic of Germany shall be unconstitutional."

35. Pierre Rosanvallon, *Counter-Democracy: Politics in an Age of Distrust,* trans. A. Goldhammer (Cambridge: Cambridge University Press, 2008).

5. Constituent Power

1. See, e.g., George Lawson, *Politica sacra et civilis* [1678], ed. C. Condren (Cambridge: Cambridge University Press, 1992), 47.

2. John Locke, *Two Treatises of Government* [1680], ed. P. Laslett (Cambridge: Cambridge University Press, 1988), vol. 2, § 222.

3. Julian H. Franklin, *John Locke and the Theory of Sovereignty: Mixed Monarchy and the Right of Resistance in the Political Thought of the English Revolution* (Cambridge: Cambridge University Press, 1978); Edmund S. Morgan, *Inventing the People: The Rise of Popular Sovereignty in England and America* (New York: Norton, 1988).

4. Declaration of Independence, 4 July 1776, Preamble.

5. Emmanuel-Joseph Sieyès, *What Is the Third Estate?* [1789], in his *Political Writings,* trans. M. Sonenscher (Indianapolis, IN: Hackett, 2003), 92–162.

6. Sieyès, *What Is the Third Estate?,* 136, 137.

7. Jean-Jacques Rousseau, *The Social Contract* [1762], in *The Social Contract and Other Later Political Writings,* ed. V. Gourevitch (Cambridge: Cambridge University Press, 1997), 39–152, 114: "Sovereignty cannot be represented. . . . The deputies

of the people therefore are not and cannot be its representatives, they are merely its agents; they cannot conclude anything definitively."

8. Lucia Rubinelli, "How to Think beyond Sovereignty: On Sieyes and Constituent Power," *European Journal of Political Theory* 18 (2019): 47–67, 51.

9. Lucia Rubinelli, *Constituent Power: A History* (Cambridge: Cambridge University Press, 2020), 66.

10. Sieyès, *What Is the Third Estate?,* 139, 140.

11. William H. Sewell Jr., *A Rhetoric of Bourgeois Revolution: The Abbé Sieyes and* What Is the Third Estate? (Durham, NC: Duke University Press 1994), 39; Marcio Pereira, "Machines de travail: Constituent Power and the Order of Labor in Sieyes's Thought," *Constellations* 25 (2018): 669–679.

12. Sieyès, *What Is the Third Estate?,* 110.

13. Sewell, *A Rhetoric of Bourgeois Revolution,* 152.

14. See Andrew Arato, *Post Sovereign Constitution Making: Learning and Legitimacy* (Oxford: Oxford University Press, 2016). Compare Joel Colón-Ríos, *Constituent Power and the Law* (Oxford: Oxford University Press, 2020).

15. Raymond Carré de Malberg, *Contribution à la Théorie générale de l'État* [1922] (Paris: Dalloz, 2004), 483–504, 504. See further Olivier Beaud, *La puissance de l'État* (Paris: Presses universitaires de France, 1994), 313–328.

16. François Furet, "The French Revolution Is Over," in his *Interpreting the French Revolution,* trans. E. Forster (Cambridge: Cambridge University Press, 1981), 1–79.

17. See Christoph Möllers, "Pouvoir Constituant-Constitution-Constitutionalisation," in *Principles of European Constitutional Law,* ed. A. von Bogdandy and J. Bast (Oxford: Hart, 2011), 169–204, 171–172.

18. Ernst-Wolfgang Böckenförde, "The Constituent Power of the People: A Liminal Concept of Constitutional Law," in his *Constitutional and Political Theory: Selected Writings,* ed. M. Künkler and T. Stein (Oxford: Oxford University Press, 2017), 168–185, 172.

19. Napoleon Bonaparte, *The Corsican: A Diary of Napoleon's Life in His Own Words* [1804], ed. R. M. Johnston (Boston: Houghton Mifflin, 1910), 182.

20. Böckenförde, "The Constituent Power of the People," 173.

21. Sieyès, *What Is the Third Estate?,* 97, 136.

22. See, e.g., Egon Zweig, *Die Lehre vom Pouvoir Constituant: Ein Beitrag zum Staatsrecht der französischen Revolution* (Tübingen: J. C. B. Mohr, 1909); Robert Redslob, *Staatstheorie der französischen Nationalversammlung von 1789* (Leipzig: von Veit, 1912).

23. Hans Kelsen, "What Is the Pure Theory of Law?," *Tulane Law Review* 34 (1959–1960): 269–276.

24. Carl Schmitt, *Political Theology: Four Chapters on the Concept of Sovereignty* [1922], trans. G. Schwab (Chicago: University of Chicago Press, 2005), 12.

25. See Lars Vinx, *The Guardian of the Constitution: Hans Kelsen and Carl Schmitt on the Limits of Constitutional Law* (Cambridge: Cambridge University Press, 2015), chap. 3.

26. Schmitt, *Political Theology*, 5, 17 (translation of first quotation modified).

27. Hermann Heller, "The Nature and Function of the State" [1934], *Cardozo Law Review* 18 (1996): 1139–1216 (part III of Heller's *Staatslehre* [1934]).

28. Hermann Heller, *Sovereignty: A Contribution to the Theory of Public and International Law* [1927], trans. B. Cooper (Oxford: Oxford University Press, 2019), 110: "An idealism . . . that at some point finally resolves the given tension in the direction of the mind is not one whit better, epistemologically or ethically, than a materialism that does the opposite."

29. See, e.g., President Lincoln's actions during the American Civil War, discussed in Chapter 11.

30. See, e.g., Bruce Ackerman's account of constitutional development, discussed in Chapter 10.

6. Constitutional Rights

1. Thomas Paine, *Rights of Man* [1791–1792], in his *Rights of Man, Common Sense and Other Political Writings,* ed. M. Philp (Oxford: Oxford University Press, 1995), 83–331, 120, 213, 210.

2. Cited in Carl Becker, *The Declaration of Independence: A Study in the History of Political Ideas* (New York: Harcourt, Brace & Co., 1922), 37.

3. John Millar, *The Origin of the Distinction of Ranks* [1771] (Indianapolis, IN: Liberty Fund, 2006), 278–279.

4. Jeremy Bentham, "Anarchical Fallacies: An Examination of the Declaration of Rights Issued during the French Revolution," in *Works,* vol. 2, ed. J. Bowring (London: Simpkin, Marshall & Co., 1843), 489–534.

5. See, e.g., Ronald Dworkin, *Taking Rights Seriously* (Cambridge, MA: Harvard University Press, 1977); Dworkin, *Freedom's Law: The Moral Reading of the American Constitution* (Cambridge, MA: Harvard University Press, 1996).

6. The American Bill of Rights, the first ten amendments adopted in 1791, was adopted ostensibly to provide assurances to anti-Federalists rather than as necessary elements of the constitutional settlement. Expressing skepticism about the value of "parchment barriers" and placing greater reliance on "balances and checks," Madison was also concerned that the enumerated rights would be taken to be a complete list of existing rights. See Jack N. Rakove, *Original Meanings: Politics and Ideas in the Making of the Constitution* (New York: Vintage Books, 1997), 144. Until 1971, the French Declaration of Rights was treated as a purely political declaration when, in a landmark ruling of the Constitutional Council (Décision no. 71-44 DC, 16 July 1971), it was held to have binding effect.

7. Paine, *Rights of Man,* 119.

8. Thomas Hobbes, *On the Citizen* [1647], ed. R. Tuck and M. Silverthorne (Cambridge: Cambridge University Press, 1998), 28–29.

9. Thomas Hobbes, *Leviathan* [1651], ed. R. Tuck (Cambridge: Cambridge University Press, 1996), 110.

10. Hobbes, *On the Citizen,* 29.

11. Hobbes, *Leviathan,* chap. 30.

12. Hobbes, *On the Citizen,* 137: "Men do not make a clear enough distinction between a *people* and a *crowd.* A *people* is a *single* entity, with *a single will;* you can attribute *an act* to it. None of this can be said of a crowd" (emphases in original).

13. Hobbes, *On the Citizen,* 150–151.

14. See Hobbes, *Leviathan,* chap. 18.

15. See Hobbes, *Leviathan,* chap. 9; Thomas Hobbes, *The Author's Epistle Dedicatory to De Corpore* [1656], in *The English Works of Thomas Hobbes of Malmesbury,* vol. 1, ed. W. Molesworth (London: J. Bohn, 1839), ix: "Civil science is no older than my own book, *De Cive.*"

16. Samuel Pufendorf, *De jure naturae et gentium* [1672], *On the Law of Nature and Nations,* trans. C. H. and W. A. Oldfather (Oxford: Clarendon Press, 1934), chap. 7, §§ 2–3.

17. John Locke, *Two Treatises of Government* [1680], ed. P. Laslett (Cambridge: Cambridge University Press, 1988), vol. 2, §§ 123–126, 136.

18. Locke, *Two Treatises of Government,* vol. 2, §§ 149, 224–226. Compare Hobbes, *On the Citizen,* 134, who argued that leaving it to the individual to decide whether the sovereign has complied with the terms of the covenant "exposes any King, good or bad, to the risk of being condemned by the judgement, and murdered by the hand, of one solitary assassin."

19. Becker, *The Declaration of Independence,* 27: "Most Americans had absorbed Locke's works as a kind of political gospel; and the Declaration, in its form, follows closely certain sentences in Locke's second treatise on government."

20. Isaiah Berlin, "Two Concepts of Liberty," in his *Four Essays on Liberty* (Oxford: Oxford University Press, 1969), 118–172, 122–131; C. B. Macpherson, *The Political Theory of Possessive Individualism: Hobbes to Locke* (Oxford: Clarendon Press, 1962), 257–262.

21. See J. T. Kloppenberg, *Uncertain Victory: Social Democracy and Progressivism in European and American Thought, 1870–1920* (New York: Oxford University Press, 1986), part II.

22. Jean-Jacques Rousseau, "Discourse on the Origin and Foundations of Inequality among Men" [1755], in his *The Discourses and Other Early Political Writings,* ed. V. Gourevitch (Cambridge: Cambridge University Press, 1997), 111–222, 173.

23. Jean-Jacques Rousseau, *The Social Contract* [1762], in *The Social Contract and Other Later Political Writings,* ed. V. Gourevitch (Cambridge: Cambridge University Press, 1997), 39–152.

24. Berlin, "Two Concepts of Liberty," 131–134.

25. Rousseau, *The Social Contract,* 53.

26. François Furet, *The French Revolution, 1770–1814,* trans. A. Nevill (Oxford: Blackwell, 1996), chap. 3; Jeremy Jennings, *Revolution and the Republic: A History of Political Thought in France since the Eighteenth Century* (Oxford: Oxford University Press, 2011), chap. 6.

7. Constitutional Democracy

1. Benjamin Constant, *Principles of Politics Applicable to all Governments* [1810], ed. E. Hoffman, trans. D. O'Keeffe (Indianapolis, IN: Liberty Fund, 2003), 20.

2. Benjamin Constant, "The Spirit of Conquest and Usurpation and their Relation to European Civilization," in his *Political Writings,* trans. B. Fontana (Cambridge: Cambridge University Press, 1988), 43–167, 74.

3. See Stephen Holmes, *Benjamin Constant and the Making of Modern Liberalism* (New Haven, CT: Yale University Press, 1984), chap. 5; Tzvetan Todorov, *A Passion for Democracy: Benjamin Constant,* trans. A. Seberry (London: Algora, 1999), 35–46.

4. Benjamin Constant, "The Freedom of the Ancients Compared with that of the Moderns" [1819], in his *Political Writings,* 307–328.

5. Marcel Gauchet, "Liberalism's Lucid Illusion," in *The Cambridge Companion to Constant,* ed. Helen Rosenblatt (Cambridge: Cambridge University Press, 2009), 23–46, 36.

6. Alexis de Tocqueville, *Democracy in America,* trans. H. Reeve, 2 vols. (New York: Vintage Books, 1990), 2:334.

7. Tocqueville, *Democracy in America,* 1:6, 7. Marx's comment is found in Karl Marx, *Critique of Hegel's "Philosophy of Right"* [c.1842], ed. J. O'Malley (Cambridge: Cambridge University Press, 1970), 29–30.

8. Tocqueville, *Democracy in America,* 1:3: "The more I advanced in the study of American society, the more I perceived that this equality of conditions is the fundamental fact from which all others seem to be derived and the central point at which all my observations constantly terminated."

9. Claude Lefort, *Democracy and Political Theory,* trans. D. Macey (Cambridge: Polity Press, 1988), 15.

10. Tocqueville, *Democracy in America,* 2:80.

11. Tocqueville, *Democracy in America,* 1:272, 273, 255, 278.

12. Tocqueville, *Democracy in America,* 1:278, 280, 276.

13. Tocqueville, *Democracy in America,* 2:319.

14. Jürgen Habermas, *Between Facts and Norms: Contributions to a Discourse Theory of Law and Democracy,* trans. W. Rehg (Cambridge: Polity Press, 1996), xlii.

15. Jürgen Habermas, *The Theory of Communicative Action*, vol. 2, *Lifeworld and System: The Critique of Functionalist Reason*, trans. T. McCarthy (Cambridge: Polity Press, 1987), 356–373.

16. Jürgen Habermas, *Legitimation Crisis*, trans. T. McCarthy (Boston: Beacon Press, 1975).

17. Habermas, *Between Fact and Norms*, 122–123.

18. Jürgen Habermas, "On the Internal Relation between Law and Democracy," in his *The Inclusion of the Other: Studies in Political Theory*, trans. C. Cronin and P. de Greiff (Cambridge: Polity Press, 1999), 253–264, 258, 261.

19. Habermas, *Between Fact and Norms*, 134.

20. See, e.g., Neil Walker, "Constitutionalism and the Incompleteness of Democracy: An Iterative Relationship," *Rechtsfilosophie & Rechtstheorie* 39 (2010): 206–233.

21. Frank Michelman, "Constitutional Authorship," in *Constitutionalism: Philosophical Foundations*, ed. Larry Alexander (Cambridge: Cambridge University Press, 1998), 64–98, 92.

22. Jürgen Habermas, "Constitutional Democracy: A Paradoxical Union of Contradictory Principles?," *Political Theory* 29 (2001): 766–781, 768, 774, 775.

23. Michelman, "Constitutional Authorship," 87: "Habermas . . . undoubtedly belongs to the family of liberal political moralists, those who judge political arrangements by asking whether the arrangements sufficiently honor elementary moral entitlements attributed to individuals."

24. Charles Larmore, "The Foundations of Modern Democracy: Reflections on Jürgen Habermas," *European Journal of Political Philosophy* 3 (1995): 55–68, 64, 65.

25. Alessandro Ferrara, "Of Boats and Principles: Reflections on Habermas's 'Constitutional Democracy,'" *Political Theory* 29 (2001): 782–791, 786.

26. Jürgen Habermas, "Historical Consciousness and Post-Traditional Identity: The Federal Republic's Orientation to the West," in his *The New Conservatism: Cultural Criticism and the Historians' Debate*, trans. S. W. Nicholsen (Cambridge, MA: MIT Press, 1989), 249–267. For historical context, see Jan-Werner Müller, *Constitutional Patriotism* (Princeton, NJ: Princeton University Press, 2007), chap. 1.

27. Lefort, *Democracy and Political Theory*, 19 (emphasis in original).

28. See Ronald Dworkin, *Taking Rights Seriously* (Cambridge, MA: Harvard University Press, 1977), chap. 4.

29. See Jeremy Waldron, *Law and Disagreement* (Oxford: Oxford University Press, 1999), chap. 13.

8. The Constitution as Civil Religion

1. G. W. F. Hegel, *Philosophy of Right* [1821], trans. T. M. Knox (Oxford: Oxford University Press, 1952), §§ 200, 236, 258.

2. See Jon Elster and Rune Slagstad, eds., *Constitutionalism and Democracy* (Cambridge: Cambridge University Press, 1988).

3. Hans Vorländer, "Integration durch Verfassung? Die symbolische Bedeutung der Verfassung im politischen Integrationsprozess," in *Integration durch Verfassung,* ed. Hans Vorländer (Wiesbaden: Westdeutscher Verlag, 2002), 9–40, 9.

4. See, e.g., Peter Häberle, "The Rationale of Constitutions from a Cultural Science Viewpoint," in *Peter Häberle on Constitutional Theory,* ed. M. Kotzur (Baden-Baden: Nomos, 2018), 229–256, 229.

5. Rudolf Smend, *Verfassung und Verfassungsrecht* (Munich: Duncker & Humblot, 1928). For excerpts, see Arthur J. Jacobson and Bernhard Schlink, eds., *Weimar: A Jurisprudence of Crisis* (Berkeley: University of California Press, 2000), 213–248.

6. Jean-Jacques Rousseau, *The Social Contract* [1762], in *The Social Contract and Other Later Political Writings,* ed. V. Gourevitch (Cambridge: Cambridge University Press, 1997), book IV, chap. 8.

7. McCulloch v. Maryland, 17 U.S. (4 Wheat.) 316, 407 (1819), Marshall C.J.

8. *Federalist* 49 (Madison).

9. Thomas Jefferson, "Letter to Samuel Kercheval, 12 July 1816," in *Thomas Jefferson: Political Writings,* ed. J. Appleby and T. Ball (Cambridge: Cambridge University Press, 1999), 210–217.

10. Justice William Johnson in Elkinson v. Deliesseline 8 Fed. Cas. 593 (1823), cited in Edward S. Corwin, "The Constitution as Instrument and Symbol," *American Political Science Review* 30 (1936): 1071–1085, 1075. The sentiment was repeated a century later by George Sutherland who, when nominated in 1922 to the Supreme Court, stated that he believed the Constitution to be a "divinely inspired instrument": cited in Michael Kammen, *A Machine That Would Go of Itself: The Constitution in American Culture* (New York: Knopf, 1987), 264.

11. Daniel Webster letter to William Hickey, 11 December 1850, cited in Kammen, *A Machine That Would Go of Itself,* 94.

12. Abraham Lincoln, "On the Perpetuation of Our Political Institutions," speech of 27 January 1838, cited in Harvey C. Mansfield Jr., *America's Constitutional Soul* (Baltimore, MD: Johns Hopkins University Press, 1991), 31.

13. See Eric Foner, *The Second Founding: How the Civil War and Reconstruction Remade the Constitution* (New York: Norton, 2019). Bruce Ackerman's thesis of "one constitution, three regimes" provides a gloss on this theme: Bruce Ackerman, *We the People,* vol. 1, *Foundations* (Cambridge, MA: Belknap Press of Harvard University Press, 1991), chap. 3.

14. Sanford Levinson, *Constitutional Faith* (Princeton, NJ: Princeton University Press, 1988), 140.

15. Corwin, "The Constitution as Instrument and Symbol," 1077–1078, 1076, 1080.

16. Kathleen Sullivan, "Constitutional Amendmentitis," *The American Prospect,* 19 December 2001.

17. Irving Kristol, "The Spirit of '87," *The Public Interest* 86 (1987): 3–9, 5.

18. There are too many examples to illustrate the point, especially since the main output is in (overly) long law review articles. By way of monographs, consider only, in addition to Balkin's book to be examined in this chapter, this selection by Yale Law School professors: Bruce Ackerman, *The Decline and Fall of the American Republic* (Cambridge, MA: Harvard University Press, 2010); Akhil Reed Amar, *America's Unwritten Constitution: The Precedents and Principles We Live By* (New York: Basic Books, 2012); Owen M. Fiss, *A War Like No Other: The Constitution in a Time of Terror* (New York: New Press, 2015); Paul Kahn, *The Reign of Law: Marbury v. Madison and the Construction of America* (New Haven, CT: Yale University Press, 1997); Robert C. Post, *Constitutional Domains: Democracy, Community, Management* (Cambridge, MA: Harvard University Press 1995); Jed Rubenfeld, *Revolution by Judiciary: The Structure of American Constitutional Law* (Cambridge, MA: Harvard University Press, 2005).

19. Jack M. Balkin, *Constitutional Redemption: Political Faith in an Unjust World* (Cambridge, MA: Harvard University Press, 2011), 2–5. See also Robert M. Cover, "Foreword: Nomos and Narrative," *Harvard Law Review* 97 (1983–1984): 4–68, 34: "I shall use 'redemptive constitutionalism' as a label for the positions of associations whose sharply different visions of the social order require a transformational politics that cannot be contained within the autonomous insularity of the association itself."

20. Balkin, *Constitutional Redemption*, 6, 11, 10.

21. Balkin, *Constitutional Redemption*, 18, 19.

22. Balkin, *Constitutional Redemption*, 51–57.

23. See J. G. A. Pocock, *The Ancient Constitution and the Feudal Law: A Study in English Historical Thought in the Seventeenth Century*, rev. ed. (Cambridge: Cambridge University Press, 1987).

24. Jack M. Balkin, *The Cycles of Constitutional Time* (New York: Oxford University Press, 2020), 4: "In every day, in every way, our Constitution is becoming a better constitution—or at least, we should interpret the Constitution to make it so."

25. Dieter Grimm, "Integration by Constitution," in his *Constitutionalism: Past, Present, and Future* (Oxford: Oxford University Press, 2016), 143–157, 152: "Where other nation states had a sound basis for integration and identity, postwar Germany faced a vacuum."

26. Dolf Sternberger, *Verfassungspatriotismus* (Frankfurt am Main: Insel Verlag, 1990), a term he coined in an article in *Frankfurter Allgemeine Zeitung*, 23 May 1979.

27. Michael Stürmer, "Geschichte in geschichtslosem Land" [History in a country without history], in *Historikerstreit: Die Dokumentation der Kontroverse um die Einzigartigkeit der nationalsozialistischen Judenvernichtung*, ed. Rudolf Augstein (Munich: R. Piper, 1987), 36.

28. Jürgen Habermas, "The Finger of Blame: The Germans and Their Memorial," in his *Time of Transitions* (Cambridge: Polity Press, 2006), 38–50, 43; Habermas,

"A Kind of Settlement of Damages: The Apologetic Tendencies in German History Writing," in *Forever in the Shadow of Hitler? Original Documents of the Historikerstreit, the Controversy Concerning the Singularity of the Holocaust,* trans. J. Knowlton and T. Cates (Atlantic Highlands, NJ: Humanities Press, 1993), 30–44.

29. See Jürgen Habermas, *The Inclusion of the Other,* trans. C. Cronin and P. de Greiff (Cambridge: Polity Press, 1999); Habermas, *The Postnational Constellation,* trans. M. Pensky (Cambridge: Polity Press, 2001).

30. Habermas, "A Kind of Settlement of Damages," 43.

31. Peter H. Merkl, *The Origin of the West German Republic* (New York: Oxford University Press, 1963), ix, 91, 54, the last citing Klaus-Berto von Dömming, Rudolf Füßlein, and Werner Matz, "Entstehungsgeschichte der Artikel des Grundgesetzes," *Jahrbuch des öffentlichen Rechts der Gegenwart, Neue Folge I,* 1 (1951), ed. P. Häberle (Tübingen: Mohr Siebeck, 2010), 14–15.

32. Eduard David, Germany's minister of interior when the National Assembly adopted the Weimar Constitution, cited in Rupert Emerson, *State and Sovereignty in Modern Germany* (New Haven, CT: Yale University Press, 1928), 231–232.

33. The Basic Law also authorized the Court to suppress extremist movements and ban political parties that seek to impair "the liberal democratic basic order." Basic Law, arts. 18, 21.

34. Merkl, *The Origin of the West German Republic,* 176, 172.

35. Merkl, *The Origin of the West German Republic,* 130.

36. Günter Frankenberg, "Tocqueville's Question: The Role of a Constitution in the Process of Integration," *Ratio Juris* 13 (2000): 1–30, 7–8.

37. Ernst Forsthoff, *Der Staat der Industriegesellschaft* (Munich: Beck, 1971), 72 (emphasis added), cited in Frankenberg, "Tocqueville's Question," 8.

38. *Lüth,* BVerfGE 7, 198, 205 (1958).

39. Grimm, "Integration by Constitution," 152.

40. Rudolf Smend, "Das Bundesverfassungsgericht" [1962], in his *Staatsrechtliche Abhandlungen und andere Aufsätze,* 3rd ed. (Berlin: Duncker & Humblot, 1994), 581–593, 593, cited in Jo Eric Khushal Murkens, *From Empire to Union: Conceptions of German Constitutional Law since 1871* (Oxford: Oxford University Press, 2013), 156.

41. Matthias Jestaedt, Oliver Lepsius, Christoph Möllers, and Christoph Schönberger, *Das entgrenzte Gericht: Eine kritische Bilanz nach sechzig Jahren Bundesverfassungsgericht* (Berlin: Suhrkamp, 2011); translated as *The German Federal Constitutional Court: The Court without Limits* (Oxford: Oxford University Press, 2020).

42. Peter Häberle, "'The Open Society of Constitutional Interpreters': A Contribution to a Pluralistic and 'Procedural' Constitutional Interpretation" [1975], in Kotzur, *Häberle on Constitutional Theory,* 129–165, 144.

43. Häberle, "Preambles in the Text and Context of Constitutions" [1979], in Kotzur, *Häberle on Constitutional Theory* 257–301, 279–280, 300–301 (emphasis in original).

44. Grimm, "Integration by Constitution," 152.

45. Grimm, "Integration by Constitution," 152.

46. Bruce Ackerman, *The Future of Liberal Revolution* (New Haven, CT: Yale University Press, 1992), 104–105, 107.

47. Montesquieu, *The Spirit of the Laws* [1748], trans. A. Cohler, B. Miller, and H. Stone (Cambridge: Cambridge University Press, 1989), book 11, chap. 6.

9. Toward a Juristocracy

1. Michael Kammen, *A Machine That Would Go of Itself: The Constitution in American Culture* (New York: Knopf, 1987), 18, referencing the words of James Russell Lowell.

2. Benjamin Constant, *Fragments d'un ouvrage abandonné sur la possibilité d'une constitution républicaine dans un grand pays,* ed. H. Grange (Paris: Aubier, 1991), 387: "Le but du pouvoir préservateur est de défendre le gouvernement de la division desgouvernants, et de défendre les gouvernés de l'oppression du gouvernement."

3. Walter Bagehot, *The English Constitution* [1867] (Oxford: Oxford University Press, 2001), 100–101.

4. Lorenz von Stein, *The History of the Social Movement in France, 1789–1850* [1850], trans. K. Mengelberg (Totowa, NJ: Bedminster Press, 1964), 228–235, 253–255, esp. 233.

5. The debate was initiated by Kelsen's 1929 article on constitutional adjudication in which he argued that a constitutional court should be established as guardian of the constitution. Schmitt rebutted that case in a book in 1931, and Kelsen responded in a review of Schmitt's book. These documents are reproduced in Lars Vinx, *The Guardian of the Constitution: Hans Kelsen and Carl Schmitt on the Limits of Constitutional Law* (Cambridge: Cambridge University Press, 2015).

6. Carl Schmitt, "The Guardian of the Constitution" [1931], in Vinx, *The Guardian of the Constitution,* 79–173, 156, 157, 167, 172.

7. Hans Kelsen, "The Nature and Development of Constitutional Jurisdiction" [1929], in Vinx, *The Guardian of the Constitution,* 22–78, 23, 24.

8. Kelsen, "The Nature and Development of Constitutional Jurisdiction," 28, 69, 73.

9. Schmitt, "The Guardian of the Constitution," 80, 82. On the U.S. Supreme Court, Schmitt is quoting John R. Commons, *Legal Foundations of Capitalism* (New York: Macmillan, 1924), 7. On his conception of the jurisdictional state, see

Carl Schmitt, *Legality and Legitimacy* [1932], trans. J. Seitzer (Durham, NC: Duke University Press, 2004), 4–8.

10. Schmitt, "The Guardian of the Constitution," 133, 132, 91, 95, 168, 171.

11. Lars Vinx, Introduction," in his *The Guardian of the Constitution,* 1–21, 1–6. See further Peter C. Caldwell, *Popular Sovereignty and the Crisis of German Constitutional Law: The Theory and Practice of Weimar Constitutionalism* (Durham, NC: Duke University Press, 1997), chap. 6.

12. Eric Voegelin, *The Authoritarian State: An Essay on the Problem of the Austrian State* [1936], trans. R. Hein (Columbia: University of Missouri Press, 1999). For Czechoslovakia, see Jiří Hoetzl and V. Joachim, *The Constitution of the Czechoslovak Republic* (Prague: Édition de la Société, 1920), 10–11.

13. For an overview of the development of constitutional review, see Yaniv Roznai, "Introduction: Constitutional Courts in a 100-Years Perspective and a Proposal for a Hybrid Model of Judicial Review," *Vienna Journal of International Constitutional Law* 14 (2020): 355–377. For a study of European development, see Francesco Biagi, *Three Generations of European Constitutional Courts in Transition to Democracy* (Cambridge: Cambridge University Press, 2020). For analysis of design factors, see Francisco Ramos, "The Establishment of Constitutional Courts: A Study of 128 Democratic Constitutions," *Review of Law & Economics* 2 (2006): 103–135.

14. See Alec Stone, *The Birth of Judicial Politics in France: The Constitutional Council in Comparative Perspective* (Oxford: Oxford University Press, 1992), chaps. 2–3.

15. Ernst-Wolfgang Böckenförde, "Constitutional Jurisdiction: Structure, Organization, and Legitimation," in his *Constitutional and Political Theory: Selected Writings,* trans. T. Dunlap (Oxford: Oxford University Press, 2017), chap. 8, 197–198.

16. Ran Hirschl, *Towards Juristocracy: The Origins and Consequences of the New Constitutionalism* (Cambridge, MA: Harvard University Press, 2004); Stephen Gardbaum, *The New Commonwealth Model of Constitutionalism: Theory and Practice* (Cambridge: Cambridge University Press, 2013).

17. Hirschl, *Towards Juristocracy,* 19: "whereas constitutional law cases represented only 2.4 percent of the SCC's [Supreme Court of Canada] caseload between 1962 and 1971 and 5.5 percent between 1972 and 1981 the proportion of constitutional cases almost quadrupled between 1982 and 1991 to 21.3 percent." See further Charles Epp, *The Rights Revolution: Lawyers, Activists, and Supreme Courts in Comparative Perspective* (Chicago: University of Chicago Press, 1998).

18. A dramatic illustration is the case of India, on which see Gautam Bhatia, *The Transformative Constitution: A Radical Biography in Nine Acts* (Noida, Utter Pradesh: HarperCollins, 2019); Tarunabh Khaitan, "The Indian Supreme Court's

Identity Crisis: A Constitutional Court or a Court of Appeals?," *Indian Law Review* 2 (2020): 1–30. But the impact is seen even in the United Kingdom, which adheres most faithfully to the principle of parliamentary sovereignty. See R(Miller) v. Prime Minister/Cherry v. Advocate General [2019] UKSC 41, in which the Supreme Court converted political practices into constitutional principles and asserted their authority to rule on the meaning of the "fundamental principles of our constitutional law."

19. Hirschl, *Towards Juristocracy*, 1.

20. C. Neal Tate and Thorbjörn Vallinder, eds., *The Global Expansion of Judicial Power* (New York: New York University Press, 1995); Epp, *The Rights Revolution;* Martin Shapiro and Alec Stone Sweet, *On Law, Politics, and Judicialization* (Oxford: Oxford University Press, 2002); Hirschl, *Towards Juristocracy;* Rachel Sieder, Line Schjolden, and Alan Angell, eds., *The Judicialization of Politics in Latin America* (London: Palgrave Macmillan 2005); Tom Ginsburg and Mila Versteeg, "Why Do Countries Adopt Constitutional Review?," *Journal of Law, Economics & Organization* 30 (2014): 587–622; Doreen Lustig and J. H. H. Weiler, "Judicial Review in the Contemporary World—Retrospective and Prospective," *International Journal of Constitutional Law* 16 (2018): 315–372.

21. See David S. Law and Mila Versteeg, "The Evolution and Ideology of Global Constitutionalism," *California Law Review* 99 (2011): 1153–1257, finding that 90 percent of all variation in the rights-related content of the world's constitutions are explained as a function of just two variables: the comprehensiveness of the constitution's rights catalog and the constitution's aspirational character.

22. Michaela Hailbronner, *Traditions and Transformations: The Rise of German Constitutionalism* (Oxford: Oxford University Press, 2015), chap. 4.

23. Johan van der Walt, *The Horizontal Effect Revolution and the Question of Sovereignty* (Berlin: de Gruyter, 2014).

24. Katharine G. Young, *Constituting Economic and Social Rights: How Rights to Food, Water, Health, Housing and Education are Changing Public Law* (Oxford: Oxford University Press, 2012).

25. Kai Möller, *The Global Model of Constitutional Rights* (Oxford: Oxford University Press, 2012), 4, 88, 89.

26. Mattias Kumm, "Who Is Afraid of the Total Constitution? Constitutional Rights as Principles and the Constitutionalization of Private Law," *German Law Journal* 7 (2006): 341–369, 344.

27. Kumm, "Who Is Afraid of the Total Constitution?," 344–345, 359.

28. Kumm, "Who Is Afraid of the Total Constitution?," 368, 346.

29. Kumm, "Who Is Afraid of the Total Constitution?," 345.

30. Kesavananda Bharati v. State of Kerala, AIR 1461 (1973); Minerva Mills Ltd v. Union of India, AIR 1789 (1980); S. R. Bommai v. Union of India, AIR 1918 (1994).

31. Yaniv Roznai, *Unconstitutional Constitutional Amendments: The Limits of Amendment Powers* (Oxford: Oxford University Press, 2017), 47–70; Silvia Şuteu, *Eternity Clauses in Democratic Constitutionalism* (Oxford: Oxford University Press, 2021); Po Jen Yap and Rehan Abeyratne, "Judicial Self-Dealing and Unconstitutional Constitutional Amendments in South Asia," *International Journal of Constitutional Law* 19 (2021): 127–148.

32. Ran Hirschl, "The Judicialization of Mega-Politics and the Rise of Political Courts," *Annual Review of Political Science* 11 (2008): 93–118, 93, 100–106.

33. Hirschl, *Towards Juristocracy,* 11, 12.

34. Hirschl, *Towards Juristocracy,* 13, 11. For a similar argument with respect to the impact of the US constitutional rights movement, see Gerald Rosenberg, *The Hollow Hope: Can Courts Bring about Social Change?,* 2nd ed. (Chicago: University of Chicago Press, 2008). And despite inclusion of social and economic rights in South Africa's 1996 Constitution, constitutionalization has signally failed to bring about redistribution: Allister Sparks, *Beyond the Miracle: Inside the New South Africa* (Johannesburg: Jonathan Ball, 2003), chaps. 9–10.

35. Yaniv Roznai suggests that since a trend similar to Israel's takes place in many other countries around the world, one might wonder why the rights revolution came to Israel only in the 1990s, long after the Ashkenazi liberal elite had lost governmental power (personal communication). On global developments, see David S. Law, "Globalization and the Future of Constitutional Rights," *Northwestern University Law Review* 102 (2008): 1277–1350. On the significance of strategic litigation, see Epp, *The Rights Revolution,* 197–205.

36. Laurence H. Tribe, *The Invisible Constitution* (New York: Oxford University Press, 2008), 9.

37. Bertolt Brecht, *Die Gedichte von Bertolt Brecht in einem Band* (Frankfurt: Suhrkamp, 1981), 387: "Alle Macht geht vom Volke aus! Aber wo geht sie hin?"

38. Landmark cases include: Buckley v. Valeo, 424 U.S. 1 (1976); McConnell v. Federal Election Commission, 540 U.S. 93 (2003); Citizens United v. Federal Election Commission, 558 U.S. 310 (2010); Shelby County v. Holder, 570 U.S. 529 (2013). See also Samuel Issacharoff, Pamela S. Karlan, Richard H. Pildes, and Nathan Persily, *The Law of Democracy: Legal Structure of the Political Process,* 5th ed. (Eagan, MN: West Publishing, 2016).

39. Ran Hirschl, "The Judicialization of Mega-Politics," 100; Richard H. Pildes, "The Constitutionalization of Democratic Politics," *Harvard Law Review* 118 (2004): 29–154, 32–34.

40. Brunner v. European Union Treaty (Maastricht) [1994] BVerfGE 89, 155; Gauweiler v. Treaty of Lisbon [2009] BVerfG, 2 BvE 2 / 08. See Jo Eric Khushal Murkens, *From Empire to Union: Conceptions of German Constitutional Law since 1871* (Oxford: Oxford University Press, 2013), chap. 7.

41. Certification of the Constitution of the Republic of South Africa 1996 [1996] ZACC 26.

42. Andrew Arato, *Post Sovereign Constitution Making: Learning and Legitimacy* (Oxford: Oxford University Press, 2016), 79–80.

43. For the most influential expression, see John Hart Ely, *Democracy and Distrust: A Theory of Judicial Review* (Cambridge, MA: Harvard University Press, 1980), presenting a participation-orientated theory that justifies judicial review for the limited purposes of unblocking the channels of political change and facilitating the representation of minorities. For implications beyond the United States, see Stephen Gardbaum, "Comparative Political Process Theory," *International Journal of Constitutional Law* 18 (2020): 1410–1457.

44. Pildes, "The Constitutionalization of Democratic Politics," 54.

45. For the role of courts in bolstering electoral democracy, see Yaniv Roznai, "Who Will Save the Redheads? Towards an Anti-Bully Theory of Judicial Review and Protection of Democracy," *William & Mary Bill Rights Journal* 29 (2020): 327–366. But note that regimes with authoritarian tendencies use courts to legitimate measures undermining electoral democracy: see David Landau and Rosalind Dixon, "Abusive Judicial Review: Courts against Democracy," *UC Davis Law Review* 53 (2020): 1313–1387.

10. Integration through Interpretation

1. McCulloch v. Maryland, 17 U.S. (4 Wheat.), 316, 407 (1819) (emphasis in original).

2. McCulloch v. Maryland, 415, 421.

3. Osborn v. U.S. Bank, 22 U.S. (9 Wheat.), 738, 866 (1824).

4. Marbury v. Madison, 5 U.S. (1 Cranch), 137 (1803), 176, 177.

5. Consider, e.g., the Ninth Amendment: "The enumeration in the Constitution, of certain rights, shall not be construed to deny or disparage others retained by the people." This suggests that certain rights vested in the people (i.e., that form part of the constitution of the state) are prior (in time, if not in authority) to the rights prescribed in the Constitution. Not surprisingly, the consensus of recent American constitutional scholarship now contests that claim: see, e.g., John Hart Ely, *Democracy and Distrust: A Theory of Judicial Review* (Cambridge, MA: Harvard University Press, 1980), 34–41.

6. Missouri v. Holland, 252 U.S. 416 (1920), 433.

7. Jeffrey M. Shaman, *Constitutional Interpretation: Illusion and Reality* (Westport, CT: Greenwood Press, 2001), 4.

8. Richard A. Posner, "Democracy and Distrust Revisited," *Virginia Law Review* 77 (1991): 641–651, 651. For corroboration, see Laurence H. Tribe, "Soundings and Silences," in *The Invisible Constitution in Comparative Perspective,* ed. Rosalind Dixon and Adrienne Stone (Cambridge: Cambridge University Press, 2018), 21–60, 22. On the other hand, perhaps much of the professors' work is

actually undertaken by their student assistants: see, e.g., Tribe, "Soundings and Silences," 201; Ely, *Democracy and Distrust,* 76.

9. See Keith Whittington, *Constitutional Interpretation: Textual Meaning, Original Intent, and Judicial Review* (Lawrence: University Press of Kansas, 1999), 64: "The written Constitution is not to be understood merely as a fundamental law structuring and limiting political powers but also as the sacred text of a community of moral and rational individuals."

10. Marbury v. Madison, 176.

11. Thomas Jefferson, "From Thomas Jefferson to William Charles Jarvis, 28 September 1820," Founders Online, https://founders.archives.gov/documents /Jefferson/98-01-02-1540.

12. Benjamin N. Cardozo, *The Nature of the Judicial Process* (New Haven, CT: Yale University Press, 1921), 17.

13. Bell v. Maryland, 378 U.S. 226 (1964), Black J (diss.).

14. Lawrence v. Texas, 539 U.S. 558 (2003), 577, 578–579.

15. Marsh v. Chambers, 463 U.S. 783 (1983).

16. Lemon v. Kurtzman, 403 U.S. 602 (1971).

17. Marsh v. Chambers, 788, 790.

18. Robert C. Post, "Theories of Constitutional Interpretation," in his *Constitutional Domains: Democracy, Community, Management* (Cambridge, MA: Harvard University Press, 1995), chap. 1.

19. Laurence H. Tribe, "Taking Text and Structure Seriously: Reflections on Free-Form Method in Constitutional Interpretation," *Harvard Law Review* 108 (1995): 1221–1303, 1224, 1225, 1235 (emphases in original).

20. Akhil Reed Amar, *America's Constitution: A Biography* (New York: Random House, 2005).

21. Ronald Dworkin, *Freedom's Law: The Moral Reading of the American Constitution* (Oxford: Oxford University Press, 1996), 2, 10.

22. Laurence H. Tribe, *The Invisible Constitution* (New York: Oxford University Press, 2008), 10 (emphasis in original).

23. Christopher Eisgruber, *Constitutional Self-Government* (Cambridge, MA: Harvard University Press, 2001), 113–114. On the circumstances of its creation, see Michael J. Klarman, *The Framers' Coup: The Making of the United States Constitution* (New York: Oxford University Press, 2016).

24. Dred Scott v. Sandford, 60 U.S. 393 (1857), 490 (emphasis in original). For details of the settlement on slavery, see Klarman, *The Framers' Coup,* chap. 4.

25. Domenico Losurdo, *Liberalism: A Counter-History* (London: Verso, 2011), 12.

26. For an extensive list of citations, see Mark A. Graber, *Dred Scott and the Problem of Constitutional Evil* (Cambridge: Cambridge University Press, 2006), 15–17. In addition, Tribe, *The Invisible Constitution,* 111, calls its holding "horrific," and Balkin argues that it must have been wrong the day it was decided because "to

believe otherwise would be to accept facts about our country that are too painful to accept": Jack M. Balkin, *Constitutional Redemption: Political Faith in an Unjust World* (Cambridge, MA: Harvard University Press, 2011), 210.

27. Graber, *Dred Scott,* 251, 18, 167, 251. On the limits of interpretation see, e.g., Madison's contortions in trying to explain the principle underpinning the provision that assesses slaves as three-fifths for the purpose of allocating legislative representation: *Federalist* 54.

28. Eisgruber, *Constitutional Self-Government,* 117.

29. Carl Schmitt, *Constitutional Theory* [1928], trans. J. Seitzer (Durham, NC: Duke University Press, 2008), 67, 59.

30. Confusingly, this distinction has also been referred to as that between "interpretivism and noninterpretivism": Thomas C. Grey, "Do We Have an Unwritten Constitution?," *Stanford Law Review* 27 (1975): 703–718; Ely, *Democracy and Distrust,* chaps. 1–2. It seems now to have fallen from favor: Thomas C. Grey, "The Constitution as Scripture," *Stanford Law Review* 37 (1984): 1–25.

31. See Hans-Georg Gadamer, *Truth and Method* [1960], trans. J. Weinsheimer and D. G. Marshall, 2nd rev. ed. (London: Sheen & Ward, 1989). Gadamer shows how the interpretation of any text alters according to the nature of the questions being asked of it. At different times and in different circumstances "people read the sources differently," and they do so "because they [are] moved by different questions, prejudices, and interests" (at xxxii).

32. See, e.g., Balkin, *Constitutional Redemption,* 19: "Courts today do not hold the Declaration [of Independence] to be part of the Constitution; they do not read the text of the Declaration as if its clauses had the force of law.... Yet there is no text that is more a part of our Constitution—or *our constitution as a people*—than the Declaration. Without its ideals our written Constitution would be an empty shell" (emphasis added). See also Balkin, "The Footnote," *Northwestern University Law Review* 83 (1989): 275–320.

33. See, e.g., Randy E. Barnett, *Restoring the Lost Constitution: The Presumption of Liberty* (Princeton, NJ: Princeton University Press, 2004); Antonin Scalia, *A Matter of Interpretation* (Princeton, NJ: Princeton University Press, 1997).

34. Bruce Ackerman, *We the People,* vol. 1, *Foundations* (Cambridge, MA: Belknap Press of Harvard University Press, 1991); *We the People,* vol. 2, *Transformations* (Cambridge, MA: Belknap Press of Harvard University Press, 1998); *We the People,* vol. 3, *The Civil Rights Revolution* (Cambridge, MA: Belknap Press of Harvard University Press, 2014). The third volume was originally intended to be called *Interpretations:* see vol. 2, 403.

35. Ackerman, *We the People,* 2:7, 3:36, 1:59.

36. Ackerman, *We the People,* 2:10, 1:34, 3:28.

37. Ackerman, *We the People,* 3:30, 2:122.

38. Brown v. Board of Education of Topeka, 347 U.S. 483 (1954).

39. Ackerman, *We the People,* 2:8, 3:5, 9. Compare Civil Rights Act 1964; Voting Rights Act 1965; Fair Housing Act 1968.

40. Ackerman, *We the People,* 2:11.

41. Post, "Theories of Constitutional Interpretation," 29–50.

42. See, e.g., Bruce M. Wilson, "Explaining the Rise of Accountability Functions of Costa Rica's Constitutional Court," in Siri Gloppen, Bruce M. Wilson, Roberto Gargarella, Elin Skaar, and Morten Kinander, *Courts and Power in Latin America and Africa* (New York: Palgrave, 2010), chap. 4; Simon Butt, "The Indonesian Constitutional Court: Implying Rights from the 'Rule of Law,'" in Dixon and Stone, *The Invisible Constitution in Comparative Perspective,* chap. 10; Gábor Attila Tóth, "Lost in Translation: Invisible Constitutionalism in Hungary," in Dixon and Stone, *The Invisible Constitution in Comparative Perspective,* chap. 19; Karl Klare, "Legal Culture and Transformative Constitutionalism," *South African Journal on Human Rights* 14 (1998): 146–188.

43. Bruce Ackerman, *The Future of Liberal Revolution* (New Haven, CT: Yale University Press, 1992), 3, 46–47.

44. Bruce Ackerman, *Revolutionary Constitutions: Charismatic Leadership and the Rule of Law* (Cambridge, MA: Belknap Press of Harvard University Press, 2019), 363.

45. For both facets at work see Ackerman, *The Future of Liberal Revolution,* 99–110. Praising the liberal advances quickly made by the Hungarian Constitutional Court, he warns that, without entrenchment, "after the first flush of revolutionary enthusiasm for the rule of law fades, so too will judicial authority" (101) and that "it is only a matter of time before the Court's abstract resolution of an unending series of burning disputes will generate an overwhelming reaction by parliamentarians, who will try to destroy such a politically exposed institution" (110).

46. See Stephen Gardbaum, "Are Strong Constitutional Courts Always a Good Thing for New Democracies?," *Columbia Journal of Transnational Law* 53 (2015): 285–320.

47. Ivan Krastev and Stephen Holmes, *The Light That Failed: A Reckoning* (London: Allen Lane, 2019), 6, 7, 22.

48. Robert C. Post and Reva B. Siegel, "Democratic Constitutionalism," in *The Constitution in 2020,* ed. Jack M. Balkin and Reva B. Siegel (New York: Oxford University Press, 2009), chap. 3; Post and Siegel, "*Roe* Rage: Democratic Constitutionalism and Backlash," *Harvard Civil-Rights Civil-Liberties Law Review* 42 (2007): 373–433.

49. Alexis de Tocqueville, *Democracy in America,* trans. H. Reeve (New York: Vintage Books, 1990), vol. 1, 248: "The law is observed because, first, it is a self-imposed evil, and, secondly, it is an evil of transient duration."

50. David M. Beatty, *The Ultimate Rule of Law* (Oxford: Oxford University Press, 2004), 159.

51. Kai Möller, *The Global Model of Constitutional Rights* (Oxford: Oxford University Press, 2012). Although constitutional review in the United States does not adopt proportionality analysis as such, the distinction made in levels of scrutiny (strict, minimal, and intermediate) provides a functional equivalent; see Shaman, *Constitutional Interpretation,* chap. 3. See also Jamal Greene, *How Rights Went Wrong* (Boston: Houghton Mifflin Harcourt, 2021), advocating adoption in the United States of this type of proportionality review.

52. Mattias Kumm, "The Idea of Socratic Contestation and the Right to Justification: The Point of Rights-Based Proportionality Review," *Law & Ethics of Human Rights* 4 (2010): 142–175.

53. See Moshe Cohen-Eliya and Iddo Parat, "Proportionality and the Culture of Justification," *American Journal of Comparative Law* 59 (2011): 463–490.

54. Beatty, *The Ultimate Rule of Law,* 170.

55. Carl Schmitt, "The Motorized Legislator" [1950], in *High-Speed Society: Social Acceleration, Power, and Modernity,* ed. Hartmut Rosa and William E. Scheuerman (University Park: Pennsylvania State University Press, 2009), chap. 5.

56. Kent Roach, *The Supreme Court on Trial: Judicial Activism or Democratic Dialogue* (Toronto: Irwin Law, 2001); Roberto Gargarella, "'We the People' Outside the Constitution: The Dialogic Model of Constitutionalism and the System of Checks and Balances," *Current Legal Problems* 67 (2014): 1–47; Aileen Kavanagh, "The Lure and Limits of Dialogue," *University of Toronto Law Journal* 66 (2016): 83–120.

11. A New Species of Law

1. John A. Hawgood, *Modern Constitutions since 1787* (London: Macmillan, 1939), 45, 46.

2. Brian Loveman, *The Constitution of Tyranny: Regimes of Exception in Spanish America* (Pittsburgh: University of Pittsburgh Press, 1993), 5, 370.

3. Clinton L. Rossiter, *Constitutional Dictatorship: Crisis Government in Modern Democracies* (Princeton, NJ: Princeton University Press, 1948), chap. 6.

4. Loveman, *The Constitution of Tyranny,* 64, 6.

5. Gabriel L. Negretto, "Authoritarian Constitution Making: The Role of the Military in Latin America," in *Constitutions in Authoritarian Regimes,* ed. Tom Ginsburg and Alberto Simpser (Cambridge: Cambridge University Press, 2014), 83–110, 84–85. See further Gabriel L. Negretto, *Making Constitutions: Presidents, Parties, and Institutional Choice in Latin America* (Cambridge: Cambridge University Press, 2013), chaps. 1–3.

6. Juan J. Linz, "The Perils of Presidentialism," *Journal of Democracy* 1 (1990): 51–69.

7. See Javier A. Couso, "The Changing Role of Law and Courts in Latin America: From Obstacle to Social Change to a Tool of Social Equity," in *Courts and*

Social Transformation in New Democracies, ed. Roberto Gargarella, Pilar Domingo, and Theunis Roux (Abingdon, UK: Routledge, 2006), 61–82.

8. Consider, e.g., the declaration of the military junta that ousted President Allende in Chile in 1973, which stated that the government "has exceeded the bounds of legitimacy by violating the fundamental rights. . . . For the foregoing reasons the armed forces have taken upon themselves the moral duty which the country imposes upon them of deposing the government, which, although legitimate in the early exercise of power, has since fallen into flagrant illegitimacy" (cited in Loveman, *The Constitution of Tyranny,* 15). For context, see Roberto Gargarella, *Latin American Constitutionalism, 1810–2010: The Engine Room of the Constitution* (Oxford: Oxford University Press, 2013), 127–129. The Chilean Constitution of 1980, adopted by plebiscite under General Pinochet's regime, currently remains in force, though is presently under review.

9. See F. A. Hayek, *Law, Legislation and Liberty,* vol. 3, *The Political Order of a Free People* (London: Routledge & Kegan Paul, 1979), 124.

10. Montesquieu, *The Spirit of the Laws* [1748], trans. A. Cohler, B. Miller, and H. Stone (Cambridge: Cambridge University Press, 1989), book XI, ch. 6: "If the executive power does not have the right to check the enterprise of the legislative body, the latter will be despotic, for it wipe out all the other powers, since it will be able to give to itself all the power it can imagine. . . . The state will perish when the legislative power is more corrupt than executive power."

11. Benjamin Constant, "The Spirit of Conquest and Usurpation and their Relation to European Civilization" [1814], in his *Political Writings,* trans. B. Fontana (Cambridge: Cambridge University Press, 1988), 43–167, 53–54.

12. Max Weber, *Economy and Society,* ed. G. Roth and C. Wittich, vol. 2 (Berkeley: University of California Press, 1978), 1400.

13. John Locke, *Two Treatises of Government* [1680], ed. P. Laslett (Cambridge: Cambridge University Press, 1998), vol. 2, §§ 160, 210.

14. "Letter from Thomas Jefferson to John C. Breckinridge, 12 August 1803," in Jefferson, *Writings* (New York: Library of America, 1984), 1138–1139.

15. See Daniel Farber, *Lincoln's Constitution* (Chicago: University of Chicago Press, 2003).

16. Ex parte Merryman, 17 F. Cas. 144 (C.C.D. Md. 1861).

17. Rossiter, *Constitutional Dictatorship,* 228.

18. Abraham Lincoln, Message to Congress in Special Session, 4 July 1861, cited in Farber, *Lincoln's Constitution,* 194.

19. Prize Cases, 67 U.S. (2 Black) 635, 670 (1863).

20. Rossiter, *Constitutional Dictatorship,* 239.

21. Farber, *Lincoln's Constitution,* 194, 195 (emphasis in original).

22. See, e.g., Richard J. Evans, *The Coming of the Third Reich* (New York: Penguin, 2003), 80–81: "The power to rule by decree was only intended for exceptional emergencies. But Ebert, as the Republic's first President [1919–1925], made very

extensive use of this power, employing it on no fewer than 136 occasions. . . . In the end, Ebert's excessive use, and occasional misuse, of the Article widened its application to a point where it became a potential threat to democratic institutions."

23. Carl Schmitt, *Dictatorship: From the Origin of the Modern Concept of Sovereignty to Proletarian Class Struggle* [1921], trans. M. Hoelzl and G. Ward (Cambridge: Polity Press, 2014).

24. Carl Schmitt, *Political Theology: Four Chapters on the Concept of Sovereignty* [1922], trans. G. Schwab (Chicago: University of Chicago Press, 2005), 5 (translation modified).

25. Schmitt, *Political Theology,* 12.

26. Schmitt, *Political Theology,* 14.

27. Schmitt, *Political Theology,* 14.

28. Rossiter, *Constitutional Dictatorship,* chap. 19.

29. Bruce Ackerman, "The Emergency Constitution," *Yale Law Journal* 113 (2004): 1028–1091. Compare David Cole, "The Priority of Morality: The Emergency Constitution's Blind Spot," *Yale Law Journal* 113 (2004): 1753–1800, arguing that Ackerman's proposals provide another mechanism legitimating the use of preventive detention.

30. Oren Gross, "Chaos and Rules: Should Responses to Violent Crises Always be Constitutional?," *Yale Law Journal* 112 (2003): 1011–1134.

31. David Dyzenhaus, *The Constitution of Law: Legality in a Time of Emergency* (Cambridge: Cambridge University Press, 2006), 7, 199, 218.

32. Dyzenhaus, *The Constitution of Law,* 215, 38, 53, 205.

33. Nomi Claire Lazar, *States of Emergency in Liberal Democracies* (Cambridge: Cambridge University Press, 2009), 13, 5, 113.

34. See my "Reason of State / State of Reason," in Martin Loughlin, *Political Jurisprudence* (Oxford: Oxford University Press, 2017), chap. 8.

35. Carl J. Friedrich, *Constitutional Reason of State* (Providence, RI: Brown University Press, 1957).

36. Dyzenhaus, *The Constitution of Law,* 3.

37. Lazar, *States of Emergency,* 17.

38. See, e.g., French Constitution (1958), art. 16: "When the institutions of the Republic, the independence of the nation, the integrity of its territory, or the fulfillment of its international commitments are under grave and immediate threat and when the proper functioning of the constitutional governmental authorities is interrupted, the President of the Republic shall take the measures demanded by these circumstances after official consultation with the Prime Minister, the presidents of the Assemblies, and the Constitutional Council." After thirty days the Constitutional Council can be asked to determine whether the conditions continue to exist. See also European Convention on Human Rights, art. 15. See Olivier Beaud and Cécile Guérin-Bargues, *L'état d'urgence: Une étude constitutionelle, historique et critique* (Paris: LGDJ, 2016).

39. See, e.g., Jack Goldsmith, "The Irrelevance of Prerogative Power and the Evils of Secret Legal Interpretation," in *Extra-Legal Power and Legitimacy: Perspectives on the Prerogative,* ed. Clement Fatovic and Benjamin A. Kleinerman (Oxford: Oxford University Press, 2013), 214–231; Ian Ostrander and Joel Sievert, "The Logic of Presidential Signing Statements," *Political Research Quarterly* 66 (2013): 141–53; Bruce Ackerman, *The Decline and Fall of the American Republic* (Cambridge, MA: Belknap Press of Harvard University Press, 2010), 68: "Over the past half-century, two new institutions—the Office of Legal Counsel and the White House Counsel—have vastly increased their constitutional authority. When added together, they form an elite professional corps that produces legal opinions of the highest technical quality . . . [and] they almost always conclude that the President can do what he wants. Presidents can then publish these respectable-looking opinions to give legal legitimacy to their power grabs. . . . Call this 'executive constitutionalism,'"

40. See Günter Frankenberg, *Political Technology and the Erosion of the Rule of Law: Normalizing the Exception* (Cheltenham, UK: Edward Elgar, 2014), chap. 6.

12. The Struggle for Recognition

1. See Liav Orgad, "The Preamble in Constitutional Interpretation," *International Journal of Constitutional Law* 8 (2010): 714–738, 716–717.

2. Domenico Lusordo, *Liberalism: A Counter-History,* trans. G. Elliott (London: Verso, 2011), 205.

3. Rogers M. Smith, *Stories of Peoplehood: The Politics and Morals of Political Membership* (Cambridge: Cambridge University Press, 2003), 45.

4. Richard Kluger, *Simple Justice: The History of* Brown v. Board of Education *and Black America's Struggle for Equality* (London: André Deutsch, 1977), 39. Note also that almost half of the delegates to the Constitutional Convention owned slaves, and of an estimated colonial population of 4 million, only 160,000 were "active citizens"—that is, possessed the property qualifications needed to elect delegates to the Philadelphia Convention and ratify their work: Eric Foner, *The Second Founding* (New York: Norton, 2019), 1.

5. Dred Scott v. Sandford, 60 U.S. 393 (1856), 410, per Taney C.J.: "But it is too clear for dispute that the enslaved African race were not intended to be included, and formed no part of the people who framed and adopted this declaration, for if the language, as understood in that day, would embrace them, the conduct of the distinguished men who framed the Declaration of Independence would have been utterly and flagrantly inconsistent with the principles they asserted, and instead of the sympathy of mankind to which they so confidently appealed, they would have deserved and received universal rebuke and reprobation."

6. Slaughterhouse Cases, 77 U.S. (10 Wall.) 273 (1869); 83 U.S. 36 (1872); U.S. v. Reese, 92 U.S. 214 (1875); Civil Rights Cases, 109 U.S. 3 (1883).

7. Plessy v. Ferguson, 163 U.S. 537 (1896), 544, 551. For context, see Steve Luxenberg, *Separate: The Story of* Plessy v. Ferguson *and America's Journey from Slavery to Segregation* (New York: Norton, 2019).

8. See Michael J. Klarman, *From Jim Crow to Civil Rights: The Supreme Court and the Struggle for Racial Equality* (Oxford: Oxford University Press, 2004), chap. 1.

9. Kluger, *Simple Justice,* 88: "In 1910, eleven Southern states spent an average of $9.45 on each white child enrolled in their public schools and $2.90 on each black child. And the disparity grew. By 1916, the per-capita outlay for black children dropped a penny to $2.89 but the white per-capita expense rose to $10.32."

10. Brown v. Board of Education of Topeka, 347 U.S. 483 (1954), 493–495.

11. Klarman, *From Jim Crown to Civil Rights,* chap. 6.

12. *Brown* was followed in the 1960s by constitutional rulings in marriage laws, voting, and criminal procedure: Loving v. Virginia, 388 U.S. 1 (1967) (laws banning interracial marriage unconstitutional); Baker v. Carr, 369 U.S. 186 (1962) (rationality of electoral districts a constitutional issue); Reynolds v. Sims, 377 U.S. 533 (1964) (electoral districts must be roughly equal); Miranda v. Arizona, 384 U.S. 436 (1966) (suspects must be informed of their rights); Gideon v. Wainwright (states must provide attorneys to defendants unable to afford one).

13. Kluger, *Simple Justice,* 758: "A head count [on the tenth anniversary of the *Brown* decision] showed that only 1.17 percent of black schoolchildren in the eleven states of the Confederacy were attending public school with white classmates."

14. Brown v. Board of Education, 494.

15. Holding that segregation "has a detrimental effect upon the colored children," the Court proceeded to justify this finding by citing seven key works by social scientists, the most famous of which is Gunnar Myrdal, *An American Dilemma: The Negro Problem and American Democracy* (New York: Harper, 1944): Brown v. Board of Education, 494n11.

16. Alexander M. Bickel, *The Least Dangerous Branch: The Supreme Court at the Bar of Politics,* 2nd ed. (New Haven, CT: Yale University Press, 1986), 236.

17. See, e.g., Michelle Alexander, *The New Jim Crow: Mass Incarceration in the Age of Colorblindness* (New York: New Press, 2010), showing that, although making up only 13 percent of the population, blacks form 40 percent of the prison population and that one-third of black men have been incarcerated.

18. Immanuel Kant, "An Answer to the Question: 'What Is Enlightenment?,'" in his *Political Writings,* 2nd ed., ed. H. Reiss, trans. H. B. Nisbet (Cambridge: Cambridge University Press, 1991), 54–60, 54.

19. See Ronald Steel, *Walter Lippmann and the American Century* (London: Bodley Head, 1980), 112.

20. Faced with an English claim to pretty much the whole of North America in 1609, "when there were only a handful of settlers clinging to the malarial swamps

of the St James River," in 1627 the French Crown, "at a time when there were only 107 French settlers in Canada, gathered in settlements in Acadia and the St. Lawrence and completely isolated from one another, asserted its rights over a territory which reached from Florida to the Arctic Circle, nearly all of which was uncharted, and virtually none of which was in practice either *res nullius* or, given the Spanish presence in the South, undiscovered": Anthony Pagden, *Lords of All the World: Ideologies of Empire in Spain, Britain and France c.1500–c.1800* (New Haven, CT: Yale University Press, 1995), 80.

21. Calvin's Case, 77 ER 377 (1608), 397.

22. "The First Charter of Virginia: 10 April 1606," Avalon Project, Yale Law School, Lillian Goldman Law Library, https://avalon.law.yale.edu/17th_century/VA01.asp.

23. John Locke, *Two Treatises of Government* [1680], ed. P. Laslett (Cambridge: Cambridge University Press, 1988), vol. 2, § 49

24. Johnson v. M'Intosh, 21 U.S. (8 Wheat.) 543 (1823).

25. James Tully, *Strange Multiplicity: Constitutionalism in an Age of Diversity* (Cambridge: Cambridge University Press, 1995), 78.

26. Robert A. Williams Jr., *The American Indian in Western Legal Thought: The Discourses of Conquest* (New York: Oxford University Press, 1990), 221, 325–326.

27. Tully, *Strange Multiplicity*, 39, 43.

28. See, e.g., John Borrows, *Freedom and Indigenous Constitutionalism* (Toronto: University of Toronto Press, 2016).

29. The classic work on the gendered aspect of constitutionalism is Mary Wollstonecraft, *A Vindication of the Rights of Men; A Vindication of the Rights of Woman* [1790–1794] (Oxford: Oxford University Press, 1993). See further Carol Pateman, *The Sexual Contract* (Cambridge: Polity Press, 1988); Beverley Baines and Ruth Rubio-Marín, *The Gender of Constitutional Jurisprudence* (Cambridge: Cambridge University Press, 2004).

30. The Constitution of the Republic of South Africa, 1996, preamble. On the participatory process, see Simone Chambers, "Democracy, Popular Sovereignty and Constitutional Legitimacy," *Constellations* 11 (2004): 153–173.

31. The Constitution of the Republic of South Africa, 1996, chap. 2 (rights), chap. 1, § 6 (languages), chap. 12 (customary law), and chaps. 6 and 7 (regional and local government).

32. Constitution of the Republic of Ecuador, 2008, Title II, Rights.

33. On Ecuador, see Carlos de la Torre, "Technocratic Populism in Ecuador," *Journal of Democracy* 24 (2013): 33–46; Steven Levitsky and James Loxton, "Populism and Competitive Authoritarianism in the Andes," *Democratization* 20 (2013): 107–136; Takis S. Pappas, *Populism and Liberal Democracy: A Comparative and Theoretical Analysis* (Oxford: Oxford University Press, 2019), 152–156, 257. On South Africa, see Allister Sparks, *Beyond the Miracle: Inside the New South Africa* (Johannesburg: Jonathan Ball, 2003); James Fowkes, "Choosing to

Have Had a Revolution: Lessons from South Africa's Undecided Constitutionalism," in *Revolutionary Constitutionalism: Law, Legitimacy, Power,* ed. Richard Albert (Oxford: Hart, 2020), 355–376, 365–368. For empirical analysis, see Adam Chilton and Mila Versteeg, *How Constitutional Rights Matter* (Oxford: Oxford University Press, 2020).

34. Granville Austin, *The Indian Constitution: Cornerstone of a Nation* (Oxford: Clarendon Press, 1966), chap. 2.

35. Partha Chatterjee, *The Politics of the Governed: Reflections on Popular Politics in Most of the World* (New York: Columbia University Press, 2004), 9.

36. Indian Constitution, 1947, arts. 15, 16.

37. Gautam Bhatia, *The Transformative Constitution: A Radical Biography in Nine Acts* (Noida, Uttar Pradesh: HarperCollins, 2019); Gary Jeffrey Jacobsohn and Yaniv Roznai, *Constitutional Revolution* (New Haven, CT: Yale University Press, 2020), chap. 5.

38. Anuj Bhuwania, *Courting the People: Public Interest Litigation in Post-Emergency India* (Cambridge: Cambridge University Press, 2017).

39. Chatterjee, *The Politics of the Governed,* 3, 38.

40. See, e.g., Menachem Mautner, *Law and the Culture of Israel* (Oxford: Oxford University Press, 2011), advancing the thesis that Israel's Supreme Court, traditionally liberalism's normative beacon, has, through its activism, "lost much stature not only among the Jewish religious group, but also among its own traditional supporters" and this deterioration "means that the Court's ability to continue playing its traditional role as a stronghold of Israel's liberalism is very much in jeopardy" (226).

41. Jürgen Habermas, "Citizenship and National Identity," in his *Between Facts and Norms* (Cambridge: Polity Press, 1996), app. II, 491–515.

42. See, e.g., Arend Lijphart, "Constitutional Design in Divided Societies," *Journal of Democracy* 15 (2004): 96–109; Sujit Choudhry, ed., *Constitutional Design for Divided Societies: Integration or Accommodation?* (New York: Oxford University Press, 2008); Hanna Lerner, *Making Constitutions in Deeply Divided Societies* (Cambridge: Cambridge University Press, 2011); Samuel Issacharoff, *Fragile Democracies: Contested Power in the Era of Constitutional Courts* (Cambridge: Cambridge University Press, 2015).

43. Mara Malagodi, *Constitutional Nationalism and Legal Exclusion: Equality, Identity Politics, and Democracy in Nepal* (New Delhi: Oxford University Press, 2013); Nepal Constitution, 2015.

44. The religious parties objected to the adoption of a constitution either because they believed effectively that the Torah was the authoritative guide for the Jewish homeland or because they were concerned that an enforceable bill of rights might be interpreted in a way that would erode special religious privileges. But the dominant secular Ashkenazi elite also were opposed while they were able to rule through parliamentary majorities; their position changed in the 1990s, argu-

ably because of a threat to their dominant position: see Ran Hirschl, *Towards Juristocracy: The Origins and Consequences of the New Constitutionalism* (Cambridge, MA: Harvard University Press, 2004), 50–56; Jacobsohn and Roznai, *Constitutional Revolution,* 187–194.

45. Basic Law: The Knesset 1985; Declaration of Establishment of the State of Israel, 14 May 1948.

46. The issue of citizenship is complicated because, regarding itself as a country of "repatriation" rather than immigration, Israel does not have citizenship tests, treats the state as made up of its residents, and has no concept of "Israeli nationality" as distinct from ethnic categories. See Liav Orgad, *The Cultural Defense of Nations: A Liberal Theory of Majority Rights* (Oxford: Oxford University Press, 2015), 125–129.

47. Mazen Masri, *The Dynamics of Exclusionary Constitutionalism: Israel as a Jewish and Democratic State* (Oxford: Hart, 2017), 21.

48. Alexander Yacobson and Amnon Rubinstein, *Israel and the Family of Nations: The Jewish Nation-State and Human Rights* (Abingdon, UK: Routledge, 2009).

49. Tamar Hostovsky Brandes, "Basic Law: Israel as the Nation State of the Jewish People: Implications for Equality, Self-Determination and Social Solidarity," *Minnesota Journal of International Law* 29 (2020): 65–107, 107: "The Law deepens the existing rift in Israeli society and facilitates the already-existing friend-enemy discourse. It reinforces an exclusionary notion of solidarity and negatively affects the prospect of creating all-encompassing solidarity, which includes all of Israel's citizens."

50. Amal Jamal, "Israel's New Constitutional Imagination: The Nation State Law and Beyond," *Journal of Holy Land and Palestine Studies* 18 (2019): 193–220, 193. See also Adam Shinar, Barak Medina, and Gila Stopler, "From Promise to Retrenchment: On the Changing Landscape of Israeli Constitutionalism," *International Journal of Constitutional Law* 18 (2020): 714–729; Jacobsohn and Roznai, *Constitutional Revolution,* 218–223.

51. Thomas Piketty, *Capital in the Twenty-First Century,* trans. A. Goldhammer (Cambridge, MA: Belknap Press of Harvard University Press, 2014), pt. III; Ganesh Sitaraman, "Economic Inequality and Constitutional Democracy," in *Constitutional Democracy in Crisis?,* ed. Mark A. Graber, Sanford Levinson, and Mark Tushnet (New York: Oxford University Press, 2018), 533–549; Yascha Mounk, *The People vs. Democracy: Why Our Freedom Is in Danger and How to Save It* (Cambridge, MA: Harvard University Press, 2018), 152–153.

52. Abraham Lincoln, First Inaugural Address, 4 March 1861, in *Selected Writings and Speeches of Abraham Lincoln,* ed. T. Harry Williams (New York: Hendricks, 1943), 117.

53. See Daniel Weinstock, "Constitutionalizing the Right to Secede," *Journal of Political Philosophy* 9 (2001): 182–203; Christopher Heath Wellman, *A Theory*

of Secession: The Case for Political Self-Determination (Cambridge: Cambridge University Press, 2005).

54. David Haljan, *Constitutionalising Secession* (Oxford: Hart, 2014), 14.

55. *Reference Re Secession of Quebec* [1998], 2 SCR 217, para. 88.

56. Susanna Mancini, "Rethinking the Boundaries of Democratic Secession: Liberalism, Nationalism, and the Right of Minorities to Self-Determination," *International Journal of Constitutional Law* 6 (2008): 553–584, 579.

57. See, e.g., South African Constitution, 1996, art. 235: "The right of the South African people as a whole to self-determination, as manifested in this Constitution, does not preclude . . . recognition of the notion of the right of self-determination of any community sharing a common cultural and language heritage." Article 72 of the Constitution of the USSR (1977) had asserted the right of every Union Republic to secede from the Soviet Union, but since it was widely recognized to be a façade constitution, no one took that seriously.

13. The Cosmopolitan Project

1. Immanuel Kant, "Perpetual Peace: A Philosophical Sketch" [1795], in his *Political Writings,* 2nd ed., ed. H. Reiss, trans. H. B. Nisbet (Cambridge: Cambridge University Press, 1991), 93–130, 103.

2. Immanuel Kant, "Idea for a Universal History with a Cosmopolitan Purpose" [1784], in his *Political Writings,* 41–53, 51.

3. Martti Koskenniemi, *The Gentle Civilizer of Nations: The Rise and Fall of International Law 1870–1960* (Cambridge: Cambridge University Press, 2002), 514.

4. Samuel Moyn, *The Last Utopia: Human Rights in History* (Cambridge, MA: Belknap Press of Harvard University Press, 2010), 3, 7.

5. Jan Klabbers, Anne Peters, and Geir Ulfstein, *The Constitutionalization of International Law* (Oxford: Oxford University Press, 2009); Ronald St. John Macdonald and Douglas M. Johnston, eds., *Towards World Constitutionalism: Issues in the Legal Ordering of the World Community* (Leiden: Nijhoff, 2005).

6. This was the basis of his debate with Dieter Grimm over a European constitution: Dieter Grimm, "Does Europe Need a Constitution?," *European Law Journal* 1 (1995): 282–302; Jürgen Habermas, "Why Europe Needs a Constitution," *New Left Review* 11 (2001): 5–26; Jürgen Habermas, "Does Europe Need a Constitution? Response to Dieter Grimm," in his *The Inclusion of the Other: Studies in Political Theory,* trans. C. Cronin and P. de Greiff (Cambridge: Polity Press, 1999), 155–161.

7. Habermas, "Why Europe Needs a Constitution," 6, 9, 16, 17.

8. Jürgen Habermas, *The Crisis of the European Union: A Response,* trans. C. Cronin (Cambridge: Polity Press, 2012), viii, 6, x, xi. Compare "Why Europe Needs a Constitution," 8, where Habermas suggests that the Euro would "soon become a unifying symbol in everyday life across the continent."

9. Jürgen Habermas, "Kant's Idea of Perpetual Peace: At Two Hundred Years' Historical Remove," in his *The Inclusion of the Other,* 165–200, 178, 183.

10. Habermas, "Kant's Idea of Perpetual Peace," 181, 190, 199.

11. Jürgen Habermas, "The Postnational Constellation and the Future of Democracy," in *The Postnational Constellation: Political Essays,* trans. M. Pensky (Cambridge: Polity Press, 2001), 58–112.

12. Jürgen Habermas, "The Constitutionalization of International Law and the Legitimation Problems of a Constitution for World Society," *Constellations* 15 (2008): 444–455, 444, 445.

13. Habermas, "The Constitutionalization of International Law," 448 (emphasis in original).

14. Habermas, "The Constitutionalization of International Law," 453.

15. See Habermas, *The Crisis of the European Union,* 37–44 (shared sovereignty as the standard for the legitimation requirements of the Union).

16. This is an extension of Habermas's argument that in the EU there is a "sharing of constituting power between EU citizens and European peoples": Habermas, *The Crisis of the European Union,* 28–37. See also Markus Patberg, *Constituent Power in the European Union* (Oxford: Oxford University Press, 2020).

17. Mattias Kumm, "The Cosmopolitan Turn in Constitutionalism: On the Relationship between Constitutionalism in and beyond the State," in *Ruling the World? International Law, Global Governance, Constitutionalism,* ed. Jeffrey L. Dunoff and Joel P. Trachtman (Cambridge: Cambridge University Press, 2009), 258–326, 261, 262.

18. Kumm, "The Cosmopolitan Turn," 272.

19. Kumm initially viewed constituent power as a product of the statist worldview that became redundant in the cosmopolitan paradigm shift, but later embraced Habermas's dualist view: Mattias Kumm, "Constituent Power, Cosmopolitan Constitutionalism, and Post-Positivist Law," *International Journal of Constitutional Law* 14 (2016): 697–711. Compare Neil Walker, "The Return of Constituent Power: A Reply to Mattias Kumm," *International Journal of Constitutional Law* 14 (2016): 906–913.

20. Kumm, "The Cosmopolitan Turn," 305.

21. Kumm, "The Cosmopolitan Turn," 322–323 (emphases in original).

22. Friedrich A. Hayek, *The Road to Serfdom* (Chicago: University of Chicago Press, 1944), 223, 232.

23. Philip Mirowski and Dieter Plehwe, *The Road from Mont Pèlerin: The Making of the Neoliberal Thought Collective,* rev. ed. (Cambridge, MA: Harvard University Press, 2015).

24. Quinn Slobodian, *Globalists: The End of Empire and the Birth of Neoliberalism* (Cambridge, MA: Harvard University Press, 2018), 4.

25. F. A. Hayek, *Law, Legislation and Liberty,* vol. 3, *The Political Order of a Free People* (London: Routledge & Kegan Paul, 1979), 149.

26. See Ludwig von Mises, *Liberalism: The Classical Tradition* [1927], ed. B. B. Greaves (Indianapolis, IN: Liberty Fund, 2005), 113: "But for the liberal, the world does not end at the borders of the state. In his eyes, whatever significance national boundaries have is only incidental and subordinate. His political thinking encompasses the whole of mankind. The starting-point of his entire political philosophy is the conviction that the division of labor is international and not merely national."

27. Ernst-Ulrich Petersmann, "Human Rights Require Cosmopolitan Constitutionalism and Cosmopolitan Law for Democratic Governance of Public Goods," *Contemporary Readings in Law & Social Justice* 5 (2013): 90–119.

28. See Gus Van Harten, *Investment Treaty Arbitration and Public Law* (Oxford: Oxford University Press, 2007).

29. Signe Larsen, *The Constitutional Theory of the Federation and the European Union* (Oxford: Oxford University Press, 2021).

30. European Court of Justice, Opinion 1 / 91, Opinion on the draft agreement between the Community and the European Free Trade Association relating to the creation of the European Economic Area: "The EEC Treaty, albeit concluded in the form of an international agreement, none the less constitutes the constitutional charter of a community based on the rule of law. The essential characteristics of the Community legal order are its primacy over the law of the Member States and the direct effect of a whole series of provisions which are applicable to their nationals and to the Member States." See further Neil Walker, "Big 'C' or Small 'c,'" *European Law Journal* 12 (2006): 12–14.

31. The implications for the standing of European member states are presented in Michael A. Wilkinson, *Authoritarian Liberalism and the Transformation of Modern Europe* (Oxford: Oxford University Press, 2021).

32. Alexander Somek, *The Cosmopolitan Constitution* (Oxford: Oxford University Press, 2014), 25.

33. Basic Law, art. 1(2).

34. Sujit Choudhry, Madhav Khosla, and Pratap Bhanu Mehta, "Locating Indian Constitutionalism," in *The Oxford Handbook of the Indian Constitution* (Oxford: Oxford University Press, 2016), 1–16, 5.

35. Networks include the Conference of European Constitutional Courts (established in 1972), the Union of Arab Constitutional Courts and Councils (1997), the Southern African Chief Justice Forum (2003), the Latin American Conference of Constitutional Justice (2005), the Association of Asian Constitutional Courts and Equivalent Institutions (2010), the Conference of Constitutional Jurisdictions of Africa (2011), and the Network of Constitutional Courts and Councils of West and Central Africa (2016). On Europe, see Maartje de Visser and Monica Claes, "Courts United? On European Judicial Networks," in *Lawyering Europe:*

European Law as a Transnational Legal Field, ed. Bruno de Witte and Antoine Vauchez (Oxford: Hart, 2013), 75–100. On the Asian network, see Maartje de Visser, "We All Stand Together: The Role of the Association of Asian Constitutional Courts and Equivalent Institutions in Promoting Constitutionalism," *Asian Journal of Law and Society* 3 (2016): 105–134. On the general trend toward global lawyering, see Neil Walker, *Intimations of Global Law* (Cambridge: Cambridge University Press, 2015), chap. 2.

36. Walter Bagehot, *The English Constitution* [1867] (Oxford: Oxford University Press, 2001), 124.

37. Somek, *The Cosmopolitan Constitution*, 179.

38. Somek, *The Cosmopolitan Constitution*, 183.

39. Somek, *The Cosmopolitan Constitution*, 202, 211.

Conclusion

1. Mark DeWolfe Howe, *Holmes-Laski Letters: The Correspondence of Mr. Justice Holmes and Harold J. Laski*, vol. 1 (London: Oxford University Press, 1953), 475 (Laski, 21.1.23). For Laski's reasons, see p. 535.

2. Sanford Levinson, *Our Undemocratic Constitution: Where the Constitution Goes Wrong (And How We the People Can Correct It)* (New York: Oxford University Press, 2006), 6 (emphasis added).

3. Bruce Ackerman, *We the People*, vol. 3, *The Civil Rights Revolution* (Cambridge, MA: Harvard University Press, 2014), 23.

4. See, e.g., Noah Feldman, *What We Owe Iraq: War and the Ethics of Nation Building* (Princeton, NJ: Princeton University Press, 2004); Andrew Arato, *Constitution Making under Occupation: The Politics of Imposed Revolution in Iraq* (New York: Columbia University Press, 2009).

5. Consider, for example, the case of South Africa, often taken as a model of "aspirational" or "transformational" constitutionalism. Far from entailing a revolutionary shift, it has been shown convincingly that this was a process by which "white elites . . . gave up their monopoly on political power to preserve their social and economic power": James Fowkes, "Choosing to Have Had a Revolution: Lessons from South Africa's Undecided Constitutionalism," in *Revolutionary Constitutionalism: Law, Legitimacy, Power*, ed. Richard Albert (Oxford: Hart, 2020), 355–376, 367.

6. Ulrich Beck and Elisabeth Beck-Gernsheim, *Individualization: Individualized Individualism and Its Social and Political Consequences* (London: Sage, 2002).

7. For a powerful illustration of the way in which developments in the European Union shaped the formation of constitutional judicial review in France see Daniel Halberstam, "How Europe Brought Judicial Review to France," in Albert, *Revolutionary Constitutionalism*, 239–263.

8. Eric Hobsbawm, *Age of Extremes: The Short Twentieth Century, 1914–1991* (London: Abacus, 1995), 112: "Taking the world as a whole, there had been perhaps

thirty-five or more constitutional and elected governments in 1920 (depending on where we situate some Latin American republics). Until 1938 there were perhaps seventeen such states, in 1944 perhaps twelve out of the global total of sixty-four."

9. Samuel Issacharoff, "Populism versus Democratic Governance," in *Constitutional Democracy in Crisis?*, ed. Mark A. Graber, Sanford Levinson, and Mark Tushnet (New York: Oxford University Press, 2018), 445–458, 445.

10. John Stuart Mill, "Considerations on Representative Government" [1861], in *Three Essays* (Oxford: Oxford University Press, 1975), 144–423, 382.

11. See, e.g., Freedom House, *Freedom in the World, 2020* (Washington, DC: Freedom House, 2021), 10: "More than half of the world's established democracies deteriorated over the past 14 years. Functioning of government, freedom of expression and belief, and rule of law are the most common areas of decline."

12. See Peter Mair, *Ruling the Void: The Hollowing Out of Western Democracy* (London: Verso, 2013), 1: "The age of party democracy has passed." For a detailed analysis, see Carolien van Ham, Jacques Thomassen, Kees Arts, and Rudy Andeweg, eds., *Myth and Reality of the Legitimacy Crisis: Explaining Trends and Cross-National Differences in Established Democracies* (Oxford: Oxford University Press, 2017), 80: "In combination it seems the omens are not good: the future for parties does not seem too bright. Fewer of us are party members; fewer of us vote in elections; of those of us who do vote we are more inconsistent in our voting behaviour."

13. See Yascha Mounk, *The People vs. Democracy: Why Our Freedom is in Danger and How to Save It* (Cambridge, MA: Harvard University Press, 2018), chap. 3.

14. Thomas Piketty, *Capital in the Twenty-First Century*, trans. A. Goldhammer (Cambridge, MA: Belknap Press of Harvard University Press, 2014), pt. III; Mounk, *The People vs. Democracy*, 218: "Since 1986 America's GDP per capita has increased by 59 percent. The country's net worth has grown by 90 percent. Corporate profits have soared by 283 percent. But those aggregate numbers hide the distribution of gains. Only 1 percent of total wealth growth from 1986 to 2012 went to the bottom 90 percent of households. By contrast 42 percent went to the top 0.1 percent."

15. T. Alexander Aleinikoff, "Inherent Instability: Immigration and Constitutional Democracies," in Graber, Levinson, and Tushnet, *Constitutional Democracy in Crisis?*, 477–493, 487: "In the United States, the percentage of foreign-born residents (14 per cent) is approaching levels not seen since 1920s. . . . In Sweden and Austria, the percentage is above 18 per cent; in Germany, 15 per cent; and in France, the United Kingdom and Spain it is over 12 per cent." Mounk, *The People vs. Democracy*, 166: "Fears about immigration are now top of mind for voters across Europe."

16. See, e.g., Tom Ginsburg and Aziz Z. Huq, *How to Save a Constitutional Democracy* (Chicago: University of Chicago Press, 2018); Graber, Levinson, and Tushnet, *Constitutional Democracy in Crisis?*; Steven Levitsky and Daniel Ziblatt, *How Democracies Die* (New York: Viking, 2018); Mounk, *The People vs. Democracy.*

17. Benjamin Arditi, *Politics on the Edges of Liberalism: Difference, Populism, Revolution, Agitation* (Edinburgh: Edinburgh University Press, 2008), chaps. 2–3; Jan-Werner Müller, *What Is Populism?* (London: Penguin, 2017); Cristóbal Rovira Kaltwasser, Paul Taggart, Paulina Ochoa Espejo, and Pierre Ostiguy, eds., *The Oxford Handbook of Populism* (Oxford: Oxford University Press, 2017).

18. Peter Wiles, "A Syndrome, Not a Doctrine: Some Elementary Theses on Populism," in *Populism: Its Meanings and National Characteristics,* ed. Ghita Ionescu and Ernest Gellner (London: Weidenfeld & Nicolson, 1969), 166–179.

19. See, e.g., the landmark text of Graber, Levinson, and Tushnet, *Constitutional Democracy in Crisis?,* which pitches the problem as a crisis of constitutional democracy. The only allusion to the argument I make is by Desmond King and Rogers M. Smith, "Populism, Racism, and the Rule of Law in Constitutional Democracies Today" (*Constitutional Democracy in Crisis?,* 459–475, 463): "Though scholars of recent populist movements have been commendably attentive to populist attitudes toward constitutionalism and the rule of law, few have explored the possibility that these movements are reactions against the dominant ideology revealed in the spate of drafting of new constitutions that occurred around the world in the last quarter century." For nuanced analysis, see Neil Walker, "Populism and Constitutional Tension," *International Journal of Constitutional Law* 17 (2019): 515–535; Paul Blokker, "Populism as a Constitutional Project," *International Journal of Constitutional Law* 17 (2019): 535–553.

20. Ginsburg and Huq, *How to Save a Constitutional Democracy,* chaps. 6–7.

21. Ivan Krastev and Stephen Holmes, *The Light that Failed: A Reckoning* (London: Allen Lane, 2019), 22.

22. Ernesto Laclau, *On Populist Reason* (London: Verso, 2005), x: "What is involved in such a disdainful rejection [of populism] is, I think, the dismissal of politics *tout court,* and the assertion that the management of community is the concern of an administrative power whose source of legitimacy is a proper knowledge of what a 'good' community is." See also Chantal Mouffe, *For a Left Populism* (London: Verso, 2018).

23. Nadia Urbinati, *Me the People: How Populism Transforms Democracy* (Cambridge, MA: Harvard University Press, 2019), 204: "The challenges to constitutional democracy come from two opposite sides: the oligarchic few, who already control the decision-making process; and the popular many, who claim that the only way they can redress the inequality of their power is by claiming the priority of the majority over all other parts of society."

24. Norberto Bobbio, "Democracy and Invisible Power," in his *The Future of Democracy,* trans. R. Griffin (Cambridge: Polity Press, 1987), chap. 4.

25. See, e.g., the ongoing dispute between the German Federal Constitutional Court and the Court of Justice of the European Union over the legality of the actions by the European Central Bank, first in its response to the Euro crisis (*Gauweiler:* BVerfG, Judgment, 21 June 2016, 2 BvR 2728 / 13; ECJ case C-62 / 14) and, more recently, its Pandemic Emergency Purchase Programme (*Weiss:* BVerfG, Judgment, 5 May 2020, 2 BvR 859 / 15; ECJ case C-493 / 17). These disputes show how the proportionality principle is used to mask policy preferences, the illusion that strict legality could prevail over "reason of state" considerations, and the inability of courts now to decline to assert jurisdiction under a political question doctrine. See Marco Dani, Agustin Menendez, Eduardo Chiti, Joana Mendes, Harm Schepel, and Michael Wilkinson, "'It's the Political Economy!' A Moment of Truth for the Eurozone and the EU," *International Journal of Constitutional Law* 19 (2021): 309–327.

26. See Max Weber, *The Protestant Ethic and the Spirit of Capitalism,* trans. T. Parsons (New York: Charles Scribner's Sons, 1948): "The development of economic rationalism is partly dependent on rational technique and law" (26). "The spirit of capitalism had to fight its way to supremacy against the whole world of hostile forces. . . . The most important opponent with which it had to struggle was traditionalism" (56, 59). Evolving from "the hard legalism and the active enterprise of bourgeois-capitalistic entrepreneurs" (139), we see "the continued life of the Word, not as a written document, but as the force of the [spirit of constitutionalism] working in daily life," which speaks directly to the individual, works through "the inner light of continual revelation," and flourishes through "this *in*visible Church of those illuminated by the spirit" (147; emphasis in original). "For the last stage it might well be truly said: 'Specialists without spirit, sensualists without heart; this nullity imagines that it has attained a level of civilization never before achieved'" (182).

27. Alexis de Tocqueville, *Democracy in America,* trans. H. Reeve, vol. 2 (New York: Vintage Books, 1990), 318.

28. Nadia Urbinati, *Democracy Disfigured: Opinion, Truth, and the People* (Cambridge, MA: Harvard University Press, 2014).

ACKNOWLEDGMENTS

I started this project in 2016–2017 when I was EURIAS (European Institutes for Advanced Study) Senior Fellow at the Freiburg Institute of Advanced Studies (FRIAS), but I could not then work out how best to present my argument. Conversations with Neil Walker in the spring of 2019 while I was a MacCormick Fellow at the University of Edinburgh helped, but it was only during the successive lockdowns of 2020 that I was finally able to sketch an acceptable draft. Neil kindly commented on that draft, as did Signe Larsen, Yaniv Roznai, and Samuel Tschorne, three former doctoral students who are now embarked (albeit at different stages) on highly successful academic careers. I have continued to learn from them and remain indebted to all four for their insights and critical feedback. I also thank the EURIAS / Marie Skłodowska Curie programme, FRIAS, the Edinburgh Law School, and, of course, my home institution, the Law Department at the London School of Economics, for the invaluable support I've received over this period.

Two reviewers commissioned by Harvard University Press produced reports that helped considerably to improve the book. I am especially grateful to Joseph Pomp, my editor at the Press, who immediately saw the book's potential and has throughout been an unwavering source of guidance and critical editorial support. Finally, I am once again indebted to Chris Foley for helping to turn my stilted academic prose into something a little more readable.

INDEX